"They Are All Red Out Here"

.

"They Are All Red Out Here"

Socialist Politics
in the Pacific Northwest, 1895–1925

Jeffrey A. Johnson

UNIVERSITY OF OKLAHOMA PRESS
Norman

Library of Congress Cataloging-in-Publication Data

Johnson, Jeffrey A., 1976–
    "They are all red out here" : socialist politics in the Pacific Northwest,
1895–1925 / Jeffrey A. Johnson.
        p. cm.
    Includes bibliographical references and index.
    ISBN 978-0-8061-3967-8 (hardcover : alk. paper)   1. Socialism—
Northwest, Pacific.   2. Socialist Party (U.S.)—History.   3. Communism—
Northwest, Pacific.   4. Northwest, Pacific—History.   5. Northwest, Pacific—
Social conditions.   I. Title.
    HX91.N77J65 2008
    324.273'7—dc22
                                                                                    2008021256

An early version of chapter 1 titled "'The Talking Stage of Socialism Has Passed': The Beginnings of Northwest Socialism, 1895–1900" appeared in *Idaho Yesterdays* (Spring/Summer 2006): 6–29.

An early version of chapter 2 titled "'The Political Trend Is Steadily toward Socialism': Building a Socialist Party in the Northwest, 1901–1905," appeared in *Columbia: The Magazine of Northwest History* (Spring 2008): 32–37.

The paper in this book meets the guidelines for permanence and durability of the Committee on Production Guidelines for Book Longevity of the Council on Library Resources, Inc. ∞

1 2 3 4 5 6 7 8 9 10

To my parents

Contents

Illustrations

Photographs

Map

Acknowledgments

THIS book began during my time at Washington State University. I remain grateful for the professional opportunities WSU's Department of History offered, specifically the Pettyjohn and Herman J. Deutsch Fellowships I received. These awards provided the financial means for much of the travel involved with this project. Also, a number of the excellent faculty at WSU helped this work. First, I must thank my Ph.D. advisor, LeRoy Ashby, who directed this project in its earliest stages. His patience and support will be remembered fondly. Another member of my doctoral committee, Laurie Mercier, and her expertise on labor in the West, were invaluable. Last, but not least, Orlan Svingen not only served on my committee but also proved an important friend and mentor throughout my time in Pullman.

I am further indebted to the countless archivists and librarians at the Idaho State Historical Society, Montana Historical Society, Oregon Historical Society, Augustana College, the University of Washington Library, and the Washington State Historical Society. The microfilm and interlibrary loan staff at Washington State University's Holland Library deserve special recognition, as they unquestioningly found me materials I did not think possible.

I also remain grateful for the fine work of the University of Oklahoma Press. In particular, Matt Bokovoy first showed interest in this project and has been consistently efficient, helpful, and professional. Also, I am grateful for Steven Baker's guidance and management of this book's progress. Finally, my copyeditor, Marlene Smith-Baranzini, diligently and carefully reviewed the work, and her close eye and detailed suggestions greatly improved the manuscript.

Throughout the Pacific Northwest and elsewhere, a number of individuals have helped this project in a variety of ways: Benjamin Baughman, Andres Caicedo, John Mann, Kris Goss, Robert Swartout, Michael Evans, Bret and Christina Patterson, and Dena Soled. Mathias D. Bergmann, though, deserves my special thanks. He not only dutifully read early and late drafts of this work but also has remained, for ten years, a professional and personal friend.

Finally, I am forever indebted to my parents, George and Joyce Johnson. Without their constant love and encouragement none of my successes would have come to fruition.

Sioux Falls, South Dakota
August 2007

"They Are All Red Out Here"

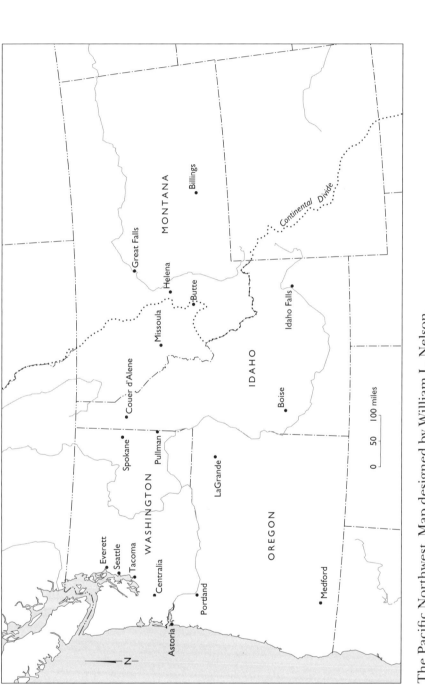

The Pacific Northwest. Map designed by William L. Nelson.

Introduction

In the first weeks of 1914 winter rains would surely have blan-kected Washington's Puget Sound region, but nothing could dampen the ardor of the region's emerging body of socialists. In Everett, a lumber-mill town on Puget Sound twenty-five miles north of Seattle, a small group of committed activists met to rebuild their defunct organization and strategize for upcoming campaigns. Five years earlier, their chronic party squabbling had led the Socialist Party of America's National Executive Commit-tee to hand down a forceful ruling disbanding the Socialist Party of Washington State. Now, in early 1914, Everett bookstore owner Frans Bostrom assumed the chairmanship of the reor-ganized state party, and the city's socialists planned an "aggres-sive" rebuilding campaign "to arouse every lagging socialist from his apathy." This resilient group, in the face of continual orga-nizational challenges, typified the dedicated, optimistic, and vig-orous party membership that spanned Washington, Oregon, Idaho, and Montana. This rising activism played out time and again in the Pacific Northwest, where industrial laborers, farm-ers, and middle-class reformers constructed a robust political alternative to the steadily changing world around them.[1]

Indeed, the preceding decades had witnessed dramatic shifts in American society, economic activity, and politics. With the end of the Civil War, as historian William Leach has pointed out, a new culture of American capitalism had emerged, leaving the popula-tion politically, religiously, and personally disconnected from one another. Capital and commodities now held center stage and first priority in American life. Amidst a capitalism seemingly gone amiss, one increasingly unfair to the working class, socialist alter-natives emerged to challenge the nation's dominant political structures. As the era's Populist and Progressive successes indi-cated, Democrats and Republicans no longer enjoyed political

hegemony, and other third-party alternatives—in this case, socialism—had emerged. In the national presidential election of 1912,
Eugene Victor Debs, the consummate face of late-nineteenth- and
early-twentieth-century socialist politics, won nearly a million
votes, and the party placed two members in Congress and countless others in local and state positions. Nationally, socialism had
grown into what historian Alan Dawley called a "sprawling, pro-
tean movement almost as diverse as the population itself." From
the eastern seaboard to the Midwest, South, and West, "socialism
could be found in abundance." As the American political scene
advanced into the twentieth century, socialism stood as a viable
political challenge to existing party systems.[2]

Surprisingly few historians have explored early-twentieth-
century grass-roots socialist activism and its repercussions in the
Pacific Northwest, one of the nation's most famously radical
regions. Forty years after historian David Shannon asserted that
"to describe the Socialist Party . . . it is necessary to survey its
regional parts," the Pacific Northwest still lacks a regional and
organizational examination of its socialist past. Mindful of this
historical omission, in this institutional study I examine the
development, dedication, and demise of socialist party politics
and activism in the Pacific Northwest from 1895 to 1925.

In many ways, the Pacific Northwest's brand of radical political
agitation mirrored the national party's experience. Like their
counterparts elsewhere, socialists in the Pacific Northwest experienced party in-fighting, sporadic electoral successes, organizational challenges from the American Federation of Labor (AFL)
and the Industrial Workers of the World (IWW), and anti-radical
opposition. Yet Pacific Northwest socialists also exhibited regional
distinctiveness: they maintained a reputation for fervent radicalism, demonstrated an exuberant sense of optimism, at times
experienced extraordinary political success, and organized enthusiastically on behalf of their cause. And while other states and locales
have often been regarded as the most energetic and determined
examples of American socialism, the Pacific Northwest was home
to some of the nation's most active and hopeful socialists.[3]

In 1906 German economist Werner Sombart asked a presumptuous question in the very title of his book *Why Is There No Socialism in the United States?* At the same time, U.S. historians found themselves fascinated by American socialism. Wisconsin economics professor John Commons presented the first serious work to explore "labor history" when, during the first three decades of the twentieth century, he and his students pioneered an organizational model of labor that focused particularly on unions and collective bargaining. During the early twentieth century, former and current party members penned the first organizational "histories" of socialism. Given their biases, however, these studies offered less-than-objective narratives. The Progressive historians of the 1920s, meanwhile, relegated socialism and other rejections of American liberalism to the historical periphery. V. L. Parrington believed that liberal thoughts were "currents," whereas *illiberal* ideas stood in the way of American progress. Other Progressive-era historians, such as Fred Haynes, dismissed the historical significance of America's "minor parties," including socialism, and argued that they and other political upstarts had "ceased to be a feature in our political history."[4]

The first syntheses of American socialism appeared in the 1950s, an unlikely time, as "consensus historians" dominated the field in both public and academic spheres. Amid the Cold War climate, cautious and conciliatory U.S. political histories emphasized the nation's political and social homogeneity and penned celebratory national narratives devoid of labor and leftist dissent. Yet during this time of tentativeness toward American radicalism, Ira Kipnis's *The American Socialist Movement, 1897–1912* (1952) and David Shannon's *The Socialist Party of America* (1955) offered the first original and chronological works to examine American socialists. As beginning points for any researcher interested in American socialism, the Shannon and Kipnis accounts offer sweeping narratives that give limited attention to socialist activity outside national party affairs. As in previous generations, consensus-era scholars, such as Daniel Bell in *Marxian Socialism in America* (1952), continued to see the socialist party as "in but not of" American society. A decade later, in contrast, James Weinstein, in *The Decline of Socialism in America, 1912–1925* (1967), typified a growing emphasis on the ideological, economic, and political conditions that brought socialism's demise. These later historians, as Richard Schneirov remarked, resembled "coroners conducting an autopsy of an exhausted and dying movement."[5]

The late 1960s and early 1970s saw the rise of a "new labor history," an attempt by historians to tackle, "from the bottom up," the place of the working class in American labor history. New labor historians, among them David Brody, Herbert Gutman, and David Montgomery, "rediscovered" the American working class. As scholars turned their attention to the role of American laborers in broader social, economic, and cultural contexts, however, they by-passed the study of labor organizations and institutions. Accordingly, socialism's broad scholarly coverage still suffered. Historians such as D. H. Leon recognized the "deficiencies" of most socialist studies and recommended that scholars give socialists "much more extensive and intensive research and sophisticated interpretation."[6]

During the next thirty years, historians expanded their approaches and broadened their perspectives, but more work remains for scholars. These studies of the region's socialists still typified what Leon recognized in 1971 as the existence of too few "detailed examples of the basic difficulty of getting socialist candidates on the ballot, of the party's success in building local organizations, their campaigning, and how socialists performed in office." Similarly, labor historians continued to neglect socialism's institutional and organizational histories. Carlos Schwantes noted in 1985 that "much more study of Pacific Northwest radicalism remains to be done."[7] More than twenty years later, Schwantes's call has still gone unanswered.

The lack of a regional socialist history, although a critical part of a broad and complex narrative of Pacific Northwestern economic, political, and social development, is nevertheless startling—particularly given the availability of resource material, including several fine first studies of Pacific Northwest radicalism. As David Brody writes, "The modern labor historian is thrown more completely on his own resources." My experience regarding original sources is no exception. In completing this study I consulted several previously untapped or rarely used sources that helped piece together the regional socialist story, including research drawn from national and regional manuscript collections, socialist party documents, and socialist newspapers and periodicals. A few place-specific studies have examined the socialist presence in the Northwest, including those by Jerry Calvert, Jonathan Dembo, Charles LeWarne, and Carlos Schwantes. Although solid institutional studies examine socialists in other states, regions, and cities, the present volume provides the first broad regional history to examine socialist party activity across Washington, Oregon, Idaho, and Montana.[8]

Several recent publications address particular aspects of Pacific Northwest labor history and culture. Works such as Laurie Mercier's study of Anaconda, Montana, Linda Carlson's examination of the company town, John Douglas Belshaw's study of Vancouver, British Columbia's working class, and William Robbins's analysis of labor in Coos Bay, Oregon, have much to tell us about the construction of working class culture and communities. While these works examine labor's rise to radicalization in specific locations or communities, more extensive and complex characterizations of the greater Pacific Northwest economy and its workers lie beyond their scope. While this volume builds on these focused social and cultural histories, it also places Pacific Northwest radicalism—and more specifically, political socialism—in the broader context of Western labor and political history.

A long-overdue history of socialism in the Pacific Northwest, *They Are All Red Out Here* departs from a formulaic or theoretical framework and does not take a polemic position. Rather, it draws on previously untapped vibrant, contemporary sources that present a more accurate portrait of socialist party form, function, and membership, and reveals the diverse personal and community experiences of the working class. On one hand, the broad organizational model of early-twentieth-century labor historians has proved an appropriate and unambiguous approach for this regionwide study. Brody argues that it once was (and I hope it remains) "in the nature of institutional history to provide for its adherents a clear framework." While I agree with him, this study expands those narrower approaches taken by older institutional studies and embraces the opportunity to restore the role of rank-and-file workers and party organizers as active participants in significantly shaping their own local histories. In a new atmosphere of harsher demands on labor, the rank and file vigorously constructed a radical and viable oppositional response to the emerging capitalist-domineered world around them; one that in many ways continually reinspired their political resolve and determination.[9]

This work examines Pacific Northwest socialism chronologically, from 1895 to 1925, which parallels the period commonly considered "the golden age of American socialism." Chapter one outlines the origins of northwest socialism, beginning in the 1890s. During the last years of the nineteenth century, it argues, the Pacific Northwest's volatile economy and "wage frontier" fostered a climate of political radicalism. The first pro-labor advocates to act publicly—utopian communitarians, Socialist Labor Party members, and Social Democratic Party organizers—emerged as the region's first "socialists." Chapter two explores the establishment of the Socialist Party of America (SPA) in 1901, which provided a permanent party structure for Pacific Northwest socialists. Chapter three traces party-building from 1905 to 1910, illustrating the increasingly problematic internal squabbling and the socialists' uncertain relationships with two other labor organizations in the region: the AFL and the IWW. Both organizations, this work contends, implicitly or explicitly challenged socialist politics, tactics, and agendas. Chapter four follows in detail the apex of regional and national socialist power—its political successes in the national elections of 1911 and 1912—and the circumstances surrounding this time of its extraordinary popular support. In spite of an invigorated party membership after the 1912 elections, successes that resonated in renewed propagandizing and rhetoric, chapter five investigates the slow and steady demise of Pacific Northwest socialism, rooted in its chronic and characteristic party infighting. Finally, chapter six explores how socialist protests against World War I and the anti-radicalism of the "Red Scare" sounded the death knell to the party's political stability. Despite its unbridled optimism and fervent activism in the region, by the mid-1920s socialist politics in the Pacific Northwest had run its course.

The region's approximately three decades of vigorous socialist politics and activism nevertheless stand as an important and intriguing period in regional and Western history. While regional party experiences often typified national party trends and challenges, the Northwest's socialists enjoyed an exceptional degree of political success and an unbridled rhetorical optimism that combined to make them some of them the most dedicated, hopeful, and successful socialists the United States has seen.[10]

1

Fanning the "Flame of Revolution"
The Beginnings of Pacific Northwest Socialism, 1895–1900

The political trend is steadily toward socialism.   Eugene V. Debs, 1900

As the nineteenth century closed, the United States witnessed the rise of a new industrial order. Not only did immigrants arrive and cities swell, but the country also underwent its greatest economic shifts since the era of Andrew Jackson. A new epoch of mechanization, mass production, and speculation brought rapid and sweeping changes in the nature of work and labor, creating what one history of the period has called "the seedbed of a new social and economic order." Further, from the late nineteenth into the early twentieth century, monumental economic, social, and cultural changes reshaped society at every level and from shore to shore. During this period of extensive transformation, the "modern" world arrived. According to historian William Leach, the nation's newly formed consumptive culture was far from benign and placed a premium on material want and wealth. It was now Carnegie, Rockefeller, and Morgan's America; and yet it also belonged to someone else—the workers.[1]

There is, consequently, a general consensus among scholars that the period from the end of Reconstruction to the New Deal stands as one of the nation's most turbulent eras. The market system expanded into the West in the context of complex and unstable economic and social relationships. As historian Alan Dawley has remarked, "Everything was in flux." And as the unstable 1890s, and particularly the Panic of 1893, illustrated, all was not well—especially for rank-and-file wage earners. Without question, industrialization and rising corporate influence brought difficult times to America's industrial and agricultural laborers, who increasingly found themselves underpaid, over-worked, and vulnerable.[2]

Pacific Northwest workers, like their counterparts in the rest of the country, responded to these striking social and economic shifts in a variety of ways. In the decade beginning in the mid-1880s, the region experienced feverish economic growth, and the so-called "bindle stiffs," the majority of rank-and-file labor-ers, provided the bulk of industrial production. Some workers joined local craft unions or national organizations such as the Knights of Labor and the American Federation of Labor. As laborers across the country boldly spoke out in response to employers' unwelcome practices, Pacific Northwest workers began to emerge, especially in reputation, as a radical workforce. Because of strained relations between workers and manage-ment, radicalized elements of labor and the Left found voices in more extreme organizations. Unionism, syndicalism, party poli-tics, and communitarianism were all alternatives for their radical expression of workplace unrest. Yet during the tumultuous 1890s, "among an array of new political possibilities," historian Richard Schneirov notes, socialism started to receive "serious consideration" from discontented workers.

Socialism in the Pacific Northwest emerged during this period as one form of sociopolitical expression and experienced mod-est growth in various forms, but its early manifestations pro-duced only pockets of political activism. The first socialist expressions were not homogenous: political activities and dif-fering ideological agendas mingled. The often-overlapping plat-forms of the Socialist Labor Party (SLP), the Social Democratic Party (SDP), Social Democracy of America (SDA), utopian com-munitarians, remnants of Populism, and pro-labor Republicans and Democrats left little room for any one group to propose truly distinct socialist politics. Not until the establishment of the Socialist Party of America in 1901 could the Pacific Northwest finally claim an organized and enduring socialist voice. However weak, the earliest years of socialism in the late-nineteenth-century Northwest illustrated the existence of broad regional radicalism, the potential for successful party politics, and socialism's rise as one expression of social and political opposition to the status quo. Regionally, rapid economic growth, a new socio-economic order, and workplace labor resistance all facilitated the emergence of a radical northwest socialism.[3]

During the last decades of the nineteenth century the Pacific Northwest economy grew rapidly. In a span of twenty years the region transitioned from an informal and seemingly impermanent backcountry economy to one based on greater industrialization and investment. The strength of its extractive industries, particularly agriculture, mining, fishing, and timber, solidified the Northwest's position as a resource hinterland for the rest of the nation. Visitors such as AFL head Samuel Gompers witnessed the changing economy and labor relations during an 1891 tour of Oregon and Washington. He believed, however, that the region was a "long way off" from the East in its economic development. Two decades later his opinion had changed. "What wondrous changes!" he wrote in 1911, "What marvelous growth and progress! Life on the Pacific Coast States is even more open and free than in the cities or even towns of the East or the Middle States." As Gompers observed, Pacific Northwest industries were booming. As elsewhere in the West, industrial mining spurred economic growth more than any other industry. Historian Patricia Limerick notes that mining "set the pace" for western economic development, and the Pacific Northwest remained an integral part of that expansion. From 1883 to 1884 between six thousand and eight thousand miners rushed to northern Idaho, and by 1891 forty mines operated in the Coeur d'Alene district. Similarly, in 1885, eighteen hundred miners toiled to the east in the rich hills of Butte, Montana. And the state's silver markets had already brought other related investments into the area with the arrival of railroads in Butte in 1881 and Helena in 1883. The Northwest simultaneously emerged as the epicenter for U.S. timber production, eventually superceding the Great Lakes region. The combined timber output of Oregon and Washington skyrocketed from 337,347 board feet in 1879 to 2,163,570 in 1899. In addition to booming lumber production, agriculture also experienced swift expansion. From 1880 to 1890, with help from expanding rail lines, Washington, Idaho, and Oregon opened an astonishing 250 million acres of agricultural land.[4]

In this new economic climate, four conditions strained the regional relationships between capital and labor and fueled political radicalism: dangerous working conditions, deflated hopes of advancement, rapid social and economic change, and racial tension among a competitive workforce. For the region's laborers, poor work conditions and relationships with employers fostered antagonism. Extractive industry laborers, namely loggers and miners, faced similar experiences as low wages, long hours, and hazardous conditions grew increasingly common.[5] Late-nineteenth-century wage issues specifically helped spur the region's first union activity. In Butte, Montana, workers demanded a universal, that is, for workers in all capacities, daily wage of $3.50. Hazardous work conditions made low wages especially disillusioning. Montana and Idaho miners faced the possibility of respiratory diseases such as silicosis, tunnel collapses, and explosions. In January 1895 a single surface explosion killed nearly sixty Butte workers, with observers reporting "bodies mangled beyond all recognition." Dangerous industries also threatened the welfare of those in surrounding communities. When the Boston and Montana Company began open roasting of copper ores near Butte, fifteen deaths occurred in two days. While these and other risks, including severed limbs and broken bones, seemed all too obvious a problem to be addressed, workers and their families encountered dismissive and patronizing responses from employers who considered physical risk a part of the job. The realities of wage work included on-the-job tension, and labor's uneasiness with dangerous or unfair conditions did not go unnoticed. Idaho governor Frank Steunenberg, former co-editor of the *Caldwell Tribune*, recognized the apprehensive relationship between labor and employers. In his 1899 annual report, he briefly addressed this uneasiness in an editorial, "Immigration and Labor," that he wrote primarily "for the benefit of the organized labor of the State—which class at the present time numbers at least 3000 of our citizens. Truly no subject is of more deep concern to mankind today than the relations, too often antagonistic, but really mutual and co-operative, of capital and labor."[6]

Corporate control of entire communities also accelerated worker unrest. This was not uncommon in company towns. In the mines of Wardner, Idaho, for example, the Bunker Hill and Sullivan Company dominated city government and life, thus ensuring their capital interests received solid support at the expense of workers' needs. Failed aspirations provided another source of worker radicalization. "For generations," historian William Leach has reflected, "America had been portrayed as a place of plenty, a garden in which all paradisiacal longings would be satisfied." A national sense of abundance saw further amplification when coupled with the allure of the mythical, untamed, and potentially profitable West. As William Robbins has offered, it was "above all the *promise* of the West that loomed largest" for settlers and emigrants.[7]

Although long-standing images and conceptions of the West as a land of endless opportunity abounded, the reality of wage work in the early twentieth century quickly dashed hopes. Often exaggerated in corporate pamphlets and propaganda, Pacific Northwest labor opportunities appeared endless. But workers of all ethnicities soon discovered the harsh realities of toiling in the Northwest. Workers' deflated hopes easily turned into contempt, and absentee eastern financiers and local mangers increasingly became the targets of their hostility. In this diverging class system, national labor leaders identified wealthy capitalists and financiers as villains.

In the last years of the nineteenth century, the nation witnessed the rise of a distinct, impersonal, intermediate "brokering class," which came to dominate the social, economic, and political climates of the new century. The consequence of this owner absenteeism for workers was a steadily growing antipathy among "have-not" laborers who found themselves increasingly at the mercy of a minority of "haves." Radical rhetoric already centered on absentee speculators. Eugene Debs, president of the American Railway Union (ARU), emphasized this widening economic gap to miners in Wallace, Idaho, when he told them: "On the Atlantic coast are a select few who are the custodians of our nation." He continued the charge during an 1897 visit to Missoula, Montana. In a speech to the state Fruit Growers Association, Debs lamented the nation's emerging "species of aristocracy."[8]

With deflated expectations of wealth and seemingly at the mercy of wage-rate dictates by eastern financiers, labor faced the challenge of a regional economy operating under "boom and bust" cycles, often controlled by external forces. Economic viability in the West, as William Robbins observed, depended on "the twin requisites of capitalism . . . predictability and a semblance of stability," neither of which the Northwest economy could claim. Price volatility, particularly in the region's extractive industries, absent safety and other regulations, and over-speculation in commodities and resources, created unsettling economic conditions. While solid economic growth in the early 1890s heartened many, railroad shipping rates, crop prices, and other commercial markets fluctuated according to national and international factors, revealing the dependence of an already volatile economy on outside forces. Throughout the West only a few exceptional locales, namely Minneapolis-St. Paul and Seattle, operated independently, otherwise, as Robbins argued, "little happened in the region that did not have the sanction of external capital." To many, the Panic of 1893 and resulting economic depression demonstrated the Pacific Northwest's clear connection to national and international markets. An isolated and dependent "wageworkers' frontier," according to Carlos Schwantes, "was ever in a state of flux." For uneasy laborers, the pace of social and economic change was worrisome.[9]

If the West marched, as Robbins purported, to a "drumbeat of incessant change," racial tension also marched in the parade of radicalism. Perceived competition with nonwhites, especially the

Chinese, worried white laborers. In workers' minds, the foundation for this concern existed in the Northwest's significantly increasing number of late-nineteenth-century immigrants entering the workforce. In the 1880s the Northern Pacific Railroad alone imported fifteen thousand Chinese laborers to the region. In economic downturns, the Chinese provided a convenient scapegoat for disaffected whites. While they did not work throughout the entire region—in an October 1899 economic report to the governor of Idaho, analysts noted that the majority of the state's labor force was made up of native-born Americans, Scandinavians, Italians, Austrians, Canadians, and Germans—many white labor leaders and workers accused the Chinese of taking jobs from able-bodied "Americans." AFL president Samuel Gompers summarized the position of many in labor circles, proclaiming that "all public spirited, intelligent Americans agree that the Chinese must not be permitted to come. . . . There are myriads of workmen to perform any of the work which is now required." Some communities legislated labor discrimination to combat this perceived "Asian evil." From 1897 to 1899, for example, Butte instituted a citywide boycott of Chinese merchants and laborers. While whites exaggerated the extent of jobs lost, they nevertheless perceived the Chinese as a threat to their economic viability. Concerns over race undoubtedly also strained the white and nonwhite labor experience.[10]

Nationally, Americans had already begun to voice their discontent with the changing world around them. "Americans had always been a restless people," wrote historian T. J. Jackson Lears, but the 1890s witnessed the rise of increasingly class-driven "isms": populism, trade unionism, and socialism. The unsettling economic climate of the late nineteenth century left the Pacific Northwest, too, susceptible to radical perspectives, as a series of national and regional events and trends highlighted the uneasy balance between capital and labor. As a result of the economic depression and labor's uneasiness in the 1890s, industrial organizing, protests, and violence grew increasingly prevalent. The march to radicalization in the Pacific Northwest was reaching full stride.[11]

One of labor's first responses to the changing northwest economy was to heighten union activity. In northern Idaho, the famed Bunker Hill Company, established in 1885, periodically witnessed labor tension and violence. State miners formalized a number of loose union locals in January 1891 and established the Miners' Union of the Coeur d'Alenes. But unionism faced an uphill battle. When miners in the communities of Wardner, Burke, Gem, and Mullan, Idaho, organized, mine operators, not surprisingly, viewed their union organizing as threats to managerial control. In February, mine owners and businessmen countered the miners' move by establishing the reactive Mine Owner's Protective Association (MOA). Now, with sides drawn and labor's new demand for a $3.50 daily wage, employers and employees stood, in Kathy Aiken's words, "poised for conflict." In 1892, when technological changes in mining and the rise of the MOA combined to lower wages, the Coeur d'Alene district experienced its first strike. Six months of strikes escalated into gunfire exchange between the strikers and mine guards, the hiring of scabs, retaliatory explosions by the miners, and threats to mines and equipment. Despite opposition from employers, as the Coeur d'Alene strike demonstrated, workers maintained their resolve and continued unionizing. During the same decade, a government observer noted that lumbermen in Washington and Oregon had also "learned the value of associated effort."[12]

Just as labor organizing gained momentum, the national Panic of 1893 struck the Pacific Northwest. Indicative of the regional economy's instability and its dependence on volatile mineral prices, silver values dropped as much as 20 percent in hours, creating instant pandemonium. Idaho wheat prices plummeted from $.82 per bushel in January 1892 to $.36 by September. Idaho businesses and banks "collapsed like paper houses in a rainstorm," observers said. In Spokane, Washington, five banks closed, as did two-thirds of those in Tacoma. Observers believed the national crisis put three million Americans out of work, and the Northwest did not escape this hardship. The governor of Oregon claimed that unemployment gripped two-thirds of the state's population. Montana felt the panic's effects too. When silver mines closed and the Northern Pacific Railroad declared bankruptcy, more than a dozen banks closed, consequently putting twenty thousand Montanans out of work. Tough times forced Helena's prolific silver investor, Samuel Hauser, to cease operation of his First National Bank.[13] The Panic of 1893 illustrated the instability of federally unregulated speculation and unbridled economic growth.

In the wake of the national economic panic, two galvanizing events led to an increasingly more vocal and radical working class. The ARU-led Pullman Strike of 1894 marked the zenith of a decade-old conflict between capital and labor. The strike against the Pullman Palace Car Company by workers stopped trains in twenty-seven states and made ARU President Eugene Debs a national figure. President Cleveland declared the strike illegal because U.S. mail moved on trains. Pacific Northwest laborers followed these events in newspapers such as the *Oregonian,* which covered the Debs story from his trial for mail interference to his six-month jail sentence for contempt of court during that trial. In 1894 Americans were startled by another event, an outgrowth of both the Panic of 1893 and laborers' discontent. Across the U.S., many unemployed and disenchanted workers joined "Coxey's Army," bands of foot "soldiers" who united to express their frustrations to lawmakers and called for federal aid through large road-building programs that would employ them. Led by "General" Jacob Coxey, an Ohio businessman dissatisfied with the lack of government action on the economy, thousands of the unemployed marched on the nation's capital, hoping to "send a petition to Washington with boots on." Among those marchers were a number of the northwest unemployed. Butte miner William Hogan led Montana's army of 330 individuals, characterized as frustrated but "determined" workers. Hogan and his followers commandeered a Northern Pacific engine and headed east with hopes of reaching Washington, but the U.S. Army halted them after 325 miles, in Forsyth, Montana. Other Coxeyites in the Pacific Northwest formed in Portland, Seattle, Tacoma, Spokane, and Yakima. Some sixteen hundred men from Seattle and Tacoma rallied at the Puyallup train depot. Portland's army numbered approximately fifteen hundred when it seized a train at Troutdale, Oregon. Although federal troops stopped the protestors near The Dalles, on the Columbia River, some of the group advanced to Boise, where they stole another train before disbanding.[14]

While the ARU and Coxeyite efforts ultimately failed, northwest workers continued radical action throughout the 1890s, notably in Idaho. In the state's mineral-rich north, a place already festering with labor tension, hostilities escalated in 1899. Despite the best efforts of the Miners' Union of the Coeur d'Alenes, Bunker Hill officials remained stingy employers, refusing to pay wage demands of $3 to shovelers and $3.50 to miners. In April, striking miners commandeered a train to take them to Wardner, where they used 3,500 pounds of dynamite to destroy the Bunker Hill and Sullivan ore concentrators, causing $250,000 in damages. Governor Frank Steunenberg declared martial law in the Coeur d'Alenes, and President William McKinley sent five hundred federal troops to quash various acts of unrest by approximately seven hundred miners. These confrontations, called the Idaho Mining Wars, and including the hasty construction of "bull pens" to house strikers and dissenting Shoshone County Populists, according to historian Dorothy Johansen, "perpetuated hatred and suspicion to breed further conflict."[15]

In the last decades of the nineteenth century, ongoing labor unrest, the sweeping effects of the deepened depression, and labor's often volatile reactions to management policies shaped an American labor force that was anxious, irritable, and motivated to act. Even the conservative Samuel Gompers articulated a nervous sentiment concerning future economic troubles in the United States: "The period of depression, or more properly speaking, the industrial panic of 1893," he wrote in 1902, "was most intense; and any student of economic and industrial history is fully aware that we shall not be entirely free from its recurrence."[16]

Historians have long debated just how the Pacific Northwest was transformed from a region of unsettled but nonexplosive labor conditions to one that would earn a reputation for radicalism. Class distinctions were undoubtedly strained during the late nineteenth century, and the first vocal advocates of socialist principles in the Northwest focused on labor's plight. As instances of radicalism and violence suggested, something in "the system" was wrong, and the 1890s provided the evidence. Historian Shelton Stromquist observed that, for workers, "the crisis of the mid-1890s confirmed their view that society was divided into two broad classes whose interests were antagonistic." Politically sophisticated socialists of the period, in fact, capitalized on this apparent class struggle. In retrospect, many of them believed that Karl Marx, who argued that capitalism developed most "shamelessly" in the United States, might have been correct.[17] Activists who agreed with him found socialism an appropriate, radical platform from which to operate. Although they were not politically successful at the polls during their founding years, America's first socialists entered the political arena at a time of economic turmoil.

During the 1890s, workers' most effective strategy for change was acting through union channels. As industrial unionists recalled later, "It was very early discovered that for the workers to make headway against the capitalists was to organize." Not all those involved in labor organizing were left-wing militants, of course. "Bread and butter" unionism—that is, craft unions for individual trades such as carpenters, typographers, and miners working for higher wages, shorter hours, and improved conditions—remained vibrant in the Pacific Northwest. The Knights of Labor, a somewhat radical group of industrial unionists, held their first organizing meetings in the Northwest during the 1880s and remained prominent in regional labor negotiations through the 1890s, particularly in Oregon, Idaho, and eastern Washington. The AFL, established in 1886, enjoyed greater prominence than the others. As the turn of the century neared, local chapters of the trade-specific AFL began to supercede the Knights in the Northwest.[18]

In addition to bread-and-butter national unions, regional and local organizations also voiced labor concerns with increasingly volatility. Montana miners unionized in 1878 as the Butte Work-ingman's Union. In 1885 miners in that city reorganized as the Butte Miner's Union (BMU), and soon grew to dominate union activity in many communities of the Intermountain West. By 1893 the BMU had forty-six hundred paying members, with par-ticularly strong followings in northern Idaho and western Mon-tana. The mining unions of the Coeur d'Alenes could also trace their roots to the BMU. In May 1893 the new and more radical Western Federation of Miners (WFM) held its organizational meeting in Butte, bringing the city prominence as a center for western working-class agitation. Miners from Montana, South Dakota, Idaho, Utah, Colorado, and Nevada convened in Butte to establish the union, which ultimately endorsed radical organ-izations such as the Socialist Party of America, and later, the Industrial Workers of the World. In its first decade of existence, the WFM and its subsidiaries battled employers, and few months passed without "violence, loss of property and life, and military intervention," according to Melvyn Dubofsky. By 1900, organ-ized labor had begun to emerge as a significant socio-economic force. The *American Federationist*, the AFL's official publication, proudly announced, "the union label has become a permanent factor in industrial reform."[19]

Mirroring the national trend, employers and regional capital-ists cracked down on union activity. Employer reaction to union membership was particularly harsh following violent instances like those of the Coeur d'Alene Mining Wars of the 1890s. For example, Idaho bureaucrats collected data on union and non-union members and instituted a permit system to regulate their mine employment. When applying for permits, miners had to disassociate themselves from violence and particular unions. Part of the permit pledge read: "I did not participate actively or otherwise in the riots which took place at Wardner on the 29th of April, 1899. [I believe] . . . that the crimes committed at Ward-ner on said date were actively incited, encouraged and perpe-trated through and by means of the influence and direction of the Miners' Union of the Coeur d'Alene."[20] By 1899, officials had granted 1,036 permits, with 467 miners declaring no union affiliation. In this period of active labor unrest, trade unionism brought suspicion and reaction from employers and government alike.

For more radically minded workers in the Pacific Northwest, even the politically aggressive union system remained disappointingly unresponsive. Instead of forcing issues, unionism, excluding the WFM, adopted an openly apolitical position. Indeed, in 1895 the AFL decreed that it had "no political platform." Rather, the organization endorsed Republicans and Democrats alike, as both mainstream parties claimed to represent labor. Thus, radical labor-reform activists suffered a political void, and with apolitical unionism and a dominant party system inhibiting their political hopes, radical laborers in the Northwest became frustrated. National leaders recognized this. During a trip to the Pacific Coast, Henry White, general secretary of the United Garment Workers of America, commented that "the far western mining states," while increasingly involved in politics, nonetheless "found that getting control of political power was not as easy as it looked." "The snares of politics," he continued, "proved too much for the guileless workers."[21]

Still, budding socialists and their political movements did not operate wholly outside the struggling union ranks. Before a distinct socialist party materialized, socialist advocates intermingled ideologically and socially with rank-and-file labor advocates. In Oregon, the Central Labor Council hosted a congress in 1895, at which delegates from across the state met to outline plans to draft and support pro-labor legislation. Attendees included members of farm alliances, craft unions, and a group calling themselves the "Academy of Socialism." Because socialist delegates enjoyed equal voice in convention proceedings, the labor congress typified the mix of factions. Yet its inclusiveness raised another challenge: mainstream labor leaders found the socialist relationship with trade unionism a divisive and delicate issue. A number of socialists, however, endorsed cooperation with trade unionists. Pro-union socialists praised the American Federation of Labor and other labor organizations for their progressive positions. Many felt that these political and economic organizations were "drifting together," while others pointed to unionism's recent failures in strikes, injunctions, and clashes with militias as evidence of its weaknesses. "Active socialists in the trade unions," still others claimed, complacently overlooked "the necessity of independent political action."[22]

During the 1890s Eugene Debs grew increasingly prominent in Pacific Northwest labor issues. A national union leader who espoused socialist rhetoric, Debs typified the blurred line between unionists and socialists. His speeches to union workers around the country consistently appeared in northwest newspapers, and his rhetoric grew increasingly radical. In early 1897 he addressed the miners in Burke, northern Idaho, reminding the crowd of three hundred that "We hang separately or hang together." He encouraged the miners to reevaluate labor's relationship to "corporations and trusts." In Wallace, Idaho, Debs spoke for two hours on the merits of a classless America, where workers would not be "chattels," but human beings. According to newspaper accounts, Debs became "political" in his speech, comparing the spirit of labor to the ardor of the American Revolution. Taking his socialistic rhetoric to its logical conclusion, the Spokane *Spokesman-Review* noted, he proclaimed, "We should have *no* classes." On June 11, 1897, to commemorate the fifth anniversary of the famed 1892 Coeur d'Alene strike, Debs returned to Wallace to deliver a Miner's Union Day address and then traveled to Spokane, specifically to address "socialistic questions."[23] As the shift in the thrust and tone of his speeches to Pacific Northwest laborers made clear, Debs and others sought radical voices outside apolitical unionism. Socialism, in its early and various forms, offered one such source.

The American propensity for dissent, and the rise of socialism, were part, of course, of broader political and social responses to the twentieth century's changing conceptions of capitalism and democracy. After the Civil War, historian William Leach described "a fierce conflict [that] swept over the country, setting farmers and workers against businessmen over how democracy in industrial America should be organized." The 1880s and 1890s ushered in unionism, populism, and eventually socialism as responses to this new reality. In the late-nineteenth-century Northwest, socialism took a number of forms. Its manifestations ranged from casual organizers to structured cooperatives and new political parties. But almost all nineteenth-century attempts to organize and spread socialism, whether through political or social activities, met with limited success. At the national level, the earliest socialist party organizing effort, in 1877, had established the Socialist Labor Party. Dogmatic German, Bohemian, and Scandinavian immigrants filled the ranks of the SLP, which faced an uphill battle as it failed to attract many native-born workers. The demise of the Knights of Labor after 1896 temporarily swelled socialism's numbers, but SLP membership still included a narrow cross-section of immigrants.

In the Pacific Northwest, the party experienced only pockets of activity, mostly in western Washington. Charles Drees, Tacoma Trades Council president, formed Washington's first section, also called a local or chapter, in 1890, with nineteen members. The section did not survive long. When the SLP held its national convention in 1896, a committee identified two hundred sections in twenty-five states, but none in the Pacific Northwest. In 1898, SLP members in Everett reorganized, but with only marginal success. The section secretary largely busied himself with logistical concerns and rallying delinquent members. In spite of this slow start, Washington hosted the Northwest's first state SLP convention in 1898. At the convention, "fusion"—the possibility of joining forces with other socialists—emerged as the hottest issue. Skeptics pointed to the Populist Party's fate after its failed 1896 fusion with the Democrats and William Jennings Bryan's unsuccessful presidential candidacy. Despite such divisions, the 1898 SLP convention nominated the first socialist candidates for state offices.[24]

By 1900, however, Washington SLP members remained the only politically active socialists in the Pacific Northwest. Based in

Seattle, the state committee now boasted six sections and claimed a membership "free of muddle head[s] and traitor[s]." According to SLP officials, Washington was "as clear, as active, as much in the thick of the fight as any State in the Union." The Pacific Northwest sent one delegate, W. S. Dalton, to the SLP's 1900 national convention.[25] But the party failed to make much progress in northwest politics, and steadily lost out to the more organized and inclusive Socialist Party of America.

Paralleling the SLP, a new but short-lived socialist experiment, the International Working-Men's Association, also formed. Described as a "curious mixture of anarchism and socialism," it was established in 1881 and found some promising northwest support. In 1887 it numbered six thousand members in Washington Territory and two thousand in Oregon. But the International Working-Men's Association faded quickly, as its calls for fusion with the SLP fell on deaf ears. It disbanded in the 1890s.[26]

Not all late-nineteenth-century socialist experiments were political forays. Washington was home to a number of utopian communities that implicitly or explicitly espoused socialist principles. Incorporated in 1887, for example, the Puget Sound Cooperative Colony, near Port Angeles, emerged as the region's first communal living enterprise. Initially a cooperative labor organization, the colony later became a joint-stock company. Formed primarily in response to Seattle's anti-Chinese labor hostilities during the 1880s, the founders envisioned a white-only membership. They structured the colony according to socialist principles, and leaders divided profits on a cooperative basis. The colony's declaration of principles articulated their goal: to establish a class system "without class distinctions or special privileges." The colony gained its greatest notoriety from its reputation, although unfounded, for practicing free love and promiscuity. Debts, however, hindered the colony's growth throughout the 1890s, and in 1904 it closed.[27]

In 1896 another short-lived socialist colony, Glennis, failed near Tacoma. Established in 1894, Glennis never had more than thirty members. After it disbanded, a number of its former residents established a more permanent colony, Home. The new colony functioned with few regulations regarding membership or personal conduct, and nearby Puget Sound residents called it a colony of anarchists and "free-lovers." The colony, however, did not live up to its licentious reputation. Aside from a few advocates, free love was rarely practiced there. But Home did serve as a passing station for countless anarchists and radicals, and also published newspapers and anarchist journals. One periodical, *Discontent: Mother of Progress,* debuted on May 11, 1898, not as an official colony journal, but as a voice for anarchist agendas. By 1899, despite its unfavorable public reputation, Home's population had grown to fifty-five residents; by April 1901 it reached ninety-four, and rose to 120 in 1905.[28]

While experimental living at both the Puget Sound Cooperative Colony and Home remained intrinsically socialistic, two more outwardly socialist colonies materialized in the Northwest. The Brotherhood of the Cooperative Commonwealth (BCC) was organized in January 1897 and became the leader in establishing additional socialist colonies in Washington, intending to plant a series of colonies throughout the West. The BCC, including organizer Eugene Debs, believed it could socialize western states by founding small socialist communities of miners, loggers, and farmers. BCC organizers targeted Washington and Idaho because of their comparatively small populations and the abundance of natural resources available to new colony residents. Ultimately, the BCC spawned two colonies in Washington, which supported a total of 110 residents. The colony attempt in Idaho never materialized.[29]

Near Bellingham, approximately eighty miles north of Seattle, Skagit County socialists and BCC leaders established Equality colony, the first explicitly socialist community in Washington. On November 1, 1897, the first settlers arrived, declaring that socialism was their "bond." One spokesman proclaimed, "The talking stage of Socialism has passed . . . now action is the live word." While Equality residents held grandiose ideas of socializing the entire state, internal squabbles soon dashed those hopes and the experiment survived only until 1906. As the nearby Mount Vernon *Argus* reported on March 23, 1906, "Socialism as it is sometimes practiced came to an inglorious end Wednesday."[30]

As Equality formed, defectors from the BCC, including Eugene Debs, were also at work, organizing the new national Social Democracy of America. The SDA's membership included disenchanted SLP, ARU, and BCC affiliates. Like previous efforts, the new organization had a short life. The final Social Democracy of America convention, held in June 1898, exposed divergent perspectives within the organization. The party remained divided between those who primarily called for colonization efforts and others who demanded it take greater political action. Despite the disunity, pro-colony SDA members began looking for suitable settlement sites in Idaho, Colorado, and Washington. The *Spokesman-Review* followed the search, while SDA chairman Debs organized the party's political activism in Washington. Reporting "Debs Hints at War," the *Spokesman-Review* summarized the SDA's plan to establish a colony in Washington, take command of state politics, and restructure government. "We will have control of the taxing power and drive tax syndicates and land sharks out of the state," Debs claimed. The SDA colony planned to levy taxes according to worker means and to slash the workday to four or five hours. State residents could also expect to pay a monthly tax of approximately $.25 to support the colony's general fund. Debs foresaw legal disputes with the state and even imagined armed conflict. Yet he remained unconcerned: "If they send the military to invade our rights," he claimed, "then there will be an army of 300,000 patriots in the state ready to meet them."[31]

Debs's plan to colonize encountered both opposition and support. He believed it could stand as a peaceful "Bellamy colony," based on the socialistic principles outlined in Edward Bellamy's classic 1888 utopian novel, *Looking Backward*. Debs claimed that one hundred thousand unemployed Chicago workers could be mobilized in ten days to serve as the first colonists. One *Spokesman-Review* editorial, however, characterized his plans and rhetoric as "lawless sentiments, hinting at bloody revolution—a mighty serious matter."

Washington governor John R. Rogers shocked people throughout the state when he announced his support for Debs and the SDA. During a visit to Pullman to deliver a commencement address at Washington State Agricultural College, Rogers admitted he had written to Debs to inform him of available, irrigable land surrounding Pasco, in the state's southeastern region. The governor expressed his admiration for the SDA cause: "I see in this movement what seems to me to be a return to fundamental principles. The great body of unemployed must, in some way, be brought back upon the land. The soil is the remedy, and Mr. Debs' attempt, it seems to me is in the right direction." Debs planned to organize a small migration of unemployed easterners to the state. But when the SDA announced intentions to "devote themselves to the cause of socialism through the party and ballot," he abandoned the colony idea.[32]

But other Washington socialists did not abandon colonization plans. In September 1898 they incorporated a new and significant colony organization, which they called the Cooperative Brotherhood. Founded with support from Seattle's SDA leadership, the colony, Olalla, spread along Burley Creek on Puget Sound's Henderson Bay. The first settlers arrived on October 20, 1898, and in time the colony's common name became Burley. Its newspaper, the *Cooperator*, warned comrades, "Do not come to the brotherhood expecting to see fine brick buildings, paved streets and sidewalks, electric cars, theaters, etc. On the contrary, you might expect to find a very thinly settled and undeveloped country, and things very much in the rough."

Strict Marxists and "scientific socialists" of the period dismissed voluntary colonies like Burley as ideologically weak. Colony residents, however, remained true to socialist principles. They firmly believed in the principles of "helping and sharing" and industrial socialism. Like the other cooperative colonies, however, Burley experienced internal conflicts. After only six months disputes arose between directors and laborers. Eventually greed, personal disagreements, and resentment sank the colony. Although in 1912 trustees began the colony's dissolution, it had survived far longer than any other "experimental" communal socialistic group in the state.[33]

Colonization efforts neither socialized Washington nor changed the Pacific Northwest's political landscape. Sites like Equality, according to historian Charles LeWarne, "made little impress politically." However, these various colonization efforts may have helped later socialist candidates, because as LeWarne observed, an ongoing network of socialists continued to thrive in Washington towns located near former colonies.[34]

During the 1890s socialism took a more active role in northwest politics than in any previous decade, and those calling themselves socialists stepped up their participation. Sympathetic national observers, such as author and committed socialist Jack London, celebrated the seemingly swelling tide of socialism at the ballot box. "Here is class animosity in the political world with a vengeance," he wrote. Citing a growth of 125,000 socialist votes between 1888 and 1900, London remained convinced that "it is the revolution that flourishes and increases." Accordingly, activism expanded in the Socialist Labor Party, the Social Democrat Party, and among socialists generally. Flyers and speakers promoting socialism appeared more frequently in the Pacific Northwest. In 1901, the Reverend Charles Vail of Tacoma, touted as "One of [the] Country's most noted writers on Socialistic Questions," offered a free lecture for curious listeners.[35]

The 1890s also spurred the Northwest's first socialist newspapers, particularly in Oregon. In 1895 the Portland Academy of Socialism launched Portland's *Leader*. In 1901 Portland socialists introduced the *Pacific Coast Citizen*. Former Populist papers, such as the *Recorder*, published from 1891 to 1901, in Bandon, Oregon, also moved toward socialism. Activists in Albany produced a weekly called the *People's Press*. Established in 1894 with Populist leanings, in 1901 it became the official organ of the Socialist Party of Oregon.[36]

Increasingly organized, socialist parties also gained political prominence. Despite its small national membership, the Socialist Labor Party continued to offer candidates for office, appealing to Washington voters with characteristic class rhetoric. An SLP flyer instructed wage workers: "Let your masters vote the ticket of their class: that of the Republican or Democratic Party. You should vote the ticket of your class: that of the Socialist Labor Party . . . Do not scab on election day." Similarly, Social Democracy of America locals gained attention. In 1898 the *Spokesman-Review* reported that the SDA was "thoroughly organized" in Whitman County, Washington, and Latah County, Idaho. Reports from organizers claimed that "organizations of the social democracy are being made in every precinct." Based on agrarian support among farmers in Washington and Idaho's fertile, rolling Palouse region, the local organizations promised to "cut quite a figure in the coming election[s]."

The Social Democratic Party, an outgrowth of the split within the ranks of the Social Democracy of America, entered the northwest political arena in the last year of the nineteenth century. In May 1899 Montana's Social Democrats organized. The activists met in Butte, and twelve charter members joined Butte Local No. 1. On October 4, 1899, the SDP issued a second charter to organizers in Chico (now called Hot Springs). By 1900 Montana socialists claimed approximately one hundred members. The SDP national secretary, William Butscher, sent Oregon organizers his "best wishes for the success of Socialism" in the state. And in 1900 two former Populists, David C. Coates and H. L. Hughes, formed Spokane's SDP chapter. News of SDP activities began to appear in mainstream newspapers. The *Seattle Post-Intelligencer* reported on the King County socialist convention on October 6, 1900.[37]

Despite their increased activism, various factors prevented socialists from making headway in elections. First, socialist candidates representing different parties drew from a limited pool of supporters. Separate parties in name, ideology, and membership, the SLP and SDP ran concurrent campaigns. In 1900, Pierce County, Washington, socialists from both the SLP and the SDP offered candidates for twenty-three positions. In a Multnomah County, Oregon, congressional race, the SDP and the SLP both ran candidates, which split the socialist vote in failed efforts. When socialists ran only one candidate per office they were more successful. In Oregon, the lone socialist presidential candidate, Eugene Debs, representing the SDP, performed well in industrialized Multnomah County, finishing behind the Republican, Democratic, and Prohibition candidates, but ahead of the candidate of the Populist Party.[38]

Other obstacles plagued early socialist politics. The *Oregonian* reported in 1898 that King County Social Democrats (who had been labeled "Debsites") were "beset with difficulties." The Seattle-area party experienced several problems. Some socialist candidates refused to accept nominations, while others faced opposition from established groups. During the 1898 election, for example, the King County auditor refused socialists a place on the ticket, citing an ambiguous violation: "failure to comply with the law."[39]

In addition to a lack of cohesiveness, socialist ties to unions continued to hinder party distinctiveness because union endorsements often still went to Republicans and Democrats. Idaho socialists, especially in the north, tied their politics to the radical Western Federation of Miners. During the 1890s, John Stevens, an active organizer for the SDP in Oregon, was also a card-carrying member of the Knights of Labor. J. A. Anthony, a member of the Seattle Painter's Union, delivered lectures in Tacoma's SLP hall. As these examples indicate, socialist organizers and voters did not operate entirely autonomously, which continued to encumber party identity.[40]

The decline of Populism stood as a final obstacle to the growth of socialist politics. During its 1896 campaign for William Jennings Bryan, the People's Party, or Populists, had united western agrarian voters. But the Populists' fusion with Democrats secured a victory for William McKinley and the Republicans and cost the Populists their political identity. And as socialists attempted to assert themselves politically from 1896 to 1900, the remnants of Populism inhibited their progress. During the 1896 campaign, prominent socialists such as Eugene Debs had also endorsed Bryan, believing him the leader of "the great uprising of the masses against the classes."

Not all socialists embraced Populism. At their 1896 convention the SLP claimed "the Populist Party cannot truly represent the class interest of the wealth-producers of this country." Yet, Debs's endorsement of Bryan demonstrated the early fluidity that existed between Populists and socialists. The *Spokesman-Review* observed this political intermingling. It claimed that "most of the middle-of-the-roaders of the populist party [referring to Populists who proposed fusion with Bryan Democrats] are socialists." On May 15, 1895, Debs visited Spokane. Speaking in support of the People's Party, he embraced the "philanthropic, patriotic movement" that can "work out the emancipation of the working men." As Carlos Schwantes observed, Populism and socialism had commonalities: both aimed at "inhibiting social privilege and arguing for strong government in the economy."[41]

This relationship had political consequences, particularly for upstart socialists. Because of their support for Populist candidates, socialist candidates did not have the backing to run in the 1896 election. Instead, Prohibition and National Democratic Party candidates were the alternatives to Republican, Democratic, and Populist candidates. The rhetoric of Populist detractors exemplified socialism's unfavorable reputation. "Bryanism," announced the pro-Republican *Oregonian*, "is Socialism." The Bryan/Democrat fusion ticket, critics argued, "appeals to human envy, jealousy and unrest, by such promises as this to produce equality of condition. . . . It is the argument of socialism."[42] The Populist-socialist association, while devoid of electoral victories, helped socialists establish themselves in the political mainstream.

After the 1896 defeat, Populists limped into the 1900 elections while socialists mobilized to disassociate themselves from Populism. Because many "middle-of-the-road" socialists (less dogmatic socialists who supported Populist planks such as government ownership of railroads and were willing to abandon abolishment of the wage system) had previously voted Populist, their votes might now go to socialists. Some socialists welcomed their new political opportunities. As the pages of the new *International Socialist Review* announced: "The populist party is today but a memory." In the Pacific Northwest, the *Oregonian* agreed: "The populistic-fusionistic ticket is deader than a dead duck."[43]

Nevertheless, intermingling between Populists and socialists continued. When Bryan ran for president as a Democrat in 1900, supporters asked Debs to withdraw from the race, still believing Bryan's "movement against monopoly . . . is the first practical step toward the co-operative commonwealth." Debs refused the request, declaring he was "in this contest to stay." For the 1900 elections, Washington's Populists agreed not to offer candidates. Accordingly, delegates meeting in Spokane passed resolutions calling for endorsements of the Social Democracy ticket.[44]

The 1896 Populist-Democratic (and implicitly socialist) fusion provided an important lesson for socialists at the national level. They recognized the value of party agreement and distinctiveness. By the turn of the twentieth century, mindful of the Populist fate, socialists now issued pleas for a "united and harmonious socialist movement." While the SLP, SDP, and utopian colonists had a common "capitalist enemy," issues of ideology, leadership, and propaganda threatened socialist cohesiveness. "Only a factional and divided socialist movement can defeat socialism," proclaimed the new *International Socialist Review* in 1901. The journal's editor, A. M. Simons, later emphasized the necessity of "organic unity" among American socialists. The challenge, however, proved to be the ability to heed their own warnings.[45]

By 1900 socialists had become increasingly optimistic about the future. Assuming they could achieve political unity, they could capitalize on a swelling niche for socialist ideologies and build a stable and autonomous party. Despite what they saw nationally as "ignorant, bitter and unreasoning prejudice" within the United States political system, they celebrated the "unprecedented activity" of the late nineteenth century. "In school and college and church, in clubs and public halls everywhere," they claimed, "socialism is the central theme of discussion." Recent elections, too, had encouraged them. In the general elections of 1898 their candidates received 91,000 votes, an increase of nearly 200 percent over 1896. Jack London continued to applaud socialism's advance. "On every country its grip closes tighter year by year," he wrote. "Nor has this flame of revolution left the United States untouched."[46]

The Pacific Northwest's economic and social disorder during the 1890s had signaled strained labor relations. Socialists stood convinced that support for their cause would grow. Eugene Debs predicted the northwestern states "will forge to the front." "The political trend," he argued, "is steadily toward Socialism."[47]

Although some citizens in the Pacific Northwest had flirted with socialism through pockets of political activism and colonization experiments, no cohesive socialist movement had materialized in the late nineteenth century. At the turn of the century, however, national socialist leaders called for a "collectivist socialist party" to unify the growing yet divided movement. The socialist movement, wrote the *International Socialist Review* in 1901, "appears to be approaching a climax." That year socialists from around the country met in Indianapolis, Indiana, to discuss the feasibility of a new and expansive party.[48] Northwest socialists ultimately embraced this new organization, the Socialist Party of America, and over the next twenty years enjoyed unprecedented political strides and electoral successes.

2

Building "A Typically American Party"
Feats and Obstacles, 1901–1905

This is no spontaneous and vague uprising of a large mass of discontented and miserable people. On the contrary, the propaganda is intellectual; the movement is based upon economic necessity and is in line with social evolution. The revolutionist is no starved and diseased slave in the shambles at the bottom of the social pit, but is, in the main, a hearty, well-fed workingman, who sees the shambles waiting for him and his children. Jack London, "Revolution," 1905

Our Country is the World—Our Countrymen all Mankind. *Liberator*, Portland, Oregon, 1903

IN the summer of 1901, socialists from around the country converged on Indianapolis, Indiana, for the first national convention of the Social Democratic Party (SDP). Meeting at the Masonic Hall, the attendees faced a difficult task: overcoming the ideological and regional fragmentation that increasingly nagged American socialists. The convention came at a critical time for party politics. The new leadership recognized it as a valuable political opportunity. Writing in the *International Socialist Review* in 1900, George Herron had contended, "Now is the time of socialist salvation, if we are great enough to respond to the greatness of our opportunity"; the SDP convention appeared to be where "salvation" could occur. A. M. Simons, the *International Socialist Review* editor, agreed. "That the present moment is a critical one in the history of the socialist movement in America is commonplace," he wrote. "It would seem probable that the Indianapolis convention would mark the turning point."[1]

When the convention commenced on July 29, 1901, 124 delegates filled the hall. Only the strictest Marxists from the Socialist Labor Party (SLP), under New Yorker Daniel DeLeon's leadership, avoided the meeting and therefore did not participate in any of the significant changes delegates would agree to. This absence aside, the convention was the culmination of approximately three years of visible cooperation between advocates calling for unity within the SDP and the SLP. For optimistic socialists in attendance, according to historian David Shannon, "the question was when, not if, the American people—the American working people—would see the logic of industrial history and vote the Socialist Party into office to socialize and democratize the American economy."[2]

At that July meeting, at least in name and principle, a politically harmonious socialist party emerged. Delegates formed the Socialist Party of America (SPA), the first national party in the United States to advocate the abolition of the wage system and the emancipation of the nation's working class from the chains of capitalistic exploitation. The Unity convention, as socialists called it, seemed to symbolize a lasting alliance of America's like-minded socialist activists and politicians. Participants left the SDP's national meeting having formally adopted the "Socialist Party" moniker. In the name of political harmony, they put aside their differences, at least temporarily. News of the convention quickly reached the Northwest. The *Seattle Post-Intelligencer*, running the headline "Socialists Seek Harmony," closely followed the convention proceedings. "The rational Socialist convention," it reported, had "made an effort to harmonize, and was partially successful." As the paper revealed, however, socialist leaders still recognized their differences. At the convention, the paper observed, "Eugene V. Debs admits his party is composed of factions." Debs's admission rang particularly true because even the new party platform accepted Progressive calls for increased wages rather than an abolition of the wage system, which had long been a fundamental socialist principle. Despite the first warning signs of ideological factionalism, the new socialist party had made important organizational and political strides. Party members mobilized under the new banner of the SPA to organize locals, propagandize the masses, and offer candidates. Accordingly, during its first decade and a half, the Socialist Party experienced party growth unequaled in American history.[3]

Once established, the SPA provided the party mechanism behind some of American socialism's most impressive electoral successes. In the Pacific Northwest, particularly, the new party galvanized the region's socialist politics. However, almost immediately, it also faced challenges of cohesiveness. Despite its meaningful political strides, the party's earliest years in this region revealed significant internal divisions and external challenges.

Pacific Northwest organizers, free from an overbearing national party structure, wasted little time getting their message out. And it did not take the Unity convention to mobilize Montana's socialists. In 1899 the state's activists had already formed their first local under the auspices of the SDP. Based in Butte, the chapter had an unassuming twelve charter members. Acting under the banner of the SPA and with state committee support, however, Montana's socialists moved into the twentieth century and enjoyed exponential party growth. Modestly organized in January 1900 with six locals and one hundred members, the new state party boasted four hundred adherents by 1904. As John N. Heldt, of Helena, serving as the first state secretary, made clear, socialist sympathies extended beyond the working-class stronghold of Butte. Within two years the Montana socialists had twenty-five locals. Like their Montana counterparts, the number of socialists in Oregon also grew, especially after the SPA's creation. Accordingly, in the first years of the twentieth century locals organized throughout the state. In 1903 F. E. Latimer, editor of Portland's new socialist newspaper, the *Liberator*, visited comrades in Woodburn, Salem, Albany, Tangent, Shedds, Harrisburg, Eugene, Roseburg, Grant's Pass, Medford, and Ashland.[4]

While party growth in Montana and Oregon pointed to growing SPA influence, the new organization did not always dramatically alter socialist memberships. In fact, except for its new

name, the Socialist Party of Washington (SPW) saw few fundamental changes after the establishment of the SPA. While a new
party structure outwardly reorganized the nation's socialists it
did not necessarily translate into an increase of members.
Instead, independent political action at the grass-roots level led
Washington to become "one of the movement's strongholds." By
late 1902 the Socialist Party of Washington possessed forty-five
locals and approximately one thousand members.[5]

Along with party organizing, northwest socialists also
increased their propaganda work. One of the most significant
means of spreading party doctrine was the socialist press. The
SPA's national secretary, William Mailly, noted that the party
press "is gaining steadily in numbers and influence." The Pacific
Northwest socialist press was no exception. A number of the
region's first distinctively socialist papers appeared during the
party's early years, often with the direct involvement of state parties. Although not initially established as a specifically socialist
paper, Lewistown, Montana's *Judith Basin News* stands as the
state's first socialist newspaper. First published on September 17,
1902, with a politically independent mission, its coverage of
socialist organizing appeared with increasing regularity, and articles in early 1903 reported the organizing of new chapters at
Lewistown and Wilder. In April 1904, the paper moved from
Lewistown to Helena, changed its name to the *Montana News*,
and focused much of its space to matters of socialism and class-
consciousness. Socialist party leaders eventually assumed control
of the *Montana News* and by late 1905 its subtitle proudly
announced that it was "owned and published by the Socialist
Party of Montana."[6]

The Washington state party also worked with the socialist
press. In 1900, on the state's west side, Hermon Titus, a Harvard-
trained physician, who for almost a decade was the leader of
Washington's most radical leftists, established the *Seattle Socialist*.
The *Socialist* (as the paper was widely known), although unaffili-
ated with the SDP or SPA, aimed to "Organize the Slaves of Capital to Vote their own Emancipation." By 1902 the *Socialist*'s

circulation reached 2,500 and its reputation soared, making the newspaper "the most important SPA organ in the West." Following its lead, in 1902 the state party secretary, Joseph Gilbert, established *New Time* in Spokane.[7]

Oregon, a state that boasted some of the region's first socialist papers, also witnessed new publications. Established in 1903 in Portland, the *Liberator* preached socialist principles during its run as a short-lived weekly. Founded by T. E. Latimer, a former professor at the University of Washington, and A. E. Fowler, a Seattle cartoonist, they announced, "This is the only paper in Oregon that is owned and edited by the working class, for the working class, and will tell the truth in the interest of the working class." The paper drew praise from mainstream publications, demonstrating the socialist party's increased visibility and recognition. The mainstream *East Oregonian* described the *Liberator* as "a neat, well printed paper, ably edited and earnest in its advocacy of the doctrine of socialism. It . . . will be watched with interest by Oregon." The Socialist Party of Oregon began publication of its official newspaper in 1904 in Grant's Pass. Named the *Real Issue*, the paper's motto revealed its revolutionary attitude: "No Compromise, No Political Trading." In 1905 *Real Issue* relocated to Portland. The arrival of the *Liberator* and *Real Issue* typified an important era in Oregon's labor-minded press. According to Carlos Schwantes, 1900 marked the beginning of the "heyday" for socialist and labor papers in Oregon. That year, the weekly *Portland Labor Press* (after 1915 the *Oregon Labor Press*), the official organ of the AFL, began publication. In 1901, the *Pacific Coast Citizen*, another short-lived socialist journal, commenced circulation.[8]

As the proliferation of party newspapers indicates, northwest socialists took their ever-increasing propaganda duties seriously. Organizers placed great importance on the role of newspapers, party literature, and public rallies to enhance their prospects for electoral success. Newspapers such as the *Liberator* ordered socialists to "see to it that the Socialists in your precinct go to the polls and vote." Nationally, most socialists considered outreach

efforts, particularly those aimed at trade unions, their most crucial activity, and Pacific Northwest socialists committed considerable time and monies to this work. The *Liberator* summarized
Oregon's expenditures on propaganda and the significance of
spreading the party's message: "At a careful estimate, at least
$50,000 is being annually spent in Oregon in the cause of social-
ism. There is a socialist sentiment in Oregon that would scare the
old parties to death if it was crystallized into a concrete movement," it warned. In Washington, party leaders believed "the
main function of the socialist party was to organize and get a
strong dues-paying organization so when the crucial moment
came they would be able to do the job and take possession of the
industries." Washington socialists may even have placed newspapers and pamphlets ahead of all other work, including electoral
achievement. As Shannon asserted, the state's organizers "had
no intention of building a political party. To them the Socialist
Party was an educational or propagandist agency, not a political
group."[9]

Without question, newspaper accounts of both party happen-
ings and larger events, viewed through a socialistic lens,
remained the most visible and important organs of party
activism. But newspapers were not the only forms of early propaganda. Handbills and socialist literature also served as important tools, and printed matter regularly appeared on northwest
streets. In 1902 flyers in Helena, Montana, advertised a "Free
Lecture On Socialism, and What It Is" by Professor Walter
Thomas Mills of Chicago. The flyer urged, "Don't Miss it. It will
be interesting"; and to encourage women's attendance it
extended a "Special Invitation to the Ladies." Utopian or broadly
socialist literature, such as Edward Bellamy's 1888 book, *Looking
Backward,* also remained important to the popularization of
socialist principles, and regional radicals took these works to
heart. J. F. Mabie, one of the most active socialist organizers in
Montana, explained his conversion to socialism: "In 1902 I read
Bellamy's *Looking Backward*[.] I discovered myself and from that
time called myself a socialist."[10]

Industrial workers composed the party's core audience, but Pacific Northwest farmers were also a primary focus of attention. Party leaders recognized the sizable voting demographic among the region's agriculturalists and wanted farmers to identify with the collective working class. "The laborer, whether he toil in the field, factory, mine or office, with plow, hammer, pick or pen, is equally a member of the 'Working Class,'" announced an editorial in the *International Socialist Review*. Under the title "The Socialist Party and the Farmer," author A. M. Simons described the ways farmers would benefit from socialist systems. "The farmer," he wrote, "is much more of a producer than a consumer of the products of industry, and that even at the present time he will be materially benefited by the high wages and shorter hours which the Socialist seeks to secure for all workers, including the farmer."[11]

In the Northwest, *Socialist* founder Hermon Titus submitted a "Farmer Resolution" essay that echoed this appeal to agriculturalists and later reached a wider audience in the *International Socialist Review*. "We call upon the small farmers," he pleaded, "to look beyond their own class, to recognize the supreme class struggle between capital and wage labor and to join hands with that class which alone can bring freedom from all economical bondage." Farmers undoubtedly encountered socialists during the party's early years. By 1901 the *Yakima* (Wash.) *Herald* included special sections for socialists. In mid-1902 during a visit to Colfax, Washington, Eugene Debs addressed a gathering of approximately two thousand wheat farmers. More than other protest movements of the early twentieth century, socialist groups stood poised to capitalize on rural ferment and to attract members of the decaying Populist Party and Farmers' Alliances. In southern Idaho, in contrast to the industrial support offered in the Coeur d'Alene district, party involvement remained fundamentally agrarian. Similarly, in predominately agrarian areas such as Lewis County, Washington, socialists drew more support from farmers than any other group. Farmers, historian Marilyn Watkins argued, still believed in the spirit of Populism and, in its absence, embraced socialism as a similar solution to age-old questions surrounding production and capitalism.[12] Pacific Northwest socialists did not overlook the political potential and regional significance of agrarian protest and, in fact, made concerted efforts to incorporate them into the party fold.

As early party debate and political outreach continued, many argued that success in small, local, municipal elections stood as an important first step in the movement. Often debated in socialist journals, the issue of "municipal socialism" remained important. This socialist gradualism, that is, winning small elections and applying socialist policies at the local level, as historian William Leach argued, represented wider rejection of a new American culture that epitomized consumer capitalism gone awry. Gradualist socialist tactics stood as one such dissenting voice, and prominent national party leaders Morris Hillquit, Victor Berger, and John Spargo, among others, championed the party's evolutionary faction. For them, the ballot box offered the best means, within democratic institutions, to spread socialism. Although more radical critics of this approach dismissed municipal strategies as "slow-cialism," most socialists recognized and agitated for the municipal strategy. In an *International Socialist Review* article, Emile Vinck observed that socialists needed to "prove our practical ability in realizing reforms" on the local levels. "Municipal Socialism," he continued, "does not signify a special kind of socialism but [is] simply the application of the general principles of socialism to a particular department of political activity."[13] The strategy sought to win local elections through campaigns focused on promoting public ownership of such things as utilities and transportation systems and supporting labor-friendly social programs, such as free medical care to all.[14]

As elsewhere, socialists in the Pacific Northwest generally embraced municipal strategies and national party leaders likely encouraged them. As the 1904 elections neared, the *International Socialist Review* predicted that "a large number of Socialists will be elected to municipal positions within the next few months." Socialist papers in the Northwest adopted similar rhet-

oric. "It is entirely plausible," the *Liberator* declared optimisti-
cally, "to expect a victory as early as 1904." Yet, despite positive
attitudes and some encouraging electoral results, those victories
materialized slowly. In state elections, socialist candidates typically finished behind Republicans and Democrats, but often
ahead of Populist, Prohibitionist, and Progressive Party candidates. In Idaho, socialist candidates on the 1902 ballot finished
third in several races, illustrative of their growing and tempered
third-party legitimacy.[15]

Despite small successes at state polls, socialism's most impressive showings initially occurred in smaller municipal elections.
The Socialist Party of Washington's first political campaigns were
particularly encouraging. In 1901 two party members, Titus and
John T. Oldman ran for seats on the King County Board of Education and together received approximately 25 percent of the
vote. By 1904 Washington socialists took an even more visible
role in politics. In state elections that year, fifty-five candidates
ran for several state and King County positions. Refusing to
abandon its purist ideological agenda to the SPA, the SLP also
ran twenty-seven candidates. The SPW, however, took the lead in
attacking state Republicans and Democrats, criticizing them in
a pre-election gathering at Seattle's Carpenter's Hall. "Socialists
Scold Both Big Parties," reported the *Seattle Post-Intelligencer*. The
paper described "quite a good many people in attendance" and
noted "some applause" during the speeches.[16]

In Montana, socialist names also began regularly appearing
on ballots, signaling the party's first steps toward municipal
socialism. In 1902 George Sproule ran for Congress, becoming
the state's first socialist candidate. His Montana comrades were
no doubt pleased that he received over three thousand votes.
Following his lead, other socialists met with greater success at
the local level. Montana's early socialist politics centered in the
Deer Lodge Valley, where copper magnate Marcus Daly built his
company town, Anaconda. Given its predominately working
class population, the city embraced unionism, and by 1902 Anaconda had twenty-seven local unions with 1,050 members. With

a fair amount of success, Montana socialists courted Anaconda's union-friendly population. At its 1902 convention the Montana Federation of Labor (MFL) overwhelming supported the recent endorsements of the Western Federation of Miners (WFM) and the AFL of the socialist party. In 1903, with support from the Anaconda Central Labor Council and many of the town's working-class residents, Anaconda socialists held their city convention to prepare for local elections. Ninety-two delegates nominated a number of municipal candidates, including cigar maker John Frinke for mayor. With the backing of the new *Anaconda Labor-Socialist*, Frinke won with an impressive 46 percent of the vote. In addition to the mayoralty, Anaconda socialists also won city treasurer and police judge positions.

Despite achieving an important electoral victory for socialism, Mayor Frinke faced almost immediate challenges. First, nonsocialists on the Anaconda city council battled with his new administration. Further, the Anaconda Company rewarded employees sympathetic to Frinke with pink slips, that is, dismissal from work. Company and WFM records vary widely, and estimates of terminations numbered anywhere between fifty and five hundred men. Faced with such stiff personal and political competition, Frinke and his socialist comrades lost badly in their 1905 bids for reelection. Although Frinke's embattled administration was "merely custodial," according to historians Jerry Calvert and John Enyeart, Frinke's 1904 election represented the first significant socialist electoral victory in the American West.[17]

Socialists in western states also saw marked increases in voter support during national elections. Under the auspices of the SDP, Debs's presidential candidacy in 1900 had garnered only 4,181 votes (1.2 percent) in the Pacific Northwest and 86,936 (0.62 percent) nationally. Conversely, despite continued competition from the Socialist Labor Party, the new SPA proved an increasingly organized and viable political player. In the 1904 elections the SPA appeared on the ballot in forty-three states, seven more than in 1900. The declining SLP, meanwhile, appeared on ballots in only fourteen states, six fewer than in 1900. When the first returns from the 1904 election were tallied, they seemed to reinforce Debs's earlier assertions that "the political trend is steadily toward Socialism." Socialists estimated the party's state votes at 4,200 in Idaho, 8,000 in Montana, 11,000 in Oregon, and 12,000 in Washington. Other socialist estimates claimed they would receive half a million votes nationally. In an announcement from New York, national party leaders reported between 10,000 and 15,000 socialist votes in Washington, and between 5,000 and 10,000 in Idaho, Montana, and Oregon. These estimates proved fairly accurate. The final socialist vote in the Northwest states was 4,949 (6.8 percent) in Idaho, 5,675 (8.9 percent) in Montana, 7,479 (8.3 percent) in Oregon, and 10,023 (6.9 percent) in Washington. In 1904 the average percentage of socialist support in the Northwest was 7.73, considerably higher than the national average of 2.98. Northwest socialists, as their electoral percentages indicate, forged to the front of regional politics and outpaced socialist support in other regions.[18]

The SPA's first national election, an impressive gain over 1900, brought the party much-needed attention from mainstream newspapers. In the Pacific Northwest, an *Oregonian* headline declared, "Socialist Vote Increases." The paper reported that "one of the noteworthy exhibits" of the 1904 election was "the relatively large vote cast for the Socialist ticket." In several Oregon counties Debs ran ahead of Democrat Alton Parker. The *International Socialist Review* spoke highly of "the growth in . . . the Pacific States" and pointed to the region as one pure in ideology and representative of party growth. Recapping the "Lessons from the Socialist Vote," the journal boasted, "The socialist vote has shown the strongest and most persistent growth in those localities where the membership has been most thoroughly trained in the principles of socialism."[19] By 1904 the region's socialists had reason for optimism.

While northwest socialists experienced important party growth and electoral strides in its first years, both internal and external difficulties had already surfaced. To socialists in the East, however,

their comrades in the West and Northwest had gained a reputation for radical, cohesive politics. In 1902 Eugene Debs accounted
for this "revolutionary spirit of the proletariat of the rugged and
sparsely settled mountain States." He called the class-conscious
union movement in the West "historic in origin and development
and every Socialist should recognize its mission and encourage its
growth." A correspondent for Philadelphia's *Socialist* wrote of the
West that "the socialist movement is seen to most advantage in the
state of Washington and [in] British Columbia . . . [where] [t]he
bulk of its members are proletarians, who make it their business
to understand the question thoroughly." Some of the first historical studies of socialism echoed this radical sentiment. Historian
David Shannon, for example, similarly characterized the revolutionary nature of western socialism. "In the Rocky Mountains and
the Pacific Northwest," he wrote, "the Socialist movement was
dominated by revolutionaries. Here was the stronghold of Bill
Haywood and the IWW. Here was clearly the most radical section
of the Socialist Party."[20] While radicalism existed in the Northwest,
those outside of the region were quick to characterize its exceptional and cohesive radicalism.

From its inception, however, the Socialist Party of America was
not harmonious. As the 1901 Unity convention had indicated,
serious ideological divisions existed among America's socialists.
The new SPA included southern agriculturalists, non-Marxist
Christians, "by the book" Marxists, former Populists, and syndicalists sympathetic to trade unionism. Schwantes wrote that the
establishment of the SPA "brought only the *illusion* of unity to
the movement." On the national level, differences and rivalries
still divided socialists. The SPA, according to Shannon, was "a
typically American party in the sense that it extended from coast
to coast." However, he observed that in most regions of the country, socialists advocated a "variety of social philosophies."[21]

The party's first internal test dealt with the relationship
between state committees and the national party. Regional
organizations enjoyed a great deal of autonomy from the
national organization. Based in Springfield, Massachusetts, the

SPA leadership was far removed from the activism of the West and Northwest. This physical distance from the SPA hierarchy contributed to the party's regional distinctiveness as northwest leaders remained beyond a watchful and sometimes domineering national party. Yet organizational independence was one factor in socialism's earlier divisiveness and was thus a condition of the new SPA's party structure. According to Schwantes, "The years of wrangling" before the establishment of the SPA "allowed state organizations to win a high degree of autonomy." The 1901 convention gave "the state committees sole control of all matters pertaining to organization within the respective states." Debated at the Unity convention in Indianapolis, this autonomy clause was inserted only after "long and heated debate."[22]

As a consequence, the SPA demanded only that state organizations submit monthly reports and dues payments. But as the new party discovered, the lack of checks and balances between the national leadership and regional activists created organizational turmoil. State organizations, often delinquent in reports and dues payments, faced little enforcement from the national secretary and the executive committee. National secretary William Mailly recognized his inability to act. "The existing political system [the national constitution] requires that state autonomy must necessarily continue to be the basis of organization," he reported, "but its boundaries and limitations must be more definitely prescribed." On the one hand there were cases of state leaders "neglecting their duties or perverting their powers," yet the "national officers are powerless to act." Therefore, since the 1901 Unity convention, the *International Socialist Review* pointed out, it had been "impossible . . . to determine the number of locals and membership of the party in the United States." The *Review* also reported that in some states "the work of organization" was "totally neglected."[23]

Although no evidence pointed to delinquent state organizations in the Pacific Northwest, disorganization existed. In 1903, Clackamas County socialists realized their need for a state convention because local party leaders kept no records of locals in good standing, and when challenged, quickly blamed the confusion on "a general misunderstanding of party and state requirements." The Northwest was not totally out of touch with the SPA, however, as the region's participation in the 1904 national convention showed. Socialists from the region took an increasingly prominent role in the party's organizational affairs. Not only was Hermon Titus one of nine signatories to the national party's constitution, but the Pacific Northwest also sent eight delegates to the meeting.[24]

Northwest socialists, although largely independent of the SPA's executive committee, still faced infighting similar to the national bickering between radicals and moderates. Despite their radical reputation, the region's socialists did not always fit the extremist label; many Pacific Northwest socialists remained restrained advocates of immediate demands and municipal socialism. Those "other Socialists," according to Schwantes, "derived their anti-capitalism more from the New Testament or *Looking Backward* than *Das Kapital*."[25] The northwest party's fragmentation, like that of the national movement, arose primarily from doctrinal differences.

Washington's socialists provided the party's strongest example of early internal divisions. Since its inception, the SPW remained bitterly split between moderate and radical factions. In 1900 E. Lux, a former member of the SDP, ran for mayor of Whatcom. He ran a successful campaign, receiving a plurality of 556 votes. Yet *Socialist* editor Titus, leader of the SPW's most radical wing, openly criticized Lux's moderate ideology. According to historian Jonathan Dembo, the "Reds" and Titus "tried to keep the SPW on a radical, class conscious, Marxist, revolutionary course." Titus stood in open defiance of moderate party members, the so-called "gas and water" socialists. Those "commonsense socialists" within the SPW, also called "Yellows," advocated gradual campaigns for public ownership of various institutions and union-friendly positions on issues. From the establishment of the SPA until approximately 1909, Titus led the SPW's "Red faction."[26]

Most socialists, however, agreed on the necessity of mobilizing through direct political action. The new Socialist Party of America, according to Shannon, was "firmly committed to the ballot box," and while socialists may have debated the form and extent of political involvement, the SPA hoped to win elections just as Republicans and Democrats did. However, the political goals of socialists, compared to "capitalist" parties, differed greatly. They hoped municipally gained political power would translate to socialization. "Once the government is so controlled," socialists in 1902 declared, "once, in short, that the Socialists are in power (and they can hardly be expected to accomplish much before)— they can use that government, state, national or local, in the interest of the creators of wealth."[27]

While a commitment to political action united them, socialists also agreed on a fundamental ideological point: the evils of capitalism. "Their ultimate aim," historian Alan Dawley believed, "was to replace the existing system with a more humane and harmonious one." The SPA's 1904 national platform, signed by nine party members including Debs, Berger, and Titus, explained their steadfast objections to capitalism: "Capitalism is the enemy and destroyer of essential private property. Its development is through the legalized confiscation of all that the labor of the working class produces, above its subsistence wage. The private ownership of the means of employment grounds society in an economic slavery, which renders intellectual and political tyranny inevitable."[28]

Regardless of region, socialists rallied around a set of shared political beliefs. Their commitments to electoral power and especially to anti-capitalist positions proved unifying. These common commitments, Shannon observed, united socialists despite their infighting. "Thus the old Socialist party," he wrote, "was a collection of quite diverse and often warring groups, held together by what proved later to be a poor adhesive, common hostility to industrial capitalism." Socialists hoped to expose capitalism's imperfections, evident in recent economic downturns, and rally America's workers. The SPA's 1904 national platform declared: "Socialism . . . comes to rescue the people from the fast increasing and successful assault of capitalism upon the liberty of the individual." United, workers could bring down the wage system. Socialists would have applauded author, activist, and party member Jack London for his 1905 description of their cause as "a distinctly working-class revolt. The workers of the world, as a class, are fighting the capitalists of the world, as a class." Party members shared a "belief in a better and more moral cooperative society, which could be built through the efforts of a united, class-conscious working class," historian Melvyn Dubofsky contended. Yet socialists remained at odds over their goals and the appropriate paths to radicalization.[29]

From 1901 to 1905, the socialist relationship to unionism—the already familiar "fusion" issue—also surfaced as an important challenge to the party. In an essay titled "Economic Versus Political Power of Labor," F. G. R. Gordon articulated the two perspectives. Socialists, he claimed, "declare that the only way to emancipate the wage workers is through political revolution." Simultaneously, Gordon noted, "the pure and simple trade unionist just as stoutly maintains that the wage class will be emancipated by his economic organization." Northwest socialists, like their comrades elsewhere, debated the extent and direction of their movement's relationship to "bread and butter" labor unions. The question of whether they should provide party support for organized labor not only strained socialists' standing with union members, but the debate also kept them at odds with one another.[30]

During the party's first years, the blurred lines between socialism and unionism complicated socialist politics. Intermingling of socialists and unions, particularly the AFL, continued, as socialists joined unions and vice versa. In 1902 Eugene Debs said openly: "I am the friend, not the enemy of the American Federation of Labor." Debs welcomed this relationship, because the AFL subsidiary in the West, the Western Federation of Miners, he noted, had recently "adopted the platform of the Socialist Party and pledged the support of their organizations to the International Socialist movement." But as others voiced their concern about the usefulness of this move, the socialist-AFL relationship proved increasingly contentious. The "fusion" matter became a great source of conflict within the SPA's ranks. "One of the issues which kept the factions of the Socialist party at odds," David Shannon suggested, "was the question of what attitude it should take toward the American Federation of Labor."

Fueling this debate were the attitudes of various party members, particularly during times of grass-roots socialist activism. In 1903, for example, blacksmiths, saloonkeepers, and carpenters in Caldwell, Idaho, aligned themselves with the pro-socialist American Labor Union in defiance of the town's AFL leaders. Because some moderate socialist sympathizers, both within and outside the SPA, still supported trade unionism, party radicals grew increasingly uneasy. According to Shannon, "the conservatives, putting their faith in the power of the ballot, held that the party had to gain the support of the AFL rank and file." It became clear that these differing perspectives, even in the party's infancy, could make unionism the SPA's most divisive issue. According to Schwantes, "The continuing controversy . . . threatened to tear the new party asunder."[31]

The lack of socialist agreement on fusion had clear political implications. Many in the AFL observed the SPA infighting regarding the party's role toward organized labor, and to AFL critics, the socialists hardly looked like a cohesive party. A 1903 *American Federationist* article criticized the socialist failure to unify. "Almost every socialist writer and orator declares that the wage class are in a vast majority," it observed, "and to gain control of government its members only have to vote together for the socialist party. Of course, you can take your choice as to which socialist party." To some unionists the socialist party's divided position on fusion was dispiriting. To complicate matters, other unionists opposed political socialism. AFL president Samuel Gompers told socialists, "Economically, you are unsound; socially, you are wrong; industrially, you are an impossibility."[32] Political disagreements and the tenuous relationship

between socialists and unionists mired the union support necessary to launch a working-class revolt and strengthen socialist
politics.

In Washington State, the SPW experienced its share of the
fusion debate. Amidst the infighting between Reds and Yellows,
the fusion issue fueled disagreements. Not surprisingly, Yellows
advocated cooperation with business and labor leaders in the
name of electoral success. Meanwhile, the SPW's Red faction
rejected cooperation with these alliances, believing it diluted
socialist convictions. Hermon Titus, on behalf of the SPW's radical wing, publicly aired his criticisms of unionism's political
ineptitude in the *International Socialist Review*. "The growing
power of concentrated capital renders even the best organized
labor unions more and more impotent and must make it evident
that only by unified action on the political field can labor achieve
any permanent benefit for itself," he wrote. "Nothing short of
the Socialist program, abolishing the wage system itself, will be
of any use as a political demand."[33]

The AFL's dedication to limiting its involvement in political
matters complicated socialist campaigns, and Pacific Northwest
socialists still failed, as Republicans and Democrats did, to court
important union endorsements. Unsupportive organizations
that represented large elements of the working class further hindered socialist success. Many union members still openly resisted
socialist politics. The pages of the AFL's *American Federationist*
announced, "The great trade union leaders of this nation, with
hardly an exception, are opposed to socialist parties."[34] For
socialists, anti-union sentiment within the party, coupled with
unions determined to stay out of politics, made union members
and their votes difficult to secure.

Despite infighting over ideological interpretation, methods of
tactical maneuvering, and the role of trade unionism, socialists in
the Northwest built state organizations and achieved modest electoral successes. From 1901 to 1905 party memberships rose and
socialist candidates captured increasingly more votes. The SPA
appeared united over fundamental political and ideological posi-

tions, namely an aversion to capitalism and a commitment to electoral strategies. But challenges to party cohesiveness and future political achievement were apparent. Despite the first hints of problems within the party that would plague their efforts, Pacific Northwest socialists moved their cause forward with what continued to be their characteristic rhetorical optimism.

3

"Friends and Enemies"
Old and New Challenges, 1905–1910

Socialism is coming. Socialism is the social philosophy of the twentieth century. It has come at a time when the world is ready for it and when its acceptance by the masses is but a matter of their understanding of its mission. Appeal to Reason, February 6, 1909

FROM 1905 to 1910, Socialist Party of America members and supporters in the Pacific Northwest steadily moved the party forward as a regionally valid political force. Their activism and organizations across the region grew despite old and new challenges and lingering party squabbling. In addition, an increasingly political American Federation of Labor challenged socialist politics. Finally, the new Industrial Workers of the World, established in 1905, also threatened to encroach on the socialist's agenda and power. Amidst a myriad of internal challenges and potentially contentious "labor voices," the region's socialists managed to build party activism, power, and notoriety.

After the formation of the SPA in 1901, the Northwest's socialists maintained, with some exceptions, a high level of party activism and growth. The party played an increasingly important role in regional politics and hoped to be the sole political voice for Pacific Northwest wage workers. In 1905, as noted earlier, Jack London celebrated the national swell of socialist support. "Here is class animosity in the political world with a vengeance," he wrote. In 1888 he had noted that the United States had only two thousand "revolutionists," yet by 1904, 435,000 voters pledged their support to socialist candidates. The Pacific Northwest was no exception, with socialists' names increasingly appearing on ballots. During the 1906 elections, twenty-five states, including the four in the Northwest, offered socialist tickets. When Oregon's socialists entered nine candidates for state and federal offices that year, each finished either second or third.[1]

This increasing national and regional socialist presence helped to constitute a legitimate third-party alternative to Democrats and Republicans. At the beginning of the twentieth century, political reform came from socialists, populists, and others who were reacting to established and often corrupt party machines, bosses, and courts. Historian Stephen Skowronek has contended that the fight became one for power and control over new bureaucratic and administrative systems, and third-party political opportunities proliferated. The Pacific Northwest typified these national trends during the Progressive era as regional socialists successfully positioned themselves as *the* third-party voice for American labor. Even as socialists and their agenda remained fervently radical, their ideological and political positions did not hinder socialism's political legitimacy. In fact, as historian Stephen Diner observed, socialists seemed unchallenged in their abilities to keep "'the labor question' as a central issue in the policy debates of the Progressive Era." Notably, a few mainstream northwest newspapers commented on the party's legitimacy. "The Socialists have an issue which is likely to become more formidable as time passes," noted the *Oregonian*, "and there is no hope whatever that their party will merge with any other, or dissolve." No longer on the outside looking in, the newspaper noted of them, socialists had established themselves despite "a vigorous two-party system," and now, the paper continued, "minor parties have grown to major ones."[2]

By 1908 socialists were optimistic about the party's potential, in historian Nick Salvatore's words, hoping for "magnificent results" in the upcoming election cycle. The reform movement of the Progressive era appealed to the moderate message of some socialists. The SPA now also seemed capable of curbing its "conflicting tendencies" for the sake of political progress. "Capitalism is breaking down," announced the *International Socialist*

Review, and the party drew upon its strong organization to appeal to prospective voters. Nationally the party grew from fewer than ten thousand members in 1901 to more than forty thousand in 1908. Eugene Debs traveled across the country, hoping that one million more voters might support socialists at the polls that autumn. For the 1908 races, according to historian Ira Kipnis, socialists "threw themselves into the presidential campaign with an enthusiasm for party work which had not been shown since the 1904 election."[3]

During the 1908 campaign, Pacific Northwest socialists demonstrated a typical party optimism. The region's state secretaries submitted hopeful reports to the *International Socialist Review* on the eve of the election. "The situation in Idaho is very promising and satisfactory," reported secretary Thomas J. Coonrod. The Idaho membership had doubled since January and socialists there hoped to triple their 1904 vote and "cause the enemy to take notice." In Montana, socialists hoped for ten thousand votes and the state party organizers remained especially positive because of recent municipal victories in Red Lodge and Livingston. Oregon's state secretary, Thomas A. Sladden, dubbed his state a "seething mass of Socialism." Sladden and the state party now boasted seventy-four local chapters, compared to only thirty-three four years earlier. Oregon's "Socialists organize themselves like clouds form under the hot sun," he observed. Washington's socialists echoed their comrades' confidence. The SPW secretary, R. Krueger, promised "at least 22,000 votes." The state party had over one hundred locals and a committed membership; in 1908 they voluntarily raised party dues.[4]

When polls closed in 1908, socialists met the outcome with mixed feelings. Despite stagnation, and in some cases decline, in socialist support, Debs and the party claimed they had doubled their 1904 returns. "On the whole," Debs announced in the *International Socialist Review*, "we have every reason to feel encouraged at the general result." The mainstream press, however, more accurately reported an "apparent falling off" of the socialist vote. The party nevertheless remained "undaunted," observed the

Oregonian, despite a decrease in socialist support in the West, long regarded as a region of "supposed Socialist strongholds." Debs quickly defended the disappointing results. "The so-called falling off was not a falling off," he argued. He claimed that the unexpected and "unusually large vote" for socialists in 1904 might have established false hopes for 1908. Defections back to the Democratic party, Debs contended, left the socialists with the support only of those "whose devotion knows no waving."[5]

In contrast to the party's first years when socialist support appeared steadily on the rise, the slumping 1908 election results might have disappointed more than a few socialists. The 1908 outcome heartened the SPA's "left wing, which encouraged socialists to work to "destroy the whole capitalist system" rather than "agitate for municipal ownership, scientific reforestation, and tax reforms." Although Kipnis labeled 1907 and 1908 the party's "stagnant years," the 1908 dip, especially for northwest socialists, was less problematic. While socialists experienced a proportionally low drop between the 1904 and 1908 campaigns, the decrease was in fact negligible. Nationally, the party dipped from taking 2.98 percent of the vote in 1904 to 2.82 in 1908. In the Pacific Northwest the socialist percentage, considerably higher than the national average, dropped from 7.73 to 7.38. The four northwest states combined gained 5,693 socialist votes in 1908. Even as socialist support slowed slightly, in the Pacific Northwest the party continued to lead all other regions in electoral results. Washington was the only state to increase its percentage of socialist support. In 1904 candidate Debs received 6.9 percent in Washington and 7.7 in 1908. The significant question, though, was why the region's socialist support had leveled off in 1908.[6]

Continued party in-fighting may have contributed to the thin 1908 returns. Even when the party showed its solidarity in some important free speech fights during the era, the region's socialists, according to the *International Socialist Review*, tried to steal the "limelight" from party rivals because of "petty jealousy." "That any person should at this time consider personal squabbles of greater importance than the great battle which is now taking place seems almost incredible," it observed.[7]

During 1908, ideological and interpersonal battles again shook state organizations, and Washington remained the center of northwest infighting. Carlos Schwantes has observed that the state's most optimistic socialists must have noticed the SPW's "incessant quarrelling." While the ideological fight raged on between the state's "Reds" and "Yellows," as party radicals and moderates were soon labeled, the SPW's infighting increasingly centered on a personal conflict between radical Hermon Titus and former Populist Walter Thomas Mills. Titus despised Mills's brand of "reform socialism," propagated in the new and moderate *Saturday Evening Tribune*. With Titus in Toledo, Ohio, for some time, the SPW had moved steadily toward the ideological middle. In Titus's absence, Mills preached his "middle class friendly" socialism in the *Tribune's* pages. By 1908 Mills's moderate Yellow faction controlled the party and worked on advancing issues such as child labor, the initiative and referendum, and female suffrage. SPW radicals, however, refused to support the party's "unrevolutionary" and moderate reform agenda. Washington's factionalism grew uncontrollably and the SPA's National Executive Committee (NEC) was forced to intervene. At the 1908 national convention, representative Reds and Yellows testified before the NEC. With no workable means of unifying them, the NEC officially dissolved the SPW. The state's factionalism, then, came at a very high price. Without a unified national party behind them in 1908, the state's socialist candidates predictably suffered, and the SPW managed only 2.7 percent of the vote.[8]

Similarly, Montana socialists continued to quarrel. One of the state party's most significant organizational tests began in 1908. In 1905 the state party had sanctioned the socialist *Montana News,* published in Helena. Editors Ida Crouch Hazlett and James D. Graham hoped to capture control of both the paper and the state party. Hazlett and Graham resented Butte's party leadership, namely Lewis Duncan and J. F. Mabie, and their support for the

IWW. During the state's 1908 convention, the Butte local called for an audit of the *Montana News*'s account books. When accountants discovered a $550 deficit, the party promptly removed Hazlett from her editorship and brought suit against Graham for fraudulent spending. Fourteen Montana locals signed a fourteen-page condemnation of Graham. Yet he and Hazlett, according to historian Terrence McGlynn, were "not friendless." For their part, locals in Missoula and Laurel remained loyal to Graham and Hazlett. Montanans, like their comrades in Washington, experienced significant party quarrelling around the 1908 elections. As members took sides in the *Montana News* fallout and engaged in other convention feuding, state membership dropped 45 percent and the party languished.[9]

Increased anti-socialist sentiment stands as another possible factor behind the 1908 slide. During the period from 1905 to 1910, as socialists took an increasingly prominent role in politics and community activities, a backlash to socialism surfaced. Across the region, visible signs of opposition to its message appeared. A 1905 *Oregonian* article titled "the Menace of Socialism" quoted attorney Wallace McCamant, a Republican who would later become a judge on the Oregon Supreme Court, "Socialism is a worse menace to the Nation than was free silver ten years ago." The paper's editors agreed: "The people of the United States are not naturally inclined to Socialism." The *International Socialist Review* observed in 1906 that evidence suggested socialists were "feared and hated" across the country. *Appeal to Reason,* a national party newspaper published in Girard, Kansas, reported that Judge C. H. Hanford of Seattle "made a covert attack upon Socialism" during a speech at the 1909 Alaska-Yukon exposition in Seattle, referring to its ideological leanings as "paternalism" and "despotism."

Among conventional politicians and newspapers, some seemed especially uneasy about the way socialists gained support for their reform message. During the 1906 campaign, for example, W. M. Kellogg of Maltby, Washington, agreed to participate in a November debate because he wanted to "prevent the Socialist party from misleading and deceiving workingmen into the belief that the Socialist party will improve their condition." Similarly, Spokane's *Spokesman-Review* printed a satirical view of socialism in a 1908 cartoon. The caricature depicted an ailing Uncle Sam with a neck tumor of "socialism." Meanwhile, Theodore Roosevelt, labeled "Doctor Roosevelt," stood nearby and offered an elixir of his "reform remedy" to aid Uncle Sam's "problem." The socialist press also experienced this backlash. City officials in Spokane banned the *Appeal to Reason,* and the Seattle Public Library barred the *International Socialist Review* after a member of its board of trustees deemed the journal "hot stuff." Library officials also called the *Review*'s language "too intemperate." The "intemperate" *Review* editors had an answer. "No doubt," they quipped "the *Ladies' Home Journal* is safer . . . saner and milder mental pabulum for sissys [*sic*] in general and capitalist lackeys in particular."[10]

No matter the explanation, most socialists looked beyond party bickering and enemy attacks for the sake of their cause. Instead, they heeded the lessons of 1908 and increased their activism. At the beginning of 1909 the *Appeal to Reason* attempted to rally the party faithful. "With the beginning of the New Year," it effused, "there spreads before us a field dazzling with promise. There has never been such an opportunity to propagate the principles of our movement." Accordingly, the party displayed a great deal of resiliency and refocused on party-building. "The Socialist party," the *Appeal to Reason* encouraged, "must have the intelligent and energetic support of all its members. No half-hearted service will answer the demands of a revolutionary party." Party members, the newspaper continued, "must work with tireless activity" to ensure political success. As the party heightened its activism and prepared for coming campaigns, from 1909 to 1911 its national membership tripled.[11]

Pacific Northwest socialists exemplified the party's broader activist offensive. In 1909 Eugene Debs toured the Northwest and the party faithful met him with "big crowds and marked enthusiasm." Reinvigorated after the poor results in 1908 and encouraged by the era's reform-friendly climate, northwest socialists mobilized. In August 1910 the Portland, Oregon, local reported "a banner month" of activity. The group's efforts included recruiting ninety-four new members, holding fifteen propaganda meetings, and selling nearly two hundred dollars in literature. In a national party bulletin, the Portland chapter challenged other locals to match its activism. Montana's state organization saw a particularly high amount of rebuilding, too. "Socialism is growing," observed secretary Lewis Duncan, "but it is not growing without the efforts of socialists."[12] The state's leadership stressed the importance of each member's participation, and state socialists responded. In late 1910 alone, the Socialist Party of Montana established six chapters. By 1911 Great Falls boasted fifty-five members and Miles City claimed fifty. Activists also looked for innovative ways to educate would-be socialists. Johanne Rae of Great Falls suggested the state convention offer a "liberal cash prize" to the best essay on socialism written by a Montana high school student. Reorganization after the state's *Montana News* feud worked. By late 1910 the party had twenty-two locals and approximately five hundred members.[13]

With the socialist press playing a central role in party activism, the Pacific Northwest's "subscription hustlers" continued to muster. National publications such as the *Appeal to Reason* reflected party vitality. The newspaper billed itself as a "pioneer propaganda paper," important to local organizing efforts. "The Appeal Army is the backbone of the Socialist Party in America," it proclaimed. In the Northwest, subscriptions to the *Appeal* steadily increased. In January 1909, the newspaper had 24,364 northwest subscribers, and by October the number was 27,140. The region also continued to produce its own socialist organs. In addition to established papers such as Seattle's *Socialist,* new papers appeared, several in Oregon. In 1906 Eugene moderates established the *Herald* to argue more effectively for municipal ownership of public utilities. The state organ, the *Oregon Socialist Party Bulletin,* commenced publication in 1910 with a circulation of fifteen hundred copies. Montana's socialist press also expanded during this period. In addition to the *Butte Socialist*, from 1905 to 1910 the *Montana News*, albeit troubled, reached a statewide audience.[14]

Also rallying potential socialists were a number of continually observable signs, organizers thought, of a swelling capitalist conspiracy. The *Appeal to Reason* encouraged socialists to believe in imminent revolution: "The pot is boiling, solidarity is simmering, and before many moons there will be something doing in the United States that will make the whole capitalist world take notice." Each week the *Appeal* described the "nearing revolution" destined to occur "in accord with the American temperament to change quickly. It is the way the American people move." In the Northwest, tales of greedy capitalists flourished. Skeptics watched in 1909 as railroad magnate James J. Hill and various "interests" bought a number of hotels in Seattle, Tacoma, and Yakima. "It is what the Socialists have been telling you for years would come," the *Appeal* reminded readers. The purchases, it claimed, illustrated the negative results that occurred when "the wealth is getting into few hands" and the "big fellows" shut out small businesses. Socialists also cried foul during 1909 when, in Butte, the Amalgamated Copper Company threatened to open a miner's supply store unless the town's merchants lowered their prices. To socialists, this maneuver proved "the worker is robbed in the pay envelope and not in the prices he pays for things." Socialists charged Amalgamated either with covering up a planned wage decrease or trying to prevent demands for higher wages. Even the flowering Progressive conservation-of-natural-resources movement caught the suspicious eye of socialists. The "conservation grab game," they professed, represented a larger capitalist scheme to "grab everything for the Rockefeller interests."[15]

As state organizations regrouped, socialists voiced their characteristic optimism again in 1910. "Socialists are not pessimists," announced the *Appeal* that summer. "They do not mope," the paper continued; "they bring, instead, the greatest hope that has entered into the heart of man through all the years." An extensive Pacific Northwest tour by Debs in the fall of 1910 represented the renewed socialist vigor. During his visit, he held fourteen meetings in Montana, Idaho, Oregon, and Washington. *Appeal to Reason* correspondent George Brewer detailed the trip. In Helena, Montana, he reported, "everybody jumped in" to make the visit a success. In Butte, "the slaves of the copper trust" eagerly attended Debs's lecture with "eager faces," "undivided attention," and "uncontrollable enthusiasm." In Moscow, Idaho, Eggan's Hall was "jammed" with the largest crowd ever to attend a political event. Organizers even commissioned a special train from Colfax, Washington, to carry two hundred socialists "imbued with militant spirit of revolt" to the event. In Lewiston, Idaho, Brewer reported, socialists "astonished even themselves" with the success of their first large organized event. Crowds swelled as the tour moved to larger cities. In Spokane Debs spoke to "a frantic and enthusiastic crowd of 8,000." He encountered similarly passionate crowds of 4,000 in Seattle, 3,500 in Portland, and 2,000 in Tacoma. "The western tour," Brewer asserted, "has been the most satisfactory yet taken, from every standpoint."[16]

Although the 1910 elections failed to bring high-profile victories, socialists made strong showings. Early returns from Washington, Montana, and Idaho all reported increases in socialist support and regional newspapers took notice of party gains. In Washington, a Pierce County socialist judiciary candidate received 1,744 votes in a losing effort, more than double the average number of votes any socialist candidate received. The *Seattle Post-Intelligencer* called the socialist showing "a feature" of the recent elections. The next day the newspaper remarked emphatically that "*even* the Socialists beat [the] Nonpartisans" in the state supreme court race. These trends, though, in spite of condescending tones by mainstream observers, should not have surprised anyone.[17]

Socialist successes beyond the region also made headlines in the Pacific Northwest. In 1910, socialist Victor L. Berger won Wisconsin's fifth congressional seat, a victory that was reported in a number of established Pacific Northwest newspapers, including the *Oregonian*, the *Seattle Post-Intelligencer*, and the *Seattle Times*.

"The United States of America now gets into line with all the other civilized nations of the world, and the working class of Milwaukee has the immortal honor of starting a new chapter in American history," the new congressman announced. The *Oregonian* called Berger's victory "most notable," and northwest socialists certainly understood the significance of the first socialist congressman elected in the United States. "What a beautiful showing," wrote a Mondak, Montana, socialist. "How grand it would be if we had a thousand organizers made of as fine stuff as is found in Victor L. Berger. How soon will we be able to see such a tremendous success in Montana?" he asked.[18]

On the surface, the 1910 elections reassured many in the socialist party that they could work together in relative harmony. When the *Appeal* described "the meaning of this election," it spoke of the "great times ahead." "Hereafter," it claimed, "the Socialist party will be generally reckoned with in considering results." Yet "fermenting just beneath the surface unanimity," historian Nick Salvatore argued, "basic difficulties remained concerning . . . relations with the AFL and IWW."[19] These two challenges, one a continually slippery relationship, the other a new and radical alternative, either outwardly or subtly contested the political efficacy of the socialist party in the Northwest.

In membership and influence, the American Federation of Labor dominated the Pacific Northwest labor climate. AFL supremacy went largely unchallenged until the rise of the IWW in 1905 and 1906. Yet the AFL continued to expand its influence and unique political power through most of the early twentieth century. "The power of the AFL," noted historian Erik Olssen, "made it unique," and the Northwest's trade unionism was no exception.[20] From 1905 to 1910, the AFL and trade unionism continued to strain socialist cohesiveness, while the AFL remained an ambiguous foe to many of the region's socialists. In addition to the AFL's prominent role in labor organizing and support, the union's shifting political strategies presented a new and direct challenge to socialists. Prior to 1905, the AFL had traditionally employed an apolitical approach to issues or quietly endorsed "pro-labor" Democrats or Republicans. But during the 1906 elections the AFL became directly involved in campaigning and therefore explicitly challenged the socialist hold on labor's political voice. Walter Copsey argued in the *American Federationist* that political activity was a "necessary evolution." "Workingmen," he observed, "now realize that the ballot is a most powerful weapon with which to back up the good work done along industrial lines in the trade union." This sentiment culminated during the 1906 election cycle when AFL head Samuel Gompers announced that his union would "stand by friends and punish enemies" in the political arena.[21]

Accordingly, many state labor federations, including some in the Pacific Northwest, became politically active, asserting themselves as labor's political representatives. For that reason, in 1906 Oregon's Federated Trades Council organized the "Union Political Party." According to the *Oregonian*, the group had "formed along the lines suggested by Samuel Gompers in setting forth his idea of a national labor political organization." On November 30 the new Union party held a convention in Portland. Organizers hoped to offer candidates in 1906, but state law required parties to have won at least 25 percent of the vote in the previous congressional election in order to appear on the ballot. Echoing Gompers's rhetoric, the Oregon Union Party chose to "stand by friends and punish enemies" and "confine its political endeavors to the support of old party men favorable to organized labor." In a departure from the politically shy trade unionism of the past, P. McDonald, secretary of the Oregon State Federation of Labor, spoke of the "many good reasons" for the "entry of labor into the political field." McDonald observed that "the present parties— I speak principally of the Republicans and Democrats, are controlled by the money interests of the country . . . their legislation will always be detrimental to organized labor and in favor of capital." Similarly, the secretary of the Portland Federated Trades Council, W. H. Fitzgerald, observed, "Such a party is sorely needed and now is the right time for its organization." These sentiments are interesting on two levels. First, unionists dismissed the growing socialist party as a pro-labor party. Second, Union Party rhetoric echoed socialist critiques of capitalist politics. To observers, the idea of politically proactive trade unionism was full of possibilities. The *Oregonian* claimed the upstart party could "cut a more than considerable figure in Oregon politics" and successfully elect pro-union candidates.[22]

After 1906 the AFL continued to assert itself politically and hoped workers would vote according to principle instead of party. Gompers continued his calls for all members' political involvement, the "necessity of united and determined action," and the "splendid prospect of labor's success in 1908." The AFL kept up its "friends and enemies" strategy in 1908 and discouraged "blindly voting for either one of the two great parties." During the 1908 campaign Gompers encouraged union members to support William Jennings Bryan for president, because William Howard Taft misrepresented "the cause of labor and deceives the laboring men." The pro-Republican *Oregonian*, meanwhile, assured workers that Taft "will still be a friend of labor" and "[will] continue the good work for labor which has been done by Mr. Roosevelt." When Taft and the Republicans prevailed in 1908, the AFL's political efforts stalled. The *Oregonian* called the AFL's 1908 efforts "futile." The "assaults of the American Federation of Labor," it observed, "apparently had no effect whatsoever on the vote."[23] While the AFL's 1906 political participation failed to make major political strides, it was a clear intrusion into socialist political territory.

In addition to the political competition between the AFL and socialists, both sides continued their verbal bantering. The AFL and trade unionists maintained their criticism of socialist leaders. Gompers penned an article titled "Debs, the Apostle of Failure," in which he said "abuse by Debs was to be expected" in part because his "past history is all in the direction of harming rather than helping the labor movement." The AFL president added rhetorically, "What has Debs ever done in the interest of labor?" Gompers claimed that, after Debs served his sentence stemming from the 1894 ARU strike, the Socialist wore "an illusory halo which no one has been desirous of disturbing." Gompers further alleged that weary Republican donors funded Debs's 1908 campaign train, which the Debs campaign called the "Red Special."[24]

Socialists responded in kind with criticism of the AFL. While they recognized the need for trade unions, they believed the union should be but a first step in working-class emancipation. "Socialism advises the worker to join the union of his craft as a means of *temporarily* bettering the condition of the working class," reminded the *Appeal to Reason*. "Joining the union might aid you in getting better wages," the paper argued, but unionism "still leaves much injustice and the system of exploitation intact."

After the AFL's political endeavors of 1906 and 1908 failed to make political gains, Gompers faced harsh and personal criticisms from the *Appeal to Reason*, some of its articles going so far afield as to question his masculinity. "Gompers, the old man, or, old woman," it wrote, no longer had "the courage to stand at the head of the labor army." "The lesson" of Gompers's leadership, claimed the *Appeal*, was that "workers must act together in the Socialist party on the political field and then they will secure material relief, and in time industrial emancipation."[25] Varied regional opinions about Gompers also played out in the northwest press. According to the *Oregonian*, the 1908 anti-Bryan "avalanche" marked "the end of Samuel Gompers as a labor leader." By 1910 a number of SPA members within the AFL still hoped their influence could inspire a socialist takeover. At the AFL's annual convention in St. Louis, socialist Victor Berger urged an alliance between unionism and socialism. "Whether unionism is to form an open alliance with Socialism," announced the *Seattle Times*, or "possibly be swallowed by it, will be determined next week." Gompers, who was particularly controversial among more radical AFL affiliates in the Northwest and elsewhere, faced a fight for reelection, and Berger claimed to have the votes to oust him. Berger demanded that Gompers and the AFL "take a radical stand or give way to some more aggressive organization of the stripe of the Industrial Workers of the World." Despite "bitter opposition," Gompers narrowly secured reelection as AFL president. Still, his vision for a politically active AFL encroached on socialist politics and perhaps helped to explain the 1908 decrease in socialist support.[26]

While the AFL's rhetoric and political involvement was a challenge to socialists, in 1905 a new force emerged in American labor that especially affected Pacific Northwest socialism. The Industrial Workers of the World—popularly called the "Wobblies"—carried a message of securing universal unionism and working-class emancipation. The IWW officially entered the political front in Chicago, at its founding convention in June 1905. At its opening session, socialist William "Big Bill" Haywood famously hailed the meeting as "the Continental Congress of the working class." Among the 203 delegates sat an eclectic mix from the Western Federation of Miners, the Socialist Party of America, the Socialist Labor Party, the American Labor Union, and the AFL. The IWW quickly emerged as a much more radical alternative to the trade union organization of the AFL. According to historian Greg Hall, the IWW had two goals, "one practical and one revolutionary." It first hoped to organize workers outside the conservative AFL, regardless of their trade, gender, or race. In addition, the Wobblies preached a "one big union" philosophy that would emancipate the working class from the grasp of capitalism through such tactics as the general strike.[27]

The nation's socialists at first welcomed the IWW. The country's most identifiable socialist, Eugene Debs, attended its opening convention and called the IWW and the SPA "the two halves that represent the organic whole of the labor movement." Debs echoed much of the convention's rhetoric against the politically ineffective AFL. "The choice," he announced, "is between the A.F. of L. and capitalism on one side and the industrial workers and socialism on the other." While pro-AFL socialists argued that the AFL most capably represented the working class and suggested a merger with the union, Debs objected furiously to such sentiment and declared any talk of fusion "absolutely inexcusable." If socialists accommodated Samuel Gompers and the AFL, he argued, party members could expect to be "puked on in return."[28]

Despite early enthusiasm over their commonalities, strategic problems arose between Wobblies and socialists. Many in the IWW wanted to separate themselves from the "nonrevolutionary" politics of the socialists. Wobblies also balked at the socialist acceptance of middle- and upper-class members. By the convention's sixth day, socialist delegates waited in vain for an IWW endorsement of the SPA. Instead, the new organization's radical majority agreed with delegate Thomas Hagerty's assertion that "the ballot box is simply a capitalist concession." A far cry from giving the socialists its direct endorsement, the IWW nevertheless conceded in its constitution that a class struggle should come from the "political, as well as the industrial field." The IWW-socialist association grew more strained by 1906. According to historian Melvyn Dubofsky, Wobblies fought among themselves—more about "personality and rhetoric than on issues and programs"—and increasingly "the political socialists and trade unionists . . . were constantly at each other's throats."

Over the next few years, socialists would steadily leave the IWW, especially after some of the most revolutionary Wobblies instigated a 1908 coup barring member Daniel DeLeon and other socialists they saw as too dogmatic. The IWW also took the radical step of disavowing politics altogether, pledging to not take part in the election process. Even Debs quietly left the Wobblies in 1907, convinced they could not effectively organize workers.[29]

However strained, common sentiments in revolutionary ideology and the rights of workers were the sinews of the IWW-socialist relationship. In the Pacific Northwest, where the IWW enjoyed exceptional success, its association with the socialists remained important. While the IWW potentially represented an organizational challenge to the northwest socialist movement, their converging ideological areas of agreement kept the relationship alive. The IWW presence, in fact, was hard to ignore. The Wobblies had appeared in the region within a year of their inaugural convention and, according to Schwantes, they "represented the most alienated of Northwest laborers"—the area's migratory lumber and agricultural workers. Spokane's IWW local claimed four thousand Wobblies and often filled its eight-hundred-person hall. The IWW's arrival began a new era of radicalism in the Northwest, because its message of revolution and class equality, as Schwantes argued, "epitomized the kind of idealistic radicalism" characteristic of the region. From 1905 to 1910 the IWW's most significant fights occurred with the sympathy and support of the socialists.[30]

If IWW activism unfolded like a drama, as Robert Tyler has suggested, many of its scenes were set in the Pacific Northwest. The most recognized event linked to the Wobblies and implicitly, the socialists, was the 1905 murder of former Idaho governor Frank Steunenberg, famous for his handling of the 1899 Coeur d'Alene Mining War. The Steunenberg murder and trial also symbolized the early cooperation between the IWW and northwest socialists. Bartlett Sinclair, Steunenberg's personal representative in northern Idaho during the Coeur d'Alene troubles, spoke of Steunenberg in glowing terms, observing that "a truer friend of laboring classes never lived."

For several years after Steunenberg's handling of the Coeur d'Alene war, however, resentment festered among radicalized laborers. As the former governor arrived at his home in Caldwell on the evening of December 30, 1905, a hastily built trigger on his front gate detonated a bomb, taking off both of his legs in the explosion. Steunenberg lived only another twenty minutes. News of the murder shocked many in Idaho and throughout the region as well. "There is no known reason for the outrage," wrote Spokane's daily newspaper, "but it is charged to some members of the famous inner circle of the Coeur d'Alene dynamiters, whom he prosecuted so relentlessly in 1899 while he was governor." Blame quickly fell on the Pacific Northwest's most radical labor activists, and Idaho governor Frank Gooding issued a five thousand dollar reward for identification of the culprits. Pinkerton detectives soon received a confession from Harry Orchard, a labor spy who claimed that leaders of the IWW and the WFM had hired him to commit the murder. Idaho authorities named three WFM/IWW figures—Charles H. Moyer, George A. Pettibone, and

William "Big Bill" Haywood—as the guilty conspirators. After a well-orchestrated stake out, complete with Pinkerton company detectives and codenames, Colorado authorities kidnapped the three men in Denver and took them to Idaho on a secretive mid-night train ride to stand trial in Boise.[31]

The quick arrests of Haywood, Moyer, and Pettibone—and their denial of due process of law—infuriated many. Protests surfaced among labor unions, radicals, and socialists; the radical press dubbed the forcible extradition a "kidnapping." For socialists, the accusations and hasty "abduction" symbolized a capitalist conspiracy. Eugene Debs threatened an "armed revolution" in the event of Haywood's conviction. Debs penned a polemical piece for the *International Socialist Review* titled "Arouse Ye Slaves." President Theodore Roosevelt grew so angry he explored legal options against Debs. The president ultimately deemed Moyer, Pettibone, Haywood, and Debs "undesirable citizens."[32]

Pacific Northwest socialists quickly mobilized on behalf of Haywood, Moyer, and Pettibone. The region's workers pledged $140,000 to the defense fund. In nearby Caldwell, Idaho, the socialist local formally denounced "the attempt of the Capitalist press of the country . . . to pre-judge the case by calling our comrades 'assassins,' 'murders,' 'conspirators,' etc. before the evidence has been heard." The socialist press, too, supported the accused. For three months in 1906, Hermon Titus moved the *Socialist*, previously based in Seattle and Toledo, to Caldwell to follow and report on the pending court proceedings. Titus distributed the *Socialist*'s trial reports to every union paper in the United States, and he estimated that his accounts of the trial reached two million workers weekly.[33]

This northwest event achieved national significance for the socialist cause. The Boise trial, socialists argued, represented the nation's larger working-class struggle. "Their battle is our battle, their cause our cause," announced the *International Socialist Review*. Death sentences for the three accused men, it wrote, "would be a deadly blow at the heart of every labor organization in America." "The real battle now, as in the past, is not in Boise," a Butte socialist added. Other socialists later called the Idaho battle "the greatest fight of the last decade."[34]

On July 28, 1907, an Idaho jury acquitted Haywood and his "co-conspirators." Haywood, Moyer, and Pettibone escaped jail time, the *American Federationist* wrote, despite "the whole power of the state" and the most "resourceful" prosecuting attorneys working for a conviction. Harry Orchard, however, received a lifetime sentence for the murder.[35] While the trial did not incite a working-class revolution, as some socialists hoped, it did help to further establish the Northwest as a significant place in the labor movement and to reinforce its reputation for radicalism.

Pacific Northwest socialists and Wobblies also successfully coordinated protests in prominent cities. Engaging in "free speech fights," the region's radicals challenged local ordinances by staging street-corner demonstrations. Through this new and effective tactic they gained victories and notoriety for the Northwest's working class. The first significant free speech fight occurred in Seattle during 1906, when socialists tested newly elected mayor William Hickman Moore's plan to remove "disreputable elements" from downtown Seattle. On August 20, 1906, police arrested editor Titus, along with socialist attorney Edwin J. Brown, for obstructing the sidewalk. In September arrests mounted, and so did socialists' notoriety. Testing the resolve of Seattle police, socialists held some of the largest rallies they had ever staged, and claimed record surges in new memberships and party funds. In turn, police arrested eight men in October for holding "socialistic meetings." During their trial in early November, the accused testified that Mayor Moore had authorized their meetings. The court released each of the eight men on $100 bonds. After his return from Caldwell and the Haywood trial, Hermon Titus again tested the limits of free speech on Seattle streets, was arrested, and served forty days in jail—under deplorable conditions. He successfully appealed to the board of health, whose inspection deemed the jail "unfit for human habitation." As the Seattle struggle indicated, free-speech campaigns could be effective political tools. They brought the region's radicals much attention and publicity, from which they derived great satisfaction and a sense that they were participating in "revolutionary acts" and attacking the "master class."[36]

Seattle was not the only Pacific Northwest city where free-speech battles challenged the status quo. The next IWW/ socialist protest occurred during 1909 and 1910 in Spokane. By 1905, because of its sizeable Wobblie population, the city had earned a reputation as an enclave for radicals. But residents grew increasingly hostile toward the socialist and IWW presence. In January 1907, for example, Spokane landlords refused to renew the socialists' lease on Oliver Hall, which had been their local headquarters for the past six years. When socialists tried to rent another hall, they reported "the same curt refusal" from all potential landlords. The Spokane Chamber of Commerce went so far as to appoint a militia committee in case of city confrontation with its radical fringe. Meanwhile, after city officials ruled that a socialist meeting hall would negate the group's need to hold public rallies, they began restricting public demonstrations of Wobblies and socialists. In the ordinance, however, Spokane's city council *did* allow the holding of public religious meetings, according to the city's radicals, "admitting . . . discrimination against the I.W.W." Representatives from the AFL, the Socialist Party, and the IWW requested that the city council repeal the ordinance and allow them to conduct "orderly meetings at reasonable hours." The city council denied the request. In response to the city's blatant anti-radical measures, Spokane became the site of the most famous northwest free speech fight.[37]

In late 1909, fraudulent unemployment agencies in Spokane promised to offer positions, which were nonexistent, to the unemployed. The job-seekers complained, but city officials did nothing. That November, agitated Wobblies and socialists began to hold public demonstrations, purposefully defying the city ordinance. The police made mass arrests, and, by November 12, police locked up two hundred cold and hungry men, confining them to a makeshift "bullpen" under "shotgun guard." Other prisoners were housed like "sardines" in "sweat boxes" for twenty-four hour periods. Some four to six police officers now began supervising IWW meetings, poised to arrest the speakers for anything they judged "incendiary." Organizers in Spokane informed the *Appeal to Reason* that "the situation grows steadily graver."[38]

In socialism's earliest years, conventional newspapers lacked a partisan socialist voice. Socialists called the *Spokesman-Review*'s coverage a "joke." Elizabeth Gurley Flynn, one of the most fervent radicals involved in the Spokane free-speech campaign following the city's punitive ordinance, decided to provide the socialist press with details of the fight. Her reports helped draw national attention to the conflict. She described "the terrors of Spokane" in the pages of the *Appeal to Reason*. "The city is wild with excitement," she wrote. Authorities arrested her on December 1, 1909, as police swept the city, rounding up all IWW leaders. While in and out of prison, Flynn submitted thorough accounts of the Spokane confrontation to the *International Socialist Review*. She described how guards forced the prisoners, by then numbering between three hundred and four hundred people, to work in the nearby quarries. Those who refused the hard labor received only bread and water, rations that Flynn dubbed "slow starvation" and "legal murder." She called the hostilities a "terrible conflict" and placed the events in a national context. "It is a fight for more than free speech," she argued, "It is to prevent the free press and labor's right to organize from being throttled."[39]

As the battle stretched into December, socialists throughout the Pacific Northwest showed their support for the Spokane radicals. Across the region they adopted resolutions of "sympathy and encouragement" that illustrated, according to the *International Socialist Review*, a "great spirit of solidarity." In Oregon, socialists sponsored a mass meeting at which they condemned Spokane officials. "Spokane is wrong judicially as well as morally and ethically," they declared. Moreover, a number of socialists traveled to Spokane to help the cause. Beulah Hyde and Eleanor M. Herman of Buckley, Washington, went there, they said, to "help their comrades." Flynn observed that "men are coming in from all directions daily to go to jail." "From almost every state in the union," reported the *Review*'s editors, "socialists are on the way to help their comrades." The IWW established a special defense fund for demonstrators, while the *International Socialist Review* published the fund's address and encouraged contributions. For socialists across the region and country, Spokane stood as an excellent example of their cause. The *Appeal to Reason* compared the significance of the Spokane IWW struggle to an earlier confrontation in American history. "What the Alamo was to Mexico," it reported, "Spokane will be to plutocracy."[40]

Wobblies and socialists filled Spokane's jails for five months. In the wake of a large demonstration on March 1, 1910, the city backed down. It revoked the licenses of fraudulent unemployment offices; and officials also relented with more tolerant street ordinances, similar to Seattle's, and released the prisoners. The *Appeal to Reason* declared, "The battle for free speech has been won in Spokane." Like the Steunenberg murder and trial, the Spokane free-speech fight assumed national proportions, with the *International Socialist Review* deeming the city "the storm center of the class-struggle." The Spokane battle symbolized, according to Carlos Schwantes, "a tradition of militancy and radicalism . . . among Northwest wageworkers." Once again, this far western region demonstrated its rightful claim as home to some of the nation's most active revolutionaries.[41]

From 1905 to 1910 Pacific Northwest socialists seemingly overcame a number of significant organizational and political challenges. Factionalism, the AFL, and the IWW all had the potential to stunt party growth. Yet encouraged by electoral victories, their own rhetorical optimism, and the power of mass action, socialists in the Northwest strengthened their organizations and looked forward to further activism in the approaching political elections. The *Appeal to Reason* predicted that "the campaign of 1912 will be the most remarkable ever held in this nation. The campaigns of slavery times will be eclipsed and far and away." For socialists, and particularly those in the Northwest, the *Appeal*'s pronouncement seemed prophetic.[42]

Coxey's Army in camp at Forsythe, Montana, 1894. Photo by L. A. Huffman. Courtesy of the Montana Historical Society, Helena. Negative no. 981-802.

Idaho hard-rock miners, ca. 1900. Courtesy of the Idaho State Historical Society. Negative no. 73-129.16.

View of Butte, Montana, looking east from approximately Emmett Street, ca. 1899. From "Butte and Its Copper Mines" (1899). Courtesy of the Montana Historical Society, Helena. Negative no. 946-035.

Seated Idaho silver miners, ca. 1900. Courtesy of the Idaho State Historical Society. Negative no. 68-62.31/9.

Ida Crouch Hazlett, Montana radical, socialist organizer, and editor of the *Montana News,* in a 1904 photograph. Courtesy of the Montana Historical Society, Helena. Negative no. 942-665.

Breaking ground at a socialist colony in Skagit County, Washington, ca. 1907–1908. Photograph by Asahel Curtis. Courtesy of the Washington State Historical Society, Tacoma. Negative no. 6784.

The banner at far left advertises a Socialist Party picnic on Third, between Union and Pike streets, Seattle, 1911. Photograph by Asahel Curtis. Courtesy of the Washington State Historical Society, Tacoma. Negative no. 21766.

Butte Miners' Hall after labor unrest culminated in over twenty dynamite blasts to the building during June 23 and 24, 1914. Courtesy of the Montana Historical Society, Helena. Negative no. 946-114.

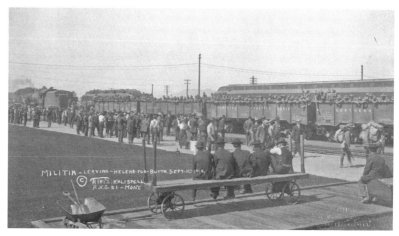

Montana State Militia leaving Helena to restore order in Butte,
September 1, 1914. Courtesy of the Montana Historical Society, Helena.
Negative no. 958-180.

Major Daniel J.
Donohue, commanding
officer of the militia,
Butte, 1914.
Courtesy of the
Montana Historical
Society, Helena.
Negative no. 958-188.

Earl Bowman, socialist
legislator in Idaho,
elected in 1914. Courtesy
of the Idaho State
Historical Society.
Negative no. D-3372.

Lewis J. Duncan,
socialist mayor of Butte,
Montana, from 1911 to
1914. Courtesy of the
Montana Historical
Society, Helena.
Negative no. 942-040.

National Guard troops pose in downtown Butte, September 6, 1914. Courtesy of the Montana Historical Society, Helena. Negative no. 958-185.

Oregon criminal syndicalism trial, March 10, 1920, Portland. Courtesy of the Oregon Historical Society. Negative no. CN009663.

Finnish socialist club picnic and band, Astoria, Oregon, 1922. Courtesy of the Oregon Historical Society. Negative no. OrHi26734.

4

"Socialist Victories and Splendid Gains"
The Height of Northwest Socialism, 1911–1912

Amid the crumbling ruins of political parties the Socialist movement stands serene and confident pointing the way out of this industrial hell into which the country has been plunged after a century of capitalist exploitation. This is the Socialist's year of opportunity. *Appeal to Reason*, July 6, 1912

Comrades, the future looks bright. *Socialist Voice*, March 11, 1911

HISTORIANS have long regarded the 1912 presidential election as the high mark of American socialism. In many respects, socialism in the United States did achieve its greatest electoral success in 1912, when socialist presidential candidate Eugene Victor Debs mustered 5.9 percent of the national vote. No other socialist contender in American history has managed to win such a significant share of electoral support. While nationally significant, this showing was even more impressive in the Pacific Northwest. The approximately 6 percent of votes that Debs received nationally was surpassed in Idaho, Montana, and Washington, where he won 10 percent. His performance in the Pacific Northwest has prompted historians to single out 1912 as "a high water mark for the region's socialist politics."[1] In fact, however, the municipal elections of the previous year helped lay the foundation for socialism's greatest electoral showing and socialists' moment of greatest optimism.

In the second decade of the twentieth century, Northwest socialists increasingly witnessed signs of regionwide growth. The *Appeal to Reason* reported gains for socialist candidates in Idaho, Oregon, and Washington and consistent socialist support in

Montana. Election results in 1910 showed sizable increases compared to 1908. In Idaho, socialists gained 4,718 votes; 619 in Oregon; and 1,812 in Washington.[2]

These results invigorated political activities for the rapidly approaching 1911 contests, and the region's socialists continued to understand the central importance of local elections. "Municipal elections are exceedingly important," said the *Appeal to Reason*. "Step by step we must conquer the political power, municipal, state and national, until we have control of the machinery of government and when that day comes it will be the last of capitalism." Mindful of this thinking, Pacific Northwest socialists enjoyed a string of victories in the 1911 local elections, giving them greater political credibility and confidence than ever before.[3]

The Northwest won its first key municipal election in eastern Washington when socialist David C. Coates was elected as one of Spokane's five city commissioners in March 1911. From *Socialist Voice* headquarters in Seattle, the newspaper described Coates, a former lieutenant governor in Colorado, as "a socialist of many years standing." Despite "bitter opposition from the capitalist papers," supporters concluded, his campaign secured victory with its "straight-forward appeal to workingmen and workingwomen to take the government from the grasp of the master class." Further, Coates's victory in Spokane offered strong evidence that socialism's appeal in Washington was not limited to the western half of the state. Recalling socialist Victor Berger's grand 1910 congressional victory in Wisconsin, the *Socialist Voice* nudged "Seattle comrades" to "make haste or Spokane and not Seattle will be the Milwaukee of Washington." After the 1911 election, even mainstream newspapers such as the *Spokesman-Review* took note of the socialist presence. "The significant fact," the *Review* pointed out, "is [that] the growth of the Socialist vote to even its present size, however inconsiderable, . . . has spread into all sections of the United States."[4]

Other northwest municipal elections in 1911 also resulted in socialist successes. In Everett, Washington, socialists celebrated after electing three aldermen. In Coeur d'Alene, they elected John T. Wood mayor and captured positions as clerk, police judge, treasurer, and city councilmen. The Coeur d'Alene victories reflected an increase of 766 votes for socialist candidates in city government. The *New York World* called this an "appreciable increase" in the Idaho vote, while a "general increase" in the socialist vote in Helena, Montana, also put an alderman in office for the first time.[5]

The 1911 elections left many socialists feeling victorious and confident even when they did not win positions. In Seattle, for example, socialists ran a hard-fought campaign for city mayor. Their candidate, Edwin J. Brown, mustered only five thousand of sixty thousand votes, yet the *Appeal to Reason* declared a "famous victory." It described the election as "enthusiastic, clean-cut, and creditable to the socialist movement." Walla Walla socialists alleged a similar victory despite electoral defeat when their mayoral candidate, Jessie Ferney, received 349 votes, the most ever won there by a socialist candidate. Similarly, Nampa, Idaho, a community that reported only 16 socialist votes in 1910, boasted 501, an increase of approximately 97 percent, in 1911.[6]

While commissioner Coates's election in Spokane that year, and impressive showings in Seattle and smaller communities encouraged socialists, a more significant breakthrough occurred in Montana. Stunning victories in Butte opened the political door for Lewis J. Duncan, a Pacific Northwest figure of national prominence. Duncan's election as mayor capped the socialists' win of every city post: treasurer, attorney, police judge, as well as five of nine aldermen positions. Now, socialists proclaimed, "Every councilman in Butte is a bona fide workingman." While few would doubt Butte's working-class ethos, in reality, socialists' electoral successes came only when campaign platforms of improving life for the rank-and-file superseded emphasis on doctrine. By contrast, the party had fared poorly prior to 1911 in Butte because citizens cared more about positive and practical change and union cooperation with the Butte Miner's Union (BMU) than ideology. A shift in socialist strategy as well as placing a remarkable candidate on the ballot brought them a memorable victory: Duncan was an evolutionary socialist, a Unitarian minister, and a Shakespearean lecturer. He received the largest plurality of votes in Butte mayoral history.[7]

As host of the Northwest's most prominent socialist administration, Butte quickly became a national reference point for how to manage successful party politics. Duncan no doubt fully understood the significance of his victory. The new mayor was cognizant that, in his words, "the very success which has been attained in Butte makes all the more critical the position of the party throughout the state." He cautioned socialists not to forget their main objective. "The important thing is the aim and purpose to revolutionize society in the interests of the working class. Our political success shall be regarded merely as a means to that political end." Although he had won the mayoralty, Duncan believed his work on behalf of socialism was far from complete. He wrote to the city clerk of the new socialist administration in Milwaukee, saying, "We are doing the best we can to educate the bourgeoisie into an understanding that their genuine interests are with us and not with the capitalists."[8]

Lewis J. Duncan's victory in Butte stirred political debate regarding the interpretation of his and other recent socialist successes. Skeptics scoffed at claims that such victories signaled the spread of socialism. Hearing doubtful sentiments, Robert F. Hoxie, professor of political economy at the University of Chicago, asked Duncan to gather more information to clarify, for his own study, Butte socialism's doctrinal "purity." Hoxie expressed concern that "there seems to be a wide-spread impression that they do not in general represent real victories for the socialist principle or triumphs of real working class organization." Duncan responded that, given his own broad appeal to nonsocialist voters, the socialist achievement in Butte was "unquestionably a victory for the socialist principle."[9] Despite Duncan's argument for his administration's legitimacy as doctrinarily "pure," many scholars, labor leaders, politicians, and journalists remained skeptical.

Across Montana, socialists rejoiced over Duncan's victory. The party's local chapter in Basin, a town between Helena and Butte, unassumingly offered its congratulations: "As Socialists we are not much given to flattery, . . ." they noted, "but we are led to remark that the comrades of Butte are especially fortunate in having elected to the office of Mayor one who can and will 'make good.'" Duncan appeared to be up to the task. He admitted to an admirer that he probably had "the hardest job of any mayor in the United States," but considered himself in "fighting trim" due to his "eat well, sleep well, and never worry" approach to life and governance.[10]

Across the Northwest other socialists offered congratulations or requested some of the new mayor's now precious time. In May 1911, the Social Science Club of Spokane embraced Duncan's election, expressing their own earnest hopes that Spokane would "be enjoying a socialist administration of municipal officers soon." Later in the year, Duncan accepted an invitation from Seattle socialists to speak at a party picnic. In 1913, Stockett, Montana, United Mine Workers requested his presence at their 1913 Labor Day celebration. Such invitations demonstrated the political weight a regional socialist mayor carried.

Duncan's victory also resonated in congratulatory reaction across the country. The head of a Massachusetts socialist club informed Duncan "how pleased I am at the growth of the movement."[11] In Orloff, California, James Pearson wrote to Duncan describing local sentiment: "We were all gladder than I can express to learn of your election." And, hopeful of a potential political opportunity, Pearson added a postscript wondering if he was "too early in applying for a position on the [Butte] police-force?" National party figures also offered their congratulations. George Kirkpatrick, author of the key socialist pamphlet "War, What For?" told Duncan he was "delighted with your election to the mayoralty. We surely need strong, well-poised men for such positions."[12]

In Butte, the new socialist administration went straight to work after what Duncan called "many years of reckless and incompetent municipal mismanagement." It became clear that the city officials would institute novel policies. Following the city plan in

Milwaukee, Duncan ensured that his government would operate the *Butte Socialist*, and the newspaper was distributed to every city household. After only two months on the job the socialist administration claimed sweeping reforms, including initiating new public works projects, changing tax and revenue laws, and assuring residents they would have "a clean city for the first time in ten years."[13]

As a result of his significant victory and his administration's accomplishments, Duncan and his programs became a shining example of municipal socialism's possibilities for northwest socialists and labor leaders. He received inquiries regarding socialist matters and governance from well beyond Montana. A North Yakima, Washington, American Federation of Labor committeeman inquired about Butte's city ordinance regarding city pay scales. Boise mayor Harry Fritchman asked about residents' reaction to Butte's new ordinance allowing "moving picture shows" to stay open on Sundays. In turn, Duncan kept in contact with socialists such as Washington's Anna Maley, telling her that "things are going fine . . . lots of work and plenty of evidences of the struggle developing right here in Butte."[14]

Because of his victory, Duncan emerged as a national leader and was regularly sought out and consulted on policy. Across the country socialists contacted him to learn more about Butte's city management. The *Milwaukee Leader* asked for his opinion on the value of socialist presses, calling him "one of the leading socialists in America." An editor for Alabama's *Birmingham Ledger* wanted his views on Butte's public park program. In order to combat the "aristocracy of southern democracy," another Alabaman, socialist W. M. Doyle, requested Duncan's "recipe" for assuring municipal victory, and the National Office of the Socialist Party of America invited Duncan and thirty-eight other socialist mayors to a 1911 Executive Committee meeting. Demonstrating his new national prominence, Duncan was also named as a delegate to the party's 1912 national convention.[15]

As 1911 ended, in addition to "the Duncan success," socialists elsewhere in the country could also celebrate meaningful political strides. Nationally they obtained and retained 1,039 positions in 337 cities and in 36 states. Socialists everywhere must have sensed this gain in party momentum. Certainly in the Pacific Northwest the Coates, Duncan, and municipal victories of 1911 suggested that socialist support was indeed on the upswing. Accordingly, northwest socialists heightened their organizational activities, hoping to capitalize on a continually tense regional labor climate.[16]

As the 1912 national elections approached, the Socialist Party of Washington boasted 183 locals and 4,286 paid-up members. This active SPW membership represented organized locals throughout the state. Not surprisingly, western Washington, with its larger metropolitan areas, drew more members. Seattle had nineteen locals, while Tacoma counted six reporting locals with a total of 209 party members. In eastern Washington's smaller agrarian communities, Cheney, Colfax, and Pullman reported active memberships. Spokane, with its larger population, possessed four locals and well over one hundred paid members.[17]

The socialist movement, however, needed to further enlarge its constituency. Party leaders and editors, ever the activists, constantly appealed for new members. A February 1912 editorial appeared in the Everett, Washington, *Commonwealth*, in which Al Roeder asked: "To all those who believe themselves socialists, near socialists, or sympathetic socialists, but who are not members of the socialist party—to you particularly this is addressed. Why are you not members of the party?" According to contributors such as Roeder, "political parties are the expression of class interests." Without an active membership, as party officials frequently stressed, the working class had no voice in politics. Regular meetings, where members could purchase newspapers and political pamphlets, were open to likely members. Organizers in Seattle urged potential members to "come inside the party and help. The revolution is almost here and the Socialist party will be one decisive factor in hastening it . . . join the local where you live."[18]

Party officials and particularly the region's socialist journals approached the 1912 local and national elections with great optimism. Everett's *Commonwealth* offered simply, "This is our year." SPW officials saw positive signs of this as party membership statewide reached 7,146 in the summer of 1912—the largest paid socialist membership in its history. The *Socialist Voice* encouraged its readership: "Comrades, the future looks bright." Even newspapers such as the *Portland Labor Press*, which favored trade unionism and the AFL over socialist politics, marveled at the "Surprising Growth of [the] Socialists' Vote." The rising vigor of the socialist vote, the paper continued, ultimately meant a "strength with which the great parties in 1912 will have to reckon."[19]

For party organizers, increased attendance at socialist events demonstrated further evidence of the "amazing growth of socialism." In 1911, for example, when Everett socialists held their annual picnic, approximately two hundred people were present; a year later fifteen hundred reportedly attended. Party coordinators contended that the larger attendance "must portend sad days for the old party politicians." In Seattle similar confidence abounded. The city's *Socialist Voice* announced that, with more systematic distribution of the *Socialist Voice* and with clear reference to Congressman Victor Berger's election, "We shall soon make Seattle another Milwaukee." Seattle socialists sensed coming victories at the polls. The *Socialist Voice*, employing an agricultural metaphor, proclaimed: "The people's hearts are right . . . we will harvest the biggest socialist crop that was ever harvested in the United States before long, and think of the thrashing time . . . by the use of the Socialist party."[20]

Like their comrades to the west, Montana's socialists, with over two thousand members, boasted a party organization the state party secretary, W. J. Beans, called "indeed alive." He added that his office could not keep up with all the necessary correspondence because party membership was growing so rapidly. In the wake of the 1911 elections, new local chapters spurred the growth of the organization. The state office received applications asking for approval of at least three new charters in 1911: the Finnish community in Helena, and the towns of Hoffman and Washoe. Before his election as mayor of Butte, state secretary Lewis Duncan celebrated the state party's widely growing membership. Not only was the Missoula local "doing herself proud and helping out the party bravely," he observed, but municipalities such as Great Falls and Miles City also reported memberships of more than fifty.[21]

Successful elections with unions also spurred socialist confidence. A dispatch from Butte celebrated recent socialist victories in the Butte Miner's Union elections. The union election on December 7, 1911, resulted in a sweep of all ten key positions, from president to warden. The *International Socialist Review* reported the election was particularly significant because "every official elected is a militant socialist, and a member of the Socialist Party." Yet unanimous support for socialism in Butte failed to occur. Anti-socialist employers fired miners affiliated with the socialist party. Party member E. L. Williams, writing from Butte, said, "Gradually the capitalists are weeding out the men active in Socialist circles in Butte by refusing to employ them."[22]

For optimistic socialists in the Northwest, however, continued labor tensions, such as those in Butte, led them to predict electoral success. As the *Appeal to Reason* reminded readers, "socialism is the product of economic conditions." Activists' confidence also seemed justified, as they could, in fact, point to low or declining wages and unfair or unhealthy work schedules and conditions. Socialists hoped these declining labor conditions would translate into coming electoral victories. "The future," claimed the *Appeal*, "belongs to socialism."[23]

Indeed, poor conditions for workers in Idaho were also widespread. The state secretary of the Idaho Socialist Party, I. F. Stewart, observed "ripe conditions" for socialism. In his estimation, "everyone is disgusted with the old order." Stewart predicted that "with the crystallization of sentiment and the rapid growth of our organization we are confident of capturing many municipal strongholds, invad[ing] the legislature, and possibly send[ing] a man to Congress this fall." Not only the miners of Coeur d'Alene experienced poor conditions. Farmers were reportedly "beginning to wake up out here." For Idaho's agriculturalists, Stewart observed, "Capitalism is really getting his land. High taxes, high cost of living, excessive freight rates, and poor markets," he reflected, painted a grim picture for Idaho's agrarian population. "The finished portrait," he remarked, "will be a poor house."[24]

Grim employment conditions in Oregon were all too apparent in Portland, where in early 1912 unemployment reportedly affected fourteen thousand people. Such large numbers of unemployed, according to socialists, meant that labor faced "a starving condition." Reports sent from Oregon to the national party described inhuman treatment of the unemployed, who were "rounded up" and ordered to leave the city.[25]

For critics of the wage system and its extremes of wealth and poverty, western Montana's copper mining industry provided further evidence of a failed capitalistic system. Writing in the *International Socialist Review* in the summer of 1912, Frank Bohn exposed "the crimes of Amalgamated," meaning F. Augustus Heinze's Amalgamated Copper Company, which for decades dominated the area economy. Bohm called it the enemy. He emphasized the economic gap between workers and "the Stockholders in the East and Europe." Of the $30 million Amalgamated earned annually, only $10 million filtered to the workers, who provided "the labor of production below and above ground." Amalgamated's "real crimes," he declared, were "bribery, thievery, social war, [and] murder."

Butte miners faced tenuous conditions. In 1911, job hazards at Amalgamated killed forty-seven men. One worker recalled that "few miners . . . live to be over fifty unless they stop work." Now in office, Mayor Duncan rebuked the corporation. "Here the whole town," he wrote, "working class and middle class alike, suffer from the depredations of the Amalgamated Copper Company." Montana's labor inequities, however, were not confined to Butte. In Great Falls, as James B. Scott wrote in the *International Socialist Review*, teamsters demanded a $.50 per day wage increase and, when they did not get it, went on strike for more than four months. During their protest the teamsters faced arrests and indictments. There, Scott declared, "The spirit of revolt is in the air." During the strike, the famous socialist "stump speaker" Tom Lewis visited Great Falls, reportedly taking "the 1,500 men and women by storm. Never in the history of Great Falls was there such an enthusiastic meeting."[26]

For visitors like Bohn and Scott, Butte and Great Falls typified vibrant socialist cities. Bohn called Butte "a place which a Socialist worker visits and investigates with a degree of satisfaction which is simply inspiring." Montana's restless labor force was important for socialism's growth, he argued, declaring that "the working class of the State of Montana are awakening, the battle cry for industrial freedom is resounding; the state is full of proletarian agitators and the masters of the bread are afraid of the rising 'mob' that threatens the destruction of their profits."[27]

By 1912, Washington State, too, witnessed widespread labor tensions. When worker strikes ripped Hoquiam, Raymond, and Gray's Harbor, newspaper headlines such as "No Use for the Dead" reminded readers of the adversarial employer-employee relationship. The *Appeal to Reason* condemned the Northern Pacific for the fate of George F. Bailey, a Tacoma resident killed while working as a switchman for the railroad. Company officials wasted no time removing Bailey from their payroll, thus abandoning his widow. The *Appeal* viewed the company's lack of empathy as a "lesson workers everywhere should heed." In Spokane, too, labor realities remained grim. A *Portland Labor Press* headline warned workers to "Stay Away From Spokane," because "scab herding employer[s]" had "paralyzed the city." Spokane's *Industrial Worker* mocked socialism's detractors in political cartoons. "'I also oppose Socialism,' said the lean and hungry working man" in one tongue-in-cheek caricature "as he looked longingly into his dinner bucket, 'It might get me a square meal and I'm sure my system couldn't stand the shock.'"[28]

As these and other circumstances in Idaho, Oregon, Montana, and Washington clearly indicated, few could deny what the *Appeal to Reason* described as "widespread destitution, misery, wretchedness, suffering, and poverty among the working class." The *Portland Labor Press* warned of a "Labor War Coming in the

Northwest" as "industrial war clouds gathered."[29] Northwest socialists hoped to capitalize on these regional gloomy labor and economic conditions and, as the 1912 elections approached, translate them into victory at the polls.

During these troubled times for labor, the Socialist Party of America held its 1912 convention in May in Indianapolis, just as it had in its formative year. By then the party had reached its political stride. Every state except South Carolina sent delegates to the meeting. The party boasted 100,845 paid members and its coffers were solid enough to provide train fare for many delegates to attend. During the sessions, socialists continued to outline their vision for a truly distinct party, separate from "capitalist" influences. Delegates resolved (perhaps symbolically, given voter confidentiality) that any member who was found to have voted for a nonsocialist candidate in the upcoming election would be guilty of "party treason" and the member would face "expulsion from the party."[30]

Pacific Northwest delegates played an important role in party debates and referendums, particularly concerning matters of radical syndicalism and sabotage (of capitalistic enterprises). At one point Lewis Duncan acted as chair and was a particularly significant delegate because he supported the Debs candidacy, despite opposition from Morris Hillquit and others. The national party convention was filled with internal dissent, and northwest socialists visibly participated in these feuds. One critical and divisive issue was the sabotage matter. A December 1911 party referendum had called for the expulsion of any member who advocated sabotage, a measure that had removed William "Big Bill" Haywood from the National Executive Council. Socialist organizations in only ten states and territories voted against the referendum for Haywood's recall, but they included Montana, Oregon, and Washington, attesting to the Pacific Northwest's particularly "radical" reputation.[31]

Several weeks before the national convention, northwest socialists mobilized for their state meetings. The SPW met in Seattle in March and adopted a platform that recognized "all the arbitrary, cruel and inhuman methods used by the capitalist class in this class war." The platform called for public ownership of municipal and monopolized utilities, reform of state health and sanitation, restriction of labor hours and conditions, and installation of the initiative and referendum statutes to better involve the citizenry in the political process. The *International Socialist Review* praised the SPW document for its "expression of the wishes and the aims of the wage-workers," and an agenda true to "the principles of international socialism." Yet like most socialist documents adopted at these conventions, the platform reflected typical party demands, including "the social ownership of [the] means of production" and "an overthrow of the present capitalist system of exploitation." In addition to their endorsement of Debs and his vice presidential running mate Emil Seidel, Washington socialists also nominated candidates for all key state positions, from governor to land commissioner.[32]

The national socialist press followed Washington's party activism and growth, praising the SPW in the *International Socialist Review* for two reasons: Washington's clear (and "revolutionary") platform and its active party membership. Washington socialists, according to observers, had "made wonderful progress . . . during the last two years." The state secretary reinforced these assessments with his account of more than six thousand paid-up members. This figure meant a ratio of one party member for every two hundred people in the state.[33]

Montana socialists held their convention in the summer of 1912 amidst similarly optimistic reports. During their Butte meeting they resolved to establish an official statewide socialist newspaper—which became the Butte-based *Montana Socialist.* Enjoying a 171-percent increase in paid membership over the previous year, Montana socialists demonstrated, according to the *International Socialist Review,* that "political warfare" was occurring in their state. "The onward sweep . . . gaining momentum every month," attested to the "rapidly awakening class-consciousness" in Montana. One attendee lauded this "real movement of, by, and for the working class." Others pointed to the success of the Duncan administration in Butte. His administration, "coming into power with a big debt on the city," had reportedly restored the city's financial stability, separated brothels from Butte's many saloons, and improved city sanitation.[34]

In smaller Montana communities such as Stockett, socialist efforts also enjoyed great energy. Stockett socialists reported that their party activity was doing well and enjoying Finnish support in the community. Activists scoffed at the rallies of the Democrats and Republicans, marked with "brass bands, cigars and free booze." In contrast, socialists distributed literature because "booze wears off." In Prairie, Montana, state leaders noticed equally vigorous party activity. A visiting speaker to Prairie later praised members of the local. "Now let me tell you something about this bunch of Prairie drylanders," he began, "You have already published the fact . . . that they built their own meeting hall twenty-five days after organizing, but that's only half the story. They built it without any money! This little local can be counted on as one of the live ones in the state, and they will be heard from good and strong in what is left of Choteau County in the coming election."[35]

Montana's socialist organizers saw encouraging statewide signs of party growth. "We are having new locals formed every few days, and the general outlook is excellent," state secretary Lewis Duncan wrote. "The January stamp sales were 1,826, and our present membership is more than 2,100, which is a gain of over 100% in the last year."[36]

The Idaho socialist party's state secretary, I. F. Stewart, also reported encouraging growth. Between September 1911 and May 1912, the number of locals had doubled to one hundred twenty. The state party estimated eighteen hundred paid members and planned a "wonderful showing" in the upcoming elections. No issue seemed trivial, as exemplified by a protest from the Twin Falls local regarding excessive postage costs passed on by the national office.[37]

"Fine reports come in from Oregon" as well, the *International Socialist Review* observed. There, state socialists also typified the political demands of their northwest comrades. Party members in Medford produced a "stout little platform" that called for municipal ownership of public utilities, abolition of binding contract labor, creation of a free employment bureau, improvement of the city's sanitary conditions, and adoption of a universal eight-hour workday.[38]

During this period of electoral success and party growth, socialist publishers and distributors of both local and regional newspapers committed themselves to educating the working class about the value of socialism. According to the *Appeal,* an "army of idle workers" was "thinking, studying, asking questions, beginning to understand the cause." A central mechanism for this "thinking" was their access to numerous socialist newspapers, journals, and pamphlets, of which the Pacific Northwest possessed many. Washington alone boasted at least seven newspapers in socialist strongholds such as Seattle and Everett, and also in smaller towns such as Kelso, Centralia, and Aberdeen. Through their concerted efforts, regional publishers during this period enjoyed reaching peaks in both the number and circulation levels of their socialist newspapers.[39]

Among Pacific Northwest socialist periodicals, the *Butte Socialist,* which began publication in December 1910, was one of the most prominent publications. By mid-1911 it boasted a weekly circulation of approximately fourteen thousand free issues. The *Appeal to Reason* described it as the "latest youngster" on the northwest propaganda scene. The Butte Socialist Publishing Company, incorporated in August 1911, aimed to establish, in addition to the local *Butte Socialist,* a statewide weekly and a larger printing plant. The new company accomplished both goals in short order. In September 1912 the *Montana Socialist* began publication, and in the summer of 1913 the new printing plant took shape, capable of handling the large printing demands required during election cycles. By 1913 Montana socialists were also producing the statewide paper, supervising the publishing plant, and working "on active propaganda all the time."[40]

Several smaller socialist papers also appeared. In Lewiston, Idaho, Alexander Humble established the *Inland Echo.* The *Echo* reported on working-class issues in Idaho, Montana, Washington, and Oregon. One Southwick, Idaho, activist understood the importance of propaganda, admitting, "we're pretty scattered out here, but I am carrying on the work. If any of the comrades have literature they would send me it would help a lot." Another small regional paper, the *3 Hour Day*, appeared in Seattle. Described by the *International Socialist Review* as a "snappy little journal," it claimed an agenda that "will appeal to every wage worker": it advocated work-hour restrictions. To help the *3 Hour Day* along, the *International Socialist Review* distributed sample copies. Portland's *Single Tax Broacher*, published only irregularly in 1912, hoped to introduce the emerging "single tax" idea to Oregonians.[41]

Some of Oregon's mainstream and socialist papers addressed the blurred lines of the AFL-socialist relationship. The state organ of the AFL, the *Portland Labor Press*, underwent an important change from 1911 to 1914. The paper shifted from previously sparse to more attentive coverage of socialist politics. A December 1911 article displayed a rare moment of pro-socialist sentiment. "The struggle between organized labor and organized capital," the author wrote, "is a war of class interest." In this appeal to "unionize the ballot box," he concluded, "If the Socialist party principles answer [*sic*] this new regime of a co-operative industrial government, embrace it." While this language demonstrated an alteration in the paper's tone, more changes came. By August 1914 the *Portland Labor Press* dedicated a weekly section to its "Department of Socialism." Meanwhile, a specifically socialist paper, the Finnish *Toveri*, of Astoria, found itself struggling to balance socialist politics with pro-AFL and pro-IWW forces. In 1911 Oregon socialists established at least two other papers—one in Medford, which the *Portland Labor Press* praised as a "brave little paper"—and the short-lived socialist *Times* in Portland.[42]

Distribution of regional and national propaganda materials remained essential to socialist activism. Organizers at the local level frequently solicited pamphlets and materials from state and national sources. One of Montana's prominent agitators, J. F.

Mabie, gladly fulfilled the request for materials from a comrade in Harlowtown, encouraging the distribution of leaflets to "some of the working men who are using their brains to find a way out of this capitalistic bog hole in which the working class is stuck." Widely circulated socialist newspapers and journals such as the *Appeal to Reason* and the *International Socialist Review* remained popular. In some cases, such as in Havre, Montana, communities led the nation in subscription orders. Even on-the-street activists often emerged as propaganda heroes. The *International Socialist Review* printed a picture and description of Seattle socialist Millard Price. Price operated the "only Socialist news cart in the North-west" and his monthly sales exceeded five thousand publications. With his less-than-subtle all-red cart, Price worked daily on First Avenue and Columbia Street from 9 A.M. to 5:30 P.M.[43]

Socialist speakers and motivational rallies remained equally vital to party growth, fundraising, and maintaining members' enthusiasm. In anticipation of the 1912 election, a number of nationally significant socialists visited the Northwest on speaking tours. These appearances by leading party figures represented another central element of northwest activism and strategy.[44]

When Eugene V. Debs, the consummate voice of American socialism, went on the campaign trail in his fourth presidential bid he did not neglect the Pacific Northwest. In the late summer of 1912, with only two months remaining until the election, he visited a number of cities, including Spokane, Seattle, Everett, Billings, Butte, and Portland. In late August his supporters filled the twenty-five hundred seats of Butte's largest opera house while many more partisans listened outside. On September 1, Debs addressed the Everett faithful in the city's five-thousand-seat coliseum. He discussed the impending socialist revolution and predicted victory in the upcoming election. Among the crowd, he said, he could "feel the throb of the social revolution that will sweep capitalism and the wage system out of existence and usher in the working class commonwealth and social republic." Debs pointed to the similarities of the Republican, Democratic, and

Progressive parties, labeling them "three wings of one . . . capitalist party." Only the Socialist party, he claimed, could topple capitalism, emancipate workingmen, and establish an "industrial and social democracy." The address excited the Everett socialists who paid the $.25 to $.75 admission fee. The *Commonwealth* called Debs's speech "the greatest address ever delivered in Everett."[45]

Debs continued his northwestern trip with a September 2 stop in Portland. Rally organizers hoped to counter a large picnic held the same day by Oregon's American Federation of Labor. Debs reportedly spoke for over two hours to an audience of between six thousand and seven thousand. The candidate's attacks focused on what he labeled the "Bull Con" party, the "pseudo socialist" Progressives, and former president Theodore Roosevelt. The event also helped with fundraising, covering "over $500" for future party activity.[46]

Other prominent socialists visited the Pacific Northwest during the 1912 campaign. Shortly after Debs's visit, the nation's only socialist congressman, Victor L. Berger of Wisconsin, also spoke at the Everett coliseum before more than two thousand area voters. In his September 22 speech, Berger espoused the doctrine of evolutionary socialism and stressed the importance of party activism. He reminded the audience that "we have nothing to hope from the two old parties," and that a viable socialist party remained the only proletarian voice. And, given the Republican-Progressive split, Berger recognized the opportunity for socialist electoral success. Addressing Theodore Roosevelt's recent Republican defection to seek the presidential candidacy on the new Progressive ticket, Berger claimed, "Teddy Roosevelt is doing this party a great service." At Debs's rally in Bellingham, the *Commonwealth* reported, were "1,500 enthusiastic people." Socialists were especially satisfied because in the same venue the Progressive candidate for governor, Robert Hodge, had managed to draw only three hundred attendees.[47]

Among the other prominent socialists appearing in the Northwest on the eve of the election were George Kirkpatrick, author of the popular pamphlet "War, What For?" who lectured at Liberty Hall in Everett. Socialist stump speaker Benjamin F. Wilson addressed mining communities in Montana and northern Idaho. Fred D. Warren, the "fighting editor" of the Kansas office of the *Appeal to Reason,* spoke in eleven Pacific Northwest cities before what the *Appeal* described as "large and appreciating audiences." In North Yakima the crowd was most "enthusiastic" and included many nonsocialists and policemen. Perhaps six thousand heard Warren's message in Portland. Indicative of the challenge socialists faced from mainstream presses, the *Portland Labor Press* expressed dismay that Warren, a man of "national prominence," did not receive coverage in other newspapers.[48]

In addition to sponsoring frequent picnics and social dances, socialist organizers across the nation rallied on the eve of the election. More than five thousand local chapters and two million party members gathered nationwide on October 13, 1912, for "Socialist Day" rallies. Socialists everywhere met to hear messages from Debs and vice presidential candidate Emil Seidel read aloud. For party members, the celebration attested to broader party growth and solidarity. According to their leaders, Socialist Day had no precedent in American history.[49]

As they prepared for the November elections, northwest socialist speakers addressed a number of important political issues. Of utmost importance, they had to distinguish themselves as a legitimate alternative to the Democratic, Republican, and Progressive parties. And, as historians Seymour Lipset and Gary Marks have noted, the Republican, Democratic, and Progressive parties "exploited and reinforced the lack of political class consciousness among American workers" at the expense of socialists, as workers voted instead along ethnic, religious, and racial lines.

By 1912, however, Progressive politics especially had begun to complicate socialists' effectiveness. That year, according to Carlos Schwantes, northwest Progressivism reached its "high tide," and party reforms continually mirrored several socialist goals. Progressive reformers in Washington's Joint Legislative Committee, for example, had previously influenced legislation in favor of workmen's compensation, eight-hour workdays for women, and woman suffrage. Not surprisingly, the *Portland Labor Press* observed that the socialist party was not "regarded as an essential feature of government in Portland." Emphasizing that their party constituted a critical alternative, as noted earlier, socialists lumped the three main opposing parties into the "capitalist" camp. For Pacific Northwest socialists, "the two old party platforms" especially failed to address the faults of the wage system and the concerns of "honest working people." Socialists appealed to frustrated voters with this plea: "If you are tired of insincerity and inefficiency of the old capitalist parties, then come and try the young, vigorous, progressive, honest socialist party." An Olga, Washington, socialist agreed: "republicans, democrats, progressives are so near alike that you cannot distinguish the difference between them." In contrast, socialists claimed, "the Socialist party goes straight to the heart of the problem" with its anti-capitalism message.

Socialists aimed their partisan attacks specifically at the Republican Party, labeling its 1912 platform "the finest piece of sophistry and unadulterated lying that has ever been offered as a political declaration." The Republican platform, socialists claimed, tried to cover up the GOP's labor record. While Republicans pledged to improve work-safety conditions, restrict the employment of women and children, and enact "comprehensive and generous" workman's compensation laws, their own congressional members, socialists gladly reminded workers, had in fact opposed such reforms.[50]

Socialists also hoped their record and position on temperance and restrictions on liquor would distinguish them from the other parties. The party officially endorsed temperance in 1912 and its national platform required socialists who held municipal positions to work to shut down saloons. By this time the national temperance movement had also reached full strength, and some northwest socialists hoped their anti-drink positions could become *their* issue. Washington's socialist candidate for governor in 1912, Anna Maley, declared, "Our party is THE party of temperance." The region's socialist administrations had already proven themselves advocates of temperance and drink restrictions. In Butte, Mayor Duncan closed a number of the town's saloons and dance halls, reportedly slashing by two-thirds the profits of those businesses. Similarly, Spokane commissioner Coates mandated "strict enforcement of saloon regulations."[51]

Like temperance, a tax debate emerged in the 1912 races. Steeped in the late-nineteenth-century writings of Henry George, the so-called "single tax"—an equalized tax on land values—gained political momentum. Single-tax proposals by various reformers divided labor advocates and socialists alike. Advocates of the tax claimed it meant a breakup of "landlordism." Socialists generally remained divided on the issue because the tax plan failed to negate totally the profit system and hence the tax was only "partially socialistic." Many farmers, meanwhile, opposed it because they perceived a heavier financial burden on their property holdings. Some northwest communities, such as Everett, passed single-tax measures.

The single-tax debate drew the most reaction and coverage in Oregon. According to the *Portland Labor Press*, support for the single tax came from both broad sections of organized labor and from "progressive men" with loose connections to labor. The single-tax work of Oregon's trade unionists, in the name of producers and to ensure fairness, was, in the words of historian Lawrence Lipin, "a radical assault on land monopoly." Beginning in 1912, under the auspices of the Graduated Single Tax League of Oregon, unionists offered a series of failed but important single-tax initiatives intended to break up monopolistic land holdings. Even the state socialist party weighed in with support for the proposition, they said, because a single tax, "in its primitive state," nevertheless "strikes at the very foundation of capitalism." Yet other outspoken socialists simultaneously criticized the single tax as a weak imitation of true socialist principles. They claimed the tax issue was a plot by property owners to "sidetrack socialism" by only halfheartedly restricting wealthy landowners.[52]

On issues of female suffrage and women's rights, Pacific Northwest socialists articulated clear positions. Capitalism and the inequities in the wage system particularly affected women, socialists argued, and prostitution typified their subjugation. Northwest socialists, accordingly, took aim at "women of the town." Lewis Duncan described prostitution as a "social disease," and his administration effectively "discontinued the old practice of blackmail on women of the red light district" with "strict enforcement" of prostitution regulations. In 1914 Duncan's administration allowed Amanda Pfeiffer, a missionary for the Florence Crittenton Rescue Circle, to patrol Butte streets in search of "erring girls." In addition to prostitution's moral implications, Socialists also criticized the "business" of prostitution. Duncan's administration refused to fine Butte's "fallen women" and accordingly, socialists claimed, the city's "big business" interests lost interest in the red-light district as a "tax-producing agency." By stamping out immoral and economically unfair professions, socialists argued, the wage system (and "wage slavery") could be abolished and the final step for the human race achieved: the "Industrial Democracy."[53]

Pacific Northwest suffrage advocates had been active since the Civil War in the midst of a population that was predominately male. Idaho enfranchised women in 1896, and Washington delivered their voting rights in 1910. However, in Oregon and Montana the battle for female suffrage still raged. Those two states granted women the vote (Oregon in 1912 and Montana in 1914), with socialists actively advocating equal suffrage. According to an editorial in the Everett *Commonwealth*, political freedom and universal enfranchisement of women had always been "an 'immediate demand' of the socialist party." Presidential candidate Debs's Portland speech, according to the *Portland Labor Press*, was "an eloquent plea for Women's Suffrage." Oregon socialists, as elsewhere in the Northwest, followed "previous education and party principle" and supported equal suffrage. Socialists actively encouraged northwest women to "think and study in order to cast your vote intelligently" in favor, of course, of socialist candidates.[54]

In the Pacific Northwest, as they did elsewhere, women engaged in socialist party activity, which included, as socialist journals noted, running for political office. Three candidates for Washington offices in 1912 were women: Anna Maley for governor, Frances Sylvester for superintendent of public instruction, and Minnie Parks for state treasurer. And it was not unusual for women to work as campaigners. Twin Falls, Idaho, boasted a women's committee, "twenty-eight strong," that distributed literature and wrote editorials. Their work, the *Appeal to Reason* said, stood as "something that can be followed elsewhere." During a Great Falls strike, moreover, thirty women marched against local stores whose policies were unfair to labor. This involvement indicated to some that "it will only be a matter of a few years" before Montana's women would serve in the "foremost ranks on the Industrial battlefield."[55]

While temperance and suffrage were important issues, socialists also faced ongoing political challenges specific to working-class associations. By 1912 the socialist relationship to the increasingly radicalized IWW continued to raise important questions among socialists about the party's direction, often with mixed sentiments. Indeed, the years from 1909 to 1915 marked the height of the IWW's "free speech" crusade, and northwest laborers in the timber and agricultural industries increasingly subscribed to the IWW's radical message. Ironically, perhaps, Wobblies themselves remained disinterested in party politics. Broadly, the IWW believed that socialist party agitators working within the parameters of traditional politics could never be anything but "prisoners" of a corrupt capitalist system. And while political indifference by Wobblies drew members to the SPA—whose membership doubled between 1909 and 1911—regional socialist leaders felt somewhat stymied. They recognized the interconnectedness of IWW-socialist party activity but did not always welcome IWW methods, particularly given false public perceptions that the two organizations were mutually and constantly cooperative. Some Portland labor leaders conceded that the IWW was "more or less a public nuisance," while others were undecided about how to handle the IWW-Socialist Party relationship. Duncan labeled the regional IWW "agitation" "ill-advised," and its approach "not welcome to socialists." Yet during the summer of 1911, "Big Bill" Haywood, a key IWW leader, spoke at two Butte engagements; one of those addresses, according to Duncan, was a "cracking good speech." Such attitudinal inconsistencies within both groups continued to prove worrisome among socialists.[56]

Within the American Federation of Labor, too, the lines between the IWW, sabotage, syndicalism, and political socialism remained blurred. The AFL, through constant, chronic maneuvering, hoped to couple, in people's minds, IWW radicalism with socialist politics, which would also tag socialists with the IWW label. Socialists, in turn, hoped to squelch this "guilt by association" rhetoric. AFL head Samuel Gompers articulated the murky lines between the IWW, sabotage, syndicalism, and political socialism: "Just when Socialists are Syndicalists, and Syndicalists Socialists, it is difficult to determine. In no country do the Socialists refuse to profit by any of the rash steps of the Syndicalists." Gompers, meanwhile, continued to emphasize the more rational approach of trade unionism. "In the presence of syndicalism and the other wild 'isms' that would paralyze society to cure it," Gompers wrote, "we say to the world that the trade unions, as affiliated to the American Federation of Labor, represent the true spirit and thought, the just activities, and the high aspirations of labor." For his part, Eugene Debs fueled the political fire in a 1912 Labor Day speech in Portland when he shouted, "I am an industrial unionist!" and then criticized trade-union activity as "puerile and ineffective."

Amidst the rhetorical posturing of Debs and others it should be noted that not all socialists remained ambivalent, as Eugene Debs was, toward the AFL. Victor Berger and Morris Hillquit stated openly that "the Socialist Party is absolutely committed to a policy of friendship to organized labor, and unequivocally recognizes the A.F.L. of today as the main representative of organized labor." Socialist gradualists even adopted the strategy of "boring within" the AFL, hoping that radicals could agitate on labor's behalf from within the organization and thereby muscle Samuel Gompers and conservatives out of power. The tactics showed some signs of success: at the 1912 AFL convention, one in four delegates was an SPA loyalist.[57] Still, as with their IWW association, the way socialist relationships with the AFL functioned and fluctuated continued to be a significant challenge for assuring party viability.

As AFL and socialist forces disagreed, Oregon followed some of their most politically charged debates. The Northwest's *Portland Labor Press,* remaining staunchly anti-socialist, was quick to label all socialists as nihilists. Regarding socialists, the newspaper claimed, "Their doctrine is in reality a new breed of anarchy." The socialist weakness, the paper continued, resulted from its alienation of rank-and-file workers in speeches that "vilif[ied] and abuse[d] the faithful." Nevertheless, at conventions and meetings socialist leaders remained divided on the AFL issue. The *Portland Labor Press* claimed that at those events, the "'trade union resolutions' have awakened a bitterness." Columnist Robert Hunter wrote that the "two great arms of the working class"—the Socialist party and the trade unions—tried "always to weaken and sometimes to destroy either the one or the other."[58]

At the Socialist Party of America's 1912 national convention, however, socialist politics and trade unionism began to find common ground. One resolution they adopted recognized that "organized workers are rapidly developing an enlightened and militant class-consciousness" at the hands of successful organization by trade unions and federations. The SPW included in its 1912 platform similar cooperative phraseology, endorsing "all unified action of the workers and pledge[d] ourselves to assist them by supplying speakers, money and other necessary support whenever possible."[59]

Along with temperance, suffrage, and unionism issues, socialists also confronted the rise of American militarism. As escalating conflict in Europe portended war, in the Pacific Northwest, socialists spoke out against the possibility of capitalist wars pitting "laborer versus laborer." A flurry of small books and pamphlets addressed socialist reasoning and its objections to war. George Kirkpatrick's "War, What For?" stood as one of the most searing indictments of war and early-twentieth-century militarism. The *Socialist Voice* claimed the pamphlet made sense "among those who think." The Socialist Party of Washington's antimilitarism extended to its formal opposition to the Boy Scouts of America. "We are absolutely opposed to the Boy Scout movement," the party's 1912 platform declared, "and the teaching of military drill with guns and other means of destruction of human life, to our school children."[60]

With socialism's recent successes in municipal elections, its ongoing activism, and its political positions more or less defined, the 1912 elections arrived. The elections symbolized an important step toward electoral success, and national socialists predicted huge gains. The *International Socialist Review* glowed, "Never in the history of the Socialist movement in America have we had so much cause for rejoicing." The *Appeal to Reason* predicted Debs would win 8,000 votes in Montana, 10,000 in Idaho, 24,400 in Washington, and 45,000 in Oregon. With the exception of Oregon, the final socialist vote exceeded his expectations and Debs polled more than 10 percent in Idaho, Montana, and Washington, and 9.7 percent in Oregon.[61]

Montana socialists showed improvements garnering votes at the ballot box, especially in Silver Bow County, which included Butte. There, the socialist vote for Debs totaled 27.9 percent, second only to victor Woodrow Wilson's 38.2 percent. County socialists, according to historian Jerry Calvert, came "from virtual oblivion" in the elections of 1908 and 1909 to now take an "impressive" second place finish. Other Montana communities also saw impressive gains. Phillipsburg reported 90 votes for Debs in this first election to carry a socialist on the ballot. Clear socialist majorities elected state representatives from Eureka and Libby. Red Lodge and Carbon County, with the help of their strong Finnish contingency, recorded a plurality in favor of gubernatorial candidate Lewis Duncan, who garnered over 12,500 votes in defeat. Regardless of Duncan's losing effort, the *International Socialist Review* applauded Montana's "remarkable gains" in 1912. Idaho, too, celebrated municipal victories in its smaller communities, including Cataldo,

Colburn, and Laclede. Naples elected three socialists: two justices of the peace and a constable.[62]

Outside Portland, where three precincts reported Debs majorities, Oregon socialists fared less successfully. Yet the local secretary for Portland compared Oregon's 1908 socialist vote (7,339) to strong gains in 1912 (14,874). In addition, Oregon elected two socialist state legislators.[63]

Washington state displayed the greatest gains in socialist support. Their support tripled its 1904 showing and almost doubled the percentage for Debs—from 6.9 percent in 1904 to 12.4 percent in 1912. Those increases were particularly impressive when compared to trendsetting Oklahoma, where, for the same period, Debs gained more than 16 percent. The SPW rejoiced at news that the socialist vote in Port Angeles and Clallam County had doubled from 300 in 1910 to 610 in 1912, and that the residents of Bangor, Washington, elected a socialist constable despite the "combined opposition of the capitalist parties." Olympia, the state capital, elected a socialist justice, and a constable won office in Thurston County. In Yakima County, the Grandview precinct elected socialist William Davey justice of the peace. As in Oregon and Montana, Washington elected two socialist state legislators. As these gains indicated, compared to the party nationally, the Socialist Party of Washington appeared strong, and fared exceptionally well.[64]

Following the 1912 contests socialists expressed satisfaction with their significant performance. Headlining "We Did Fine," the *Appeal to Reason* underscored the party's gains despite Debs's defeat. "It is well to remember," the *Appeal* noted, "that there has never been an election but that the Socialists showed a gain over the preceding election."[65] Time, they believed, was on their side. With their 1911 municipal victories and the 1912 presidential outcome, they looked to the future with confidence. As they discovered, however, organizational squabbles and international affairs would soon undermine their cause.

5

From "Socialist Supremacy" to "Disharmony and Disruption"
Party Turmoil, 1913–1916

Comrades and friends . . . we are in distress. Regardless of the shades of opinion, red, yellow, green, or pink, that may indicate to yourselves your superiority over fellow revolutionists . . . new and great issues are now confronting our organization. *Northwest Worker*, 10 February 1916

PINPOINTING when the Socialist Party of America began its decline has attracted considerable historical debate. Some scholars purport that the party's slow deterioration followed its 1912 successes. Other scholars contend that it held strong until World War I, when anti-radicalism reached new heights—an argument that has more validity in the Pacific Northwest than elsewhere.[1] The socialist outlook in the region, with some exceptions, appeared positive until after 1916. In activism, propaganda, and election results, northwest socialists continued their work and felt certain they had little reason for concern about their future. They believed that the success of 1912 ensured continued triumphs. Not until the approach of World War I and the paranoia and government crackdown on suspected socialists and communists, known as the "Red Scare," would anti-radicalism and factionalism ultimately combine to cripple the party.

After the Socialist Party of America's impressive 1912 showing at the polls, party membership held firm and, in most states, continued to rise. Nationally in 1914 the party boasted 118,045 dues-paying members, doubling the 58,011 count in 1910. Growth in the Northwest contributed to the swelling party ranks. Washington, one of the movement's leading states, boasted 202 locals and 3,330 paid members in 1913; the Socialist Party of Washington continued to have between two thousand and three thousand paid members through 1916. During 1915, membership in Washington made the biggest gains of any state in the union. In Oregon, socialists reported being "as busy as in former days" and relied heavily on party activity in Portland. "Local Portland is on the boom," declared the *Northwest Worker*, and the city's socialists held an average of six meetings per week. A visit to comrades in Portland, the *International Socialist Review* promised, "will find the hall always open and some one [*sic*] on the job."[2]

Conventional forms of activism remained important to the swelling party ranks. Reports of meetings, subscription sales, and organizing activities across the Northwest encouraged optimism among the party faithful. The creation and expansion of locals remained central to party activity, as locals continually planned and executed countless party events. The new chapter in Centralia, Washington, had five committees by 1913 that handled event planning. Everett reported "many successful socialist activities," including lectures, debates, and balls; it planned a "vigorous organization and membership campaign" for the 1914 elections. Socialists in Whitman County, Washington, prepared for that election at their January 13 convention in Colfax, pledging "a vigorous propaganda campaign" and planning to launch a socialist newspaper. Similarly active, the Portland local held meetings every Sunday and a social dance on Tuesdays. In addition, the city's meeting hall was "well located," with a seating capacity of one thousand. Idaho socialists, too, reported heightened activism. With elections looming, they observed, "the movement begins to take on a spirit of greater activity."[3]

Socialists devised innovative and inclusive membership campaigns. The interest in socialist literature in the Pacific Northwest continued beyond the 1912 elections, and organizers in Washington and Oregon were praised for their educational efforts. The *International Socialist Review* commended Washington for being "first in the field" to announce study clubs in cities such as Puyallup. In 1913 the SPW also established a "Socialist

Education Bureau," offering lectures on American history from the labor perspective. SPW state secretary Frans Bostrom ordered the distribution of $300 in books, which, according to the *International Socialist Review*, "explains why the Socialists in Washington are among the most intelligent and revolutionary in this country." Comrade C. W. Barzee of Portland started a circulating socialist library in the city, which offered socialist books and pamphlets to readers—on loan or for purchase—encouraging them to begin with Charles H. Kerr's introductory volume, "What Socialism Is."[4] Because Pacific Northwest socialists recruited across gender lines, they built an increasingly inclusive organization. They focused their first membership drives on recruiting young agitators, and after 1912 more teenage Northwesterners joined the Young People's Socialist League (YPSL), an organization directly tied to the SPA. The Seattle chapter, chartered in 1913, had fifty-three members. The Seattle YPSL constitution was "in accordance with the constructive policy of the International Socialist Movement." Everett, not far behind, formed its YPSL in late 1914, also with approximately fifty members.[5]

Pacific Northwest socialist organizations were not only increasingly diverse in their members' age-span, they also maintained a progressive attitude in their acceptance of women and non-whites in a less-than-inclusive national climate. Officially, in the true spirit of socialist equality, the party, as Sally Miller observed, was one of "few institutions in American life in the early twentieth century" with little consideration for race and gender.[6]

In her work on rural politics in Lewis County, Washington, Marilyn Watkins argued that "we still know very little about women's participation in rural political life." Regarding Pacific Northwest socialism, while Watkins's characterization generally holds true, evidence shows that party leaders made concerted efforts to recruit and involve women. A 1913 *Commonwealth* article encouraged married men to engage their wives in the cause. "In your local there are so many more married men than women. Begin now," the article urged, "Insist on her going to meeting . . . . Let us make the party doubly strong by all joining in the campaign for a fifty per cent woman membership."

Women, in fact, took on prominent roles in regional activism as organizers, speakers, and candidates. In Centralia, Washington, the *Socialist Herald* noted that "the social committee is comprised of ladies entirely . . . [putting] on box . . . and toe socials and entertainments of various kinds." The Women's Socialist Study Club of Rainer Valley hosted a picnic on Alki Beach in 1915. Social functions organized by women also doubled as important party fundraisers. Some women also wrote regularly for the party press. The *Butte Socialist* included a "women's column," while another Montana journal, the *Flathead County Socialist*, featured a "women's department." In both Oregon and Washington, women from countless locals served as "Woman's Correspondents" to report, and react to, party activities. In Washington, one writer noted with pride, "There are eighty-three of us now," forming "quite a formidable Socialist Woman's Army."[7]

Both regionally and nationally the majority of party members were native-born, yet immigrant populations also contributed to the organization in varying ways. As eastern European enclaves of German and Russian immigrants—socialists, communists, and anarchists, at least in reputation—arrived, they fed the paranoid imaginations of early-twentieth-century anti-radicalists. By 1913, on the other hand, the socialist party boasted of "foreign branches" including prominent German, Yiddish, Lithuanian, Slavic, Italian, Hungarian, Bohemian, and Polish activists. The northwest experience, however, with some notable exceptions, failed to establish a broad swell of immigrant-comprised local chapters. One organization, the Western Federation of Miners, also reflecting its racism, forbade Mexicans, Finns, and Greeks from joining its organization. Such exclusionist attitudes would surely have discouraged immigrant socialist activity, given the ties between the WFM and the SPA, particularly in places like Butte—home to the largest WFM local—the Butte Miner's Union. Western settlement patterns and outwardly visible WFM nativism may partly explain northwest socialism's limited immigrant presence, but settlement, nativism, and racism are factors more convincing than is the claim of "simply overlooked evidence" of immigrant involvement. Regardless of the reasons, the Pacific Northwest, particularly when compared to the East and even the Midwest, failed to exhibit extensive foreign-born socialist involvement.[8]

Some of the region's most visible and vigorous socialists belonged to Finnish communities. Given their previous involvement with European socialism, Pacific Northwest Finns, for example, brought their "rich socialist culture" to the United States and assumed important roles in party politics. With the 1904 establishment of the Finnish Federation, exclusively Finnish local chapters also formed under the banner of state organizations. At first, most state parties and even the SPA's National Executive Committee (NEC) failed to formally recognize the Finnish Federation; eventually, however, they recognized the dedicated socialist support growing within these communities. In 1907, accordingly, the SPA allowed a Finn member to translate materials for the Chicago national office; and in 1908 the party officially declared itself "in favor" of affiliated foreign-language federations, opening the door for many other ethnicities to organize. Based on the Finnish model, the SPA also announced that any foreign group having more than five hundred members could apply for a translator in the national office, to ensure party documents and messages reached their broadest audience. Nationally, the drive to increase the party's foreign-born segment met with success: by 1915 foreign-language federations claimed thirteen thousand members.[9]

Pacific Northwest Finns exhibited the same dedication and fervor on behalf of the socialist cause as did their American-born comrades. Astoria, Oregon, claimed the region's most notable and active Finnish-socialist community. At the turn of the century Finns comprised some two thousand of the city's residents, ably transplanting their culture and politics to Astoria. They founded the Astoria Finnish Socialist Club in 1905, and two years later established a Finnish-socialist newspaper, the *Toveri*, a key part of regional propagandizing. Until 1931 it was distributed to nearly every state in the West. Their socialist hall opened in 1910 and became a community gathering spot for lectures, meetings, and social events. Astoria Finns also published the official women's paper of the national Finnish Socialist Federation, the *Toveritar*, from 1911 to 1930. Like the *Toveri*, the *Toveritar* served a much wider audience than simply Astoria's Finns.[10]

Because the work of Finns in western Oregon may have inspired and motivated others, Finnish socialists began to form modestly sized locals in several other northwest communities as well. To encourage their activism, the Northwest's socialist organizations offered member discounts from 12.5 percent to 65 percent on dues stamps for Finns. In 1911, eleven charter members formed Montana's Finnish local, in Helena. In and around Winlock, small groups of Finnish settlers began arriving in 1903 to build farms and work in timber. By 1910 their community had grown to more than seventy-five pro-socialist families. Among them were a high number of "Red Finns," whose labor patterns and long-established sense of community aligned with organized socialist principles and drew them to support precincts in Ainslie, Veness, and Prescott. Other Finnish locals sprang up throughout the Pacific Northwest, too, notably in McCall, Idaho; Bonner, Geyser, Hamilton, Red Lodge, Roundup, Sandcoulee, and Stockett, Montana; and Hoquiam, Pearson, Raymond, Roslyn, Spokane, and Wilkeson, Washington.[11]

The vitality of party propaganda, particularly in the socialist press, stood as another sign of northwest socialism's resiliency. From 1912 to 1917, flyers, newspapers, and other print media furthered the socialist message. Pacific Northwest agitators saw to it that nationally prominent socialist journals were particularly well distributed. Many northwest socialists also subscribed to and distributed the Kansas *Appeal to Reason*. In 1913, Washington had 16,922 subscribers, ranking the state's readership ninth in the country. The other prominent national journal of the era, the *International Socialist Review*, also had an impressive circulation in the Northwest. In 1916 in Montana, George H. Curry of the Butte

Workingmen's Union sold one hundred subscriptions. These impressive sales did not surprise the *Review*'s editors, who observed, "The Butte miners have always been to the front in every educational and fighting campaign in this country." For many, there seemed a clear link between party participation and journal subscriptions. F. Olson, from Twin Falls, Idaho, ordered twenty copies of a back issue and declared, "I do not see how anyone who claims to be a Socialist can be without the *Review*." In 1916, hard at work "IWW rebels" in Seattle reportedly ordered "hundreds" of single copies and bought subscriptions to the *Review*. Seattle socialists and IWW organizers sold side by side the *Review* and IWW journals such as the *Industrial Worker* and *Solidarity*. "In other words," proclaimed the *Review*, "the Seattle locals of the I.W.W. are militant workers who not only ta[lk] solidarity, but back it up with action on the soap box and on the job."[12]

In addition to obtaining national papers like the *Appeal to Reason* and the *International Socialist Review* and devouring the works of socialist authors such as Upton Sinclair and Jack London, Pacific Northwest socialists produced—and read—their own pamphlets and other literature. Educational pamphlets, such as Oregon's "Well! Well! Well! What in Thunder do you Socialists Want Anyhow?" outlined socialist principles and provided organizing tips for activists. In Baker County, the Eastern Oregon Socialist Publishing Company offered a flyer filled with organizational outlines and tips from John B. Hunter, the county secretary. Further, pamphlet production increased in anticipation of the 1916 election. Washington leaders planned a statewide distribution campaign, with pamphlets addressing "the farmer question, increasing membership, and working class politics." Activists distributed flyers, dubbed "Benson's Bombshells," on behalf of the 1916 SPA presidential candidate, Allan Benson. In their statewide plan, SPW organizers involved one hundred locals and distributed fifty thousand leaflets a month. Other northwest organizations followed Washington's lead. Portland socialists distributed upwards of twenty thousand pamphlets weekly. Oregon organizers called it "the greatest literature campaign ever attempted." Similarly, Boise activists entered the fray and passed out one thousand Benson leaflets weekly.[13]

From 1912 to 1917 the Pacific Northwest socialist press also continued its success. Socialists across the four states published papers during the period. Presidential candidate Benson remarked that "a Socialist press is indispensable to the success of Socialism. Every dollar's worth of truth promulgated by a Socialist publication will kill a thousand dollar's worth of capitalist lies." Not only were party newspapers important as alternative news sources, they also attracted new members. In 1915 statistics from the SPA national office revealed that approximately 40 percent of new members joined because of the party press, an effective forum for outreach and organizational news. Accordingly, the *Portland Labor Press* observed that socialists were now "receiving more attention" in mainstream newspapers, compared to previous decades when "it was . . . rare . . . to find mention of Socialism in any other than a despised, misrepresented, and very objectionable expression of hatred."[14]

Washington claimed the Pacific Northwest's most vibrant socialist press, whose readership drew largely from the state's more urban western half. The most consistently published socialist newspaper, based in Everett, appeared weekly from 1912 to 1918, under four different names. Established as the *Commonwealth*, in 1914 upon party ownership it became the *Washington Socialist*. The following year its circulation had reached approximately seven thousand, and its readership included socialists in Idaho and Oregon. In July 1915, editors renamed the paper the *Northwest Worker* to reflect its wider audience. In 1917, perhaps to skirt World War I-era persecution, the paper became the unassumingly titled *Co-operative News*.

Seattle socialists produced three newspapers. Stockholders in the Socialist Publishing Association of Seattle published the *Seattle Herald*, a paper that saw limited production during 1916. Also that year, Bruce Rodgers, a former member of the *Appeal to Reason*'s editorial board, founded the *Red Feather*, which said its mission was to do "some 'corrective' work within the Socialist party."

Indicative of various divisions within the party, the *Red Feather* offered readers a range of socialist perspectives. According to the *International Socialist Review*, the *Seattle Daily Call*, established in 1918, was a "great little daily socialist rebel from the great and growing west." To the south, from 1913 to 1914, Tacoma's socialists published their weekly *Truth*. The *International Socialist Review* described it as one that "takes up all current events from the Socialist and working class viewpoint and is class conscious and revolutionary from the first to the last line." This perspective, the *Review* continued, made *Truth* "one of the liveliest periodicals in the western movement." Smaller Washington towns also had socialist papers. In Kelso, the *Socialist News*, also established in 1913, drew praise from the *International Socialist Review* as "the liveliest little party-owned sheet we have seen . . . and contains more Marxian Socialism to the square inch than most of our papers have to the square yard." The next year Port Angeles activists established the *Peninsula Free Press.* "Comrades who are interested in the movement in the northwest, take notice!" wrote the *International Socialist Review.* The *Peninsula Free Press* functioned on an "almost self-sustaining basis" and local socialists voluntarily constructed its printing plant.[15]

Montana and Idaho socialists also produced a number of papers during this period. The *Butte Socialist*, published from 1910 to 1915, led the way. Butte's capitalist newspapers, socialists charged, "dish up fake stories against Socialism and the I.W.W." The *Butte Socialist*, published by the party's county committee, was especially important because it carried socialist viewpoints that "the prostituted papers of Butte . . . dare not print." From 1915 to 1917, the state party published the *Montana Socialist*, also in Butte. Beginning in 1915, in northeastern Montana, Sheridan County radicals in Plentywood published the *Producers News.* It existed until 1937 and represented a number of political perspectives, including those of the Non-Partisan League, the Farmer-Labor Party, and the United Farmers League. In the *Producer's* earliest years, though, its editor was Charles Taylor, a self-described "Socialist in some terms," who later became a two-term

senator in the Montana legislature. Lewiston, Idaho, publisher
W. E. Reynolds reportedly published a newspaper in 1914 cen-
tering on "scientific socialism," while in 1917 the Socialist Party
of Idaho began the *Idaho Party Builder*.[16]

Oregon socialists, too, produced a number of short-lived
papers. *Discontent* (Albany, 1913), *Saturday Review* (Medford,
1913), *Hourglass* (Portland, 1915), *Oregon Herald* (Portland, 1916–
1917), and *Western Socialist* (Portland, 1919) all saw limited runs.
Also, it was not uncommon for the state's socialists to explore
outside options for disseminating party propaganda. Because
Oregon lacked a state socialist journal, vibrant Washington publications such as Everett's *Washington Socialist* gained wide distribution in Portland. Activists sold bundles of it at meeting halls
and street rallies. Oregon's state secretary noted, "The comrades
like the paper very much, and if it keeps up its color and stands
for revolutionary Socialism it will surely be the organ of the revolutionary workers on the Pacific Coast." Even nonsocialist journals provided a voice for the Oregon party. Beginning in 1913,
under an agreement with Portland's Socialist Local Number 2,
the *Portland Labor Press* introduced its "Department of Socialism,"
whose mission was to enlarge on socialist principles "as they apply
to current events and economic conditions." The column facilitated socialist discussion in the previously exclusive American
Federation of Labor (AFL) organ, and voiced a sympathetic tone
toward socialism in what formerly had been a more conservative
paper. "Socialism as a political entity," the editors granted, "has a
place in the future governments of advanced civilization."[17]

Socialist speakers stand as one final vibrant element of party
activism during 1915 and 1916. Countless members addressed
comrades and general audiences alike. In 1915 a SPA national
office study revealed that approximately 7 percent of party members joined after being influenced by lectures and meetings. The
SPA's lyceum lecture series, whose presenters often toured, was
specifically developed to attract new members. Locals chapters,
state officers, and the national party all participated "to build up
the party."[18] Accordingly, both national and regional orators

enjoyed well-attended meetings, particularly around the 1916 elections.

As the campaign season neared, a number of nationally prominent socialist figures, notably Eugene Debs, again descended upon the Pacific Northwest, working to maintain the activism of Northwesterners. From 1913 to 1915 the persistent presidential candidate made three trips to Washington, speaking in fifteen cities during his 1913 trip and returning to Everett and Seattle in early 1914. During his Everett visit on January 27, 1914, he was reportedly in "excellent form." Spectators filled the Everett Theater to capacity and immediately the *Washington Socialist* called the meeting a success. "Much enthusiasm for the Cause was aroused," it noted, saying "the visit of comrade Debs in Everett at this time cannot but result in a permanent advance of the local movement." In 1915 Debs returned to Puget Sound, delivering speeches on January 24, first in Everett and then Seattle. His evening address, observed the *Seattle Post-Intelligencer*, "taxed the capacity" of the city's Dreamland Pavilion. The *Washington Socialist* was more celebratory, calling his performance "the greatest speech of his splendid career," with "his lean body crouching with the grace of a panther. In Seattle he easily took first place as the most eminent orator in the world."[19]

Other important figures in American socialism also flocked to the Northwest. In 1913 IWW head William Haywood visited Portland. According to Portland socialist Tom Burns, "Big Bill" delivered "the ablest, cleanest, and most terrific indictment of capitalism ever heard in Portland." During the summer of 1914 Emil Seidel, former socialist mayor of Milwaukee and Debs's 1912 running mate, visited Washington. Finally, "industrialist speakers from all over the country," announced the *International Socialist Review*, "have found a hearty welcome and big audiences in Butte."[20]

From 1912 to 1916, then, activism and optimism increased in the Pacific Northwest as well as nationally. Party leaders, looking ahead to the 1916 election, hoped to double the socialist vote and believed that two million votes would place approximately twenty socialists in Congress. With high expectations for the 1916 campaign, socialist speakers once more blanketed the Northwest. Author George Kirkpatrick, cartoonist Ryan Walker, and politician Emil Seidel formed a three-speaker lecture series and visited three cities in Oregon, twelve in Washington, and eleven in Idaho. Allan Benson, the socialist party's 1916 presidential candidate, also visited the Pacific coast. In September, the candidate addressed crowds in Vancouver, Everett, Seattle, and Bellingham.[21]

As they looked ahead to local and national elections, regional socialists regained the optimism of the party's earliest years. Idaho, according to the *Appeal to Reason,* was "ripe for Socialism." The *Northern Idaho News* noticed that, following the 1912 elections, local socialists were "conducting an incessant campaign," and "preaching the propaganda month in and month out by meetings, personal work, and literature." Even this largely Democratic paper conceded that "it would not have surprised many people to see some of the socialist candidate[s] land in office." In 1913, a Montana socialist reported, "they are all red out here," and the letterhead of the Socialist Party of Montana carried the slogan "The future will be ours." In Oregon, socialists believed the new Woodrow Wilson administration would help their cause. The inevitable "failure," they wrote, "of the Wilson administration to do anything constructive for the common people will be so evident that there will be a tremendous wave toward the Socialist party." And in 1914, confident Washington socialists spoke of the "rising tide of socialism," and of a movement that had grown "by leaps and bounds."[22]

As the 1916 election neared, socialists' optimism reached new heights. A *Northwest Worker* reader predicted, "the unexpected may happen this fall." "We may have a perfect landslide," the hopeful socialist continued. "This year reminds me of 1860. No one expected to see Lincoln elected but he was." Meanwhile, Oregon socialists held their most successful state convention and a party member declared, "Our cause looks up this year all over; the state of Oregon is doing well considering everything." While states such as Oklahoma, Nevada, and Indiana received recognition for their successful organizations, Washington's socialists concluded: "when the ballots are counted the state of Washington will attract more attention that all the others combined because we will elect a man to congress and nobody will be expecting it, outside of the particular district."[23]

During the campaigns from 1912 to 1916 northwest socialists celebrated and drew on their previous victories. The political records of elected socialists, organizers believed, were central to campaigns and propaganda. Activists especially touted the Duncan administration in Butte as one of the nation's most successful socialist administrations. Sources elsewhere applauded the city's socialist government. During Duncan's tenure, according to the *Appeal to Reason,* the city paid off a bond to save eighteen thousand dollars in annual interest, established "the very best" sanitary conditions, "abolished [the] contract system of public works, while increasing wages of workers," "inaugurated milk and food inspection," and "closed dance halls." The *Portland Labor Press* also praised Butte's successful "Socialist rule." As the paper observed, the Duncan administration had cost the city sixty-two thousand dollars less than the previous administration, and sanitary regulations had decreased the number of infectious disease cases from 1,084 to 126. The *Butte Socialist,* not surprisingly, lauded the Duncan record. Headlines announced, "Butte greatly improved city under Socialist administration," and editorials recapped the "extensive and thorough" municipal improvements under the socialists. The Duncan administration, the *Butte Socialist* pointed out, not only constructed and improved Butte's streets and sewers, but also established a free city ice skating rink.[24]

Duncan's administration, however, was not the only political success party organizers could point to; J. M. Salter, Everett's commissioner of public works, proved that no socialist position was too small to utilize for campaign purposes. Salter, a former school principal and twice the editor of the *Commonwealth,* won his commissionership in 1914. Upon his election, local socialists organized an "enthusiastic gathering" for the new commissioner while his supporters immediately envisioned larger goals. The *Washington Socialist* said his election would "undoubtedly act as a stimulant throughout the whole state of Washington, urging all fighters in the great cause on to still more strenuous efforts." "Wherever people are interested in the progress of Socialism," the article continued, "interest will be directed toward Everett and its municipal affairs."

J. M. Salter's greatest political victory came when he success-fully reduced city work hours from twelve to eight per day at Everett's east-side bridge. "Changes of this nature should con-vince the most bone-headed worker that it pays to put class-conscious Socialists into office," insisted the *Washington Socialist*. Among socialist organizers, then, Salter's tenure was "proof that a Socialist is not just like the old party officials when elected." Despite reports from the *Everett Morning Tribune* that there would be socialist opposition to his candidacy, the party unanimously renominated him in 1915. Similarly, Idaho's only socialist legis-lator, state senator Earl Bowman, made important political strides for the unemployed. Bowman, elected in 1914, authored an "emergency employment law" that required Idaho county commissioners to provide the jobless with up to sixty days of work per year. The bill passed the Idaho legislature in February. According to the sponsor, the bill was "not a charity measure"; it was common sense. "I need what few dollars I earn to feed my own family," Bowman argued; "let the other fellow [be given help to] feed his."[25]

To varying degrees, the Duncan, Salter, and Bowman records illustrated socialism's political potential. In addition to recent elections and political effectiveness, other post-1912 socialist vic-tories provided encouragement. In St. John, Oregon, A. W. Vin-cent, who became the socialist mayoral candidate in 1914, defeated the Republican-Democrat candidate. More small vic-tories came in Washington, where in 1915 citizens elected social-ist school "directors" in Birmingham, Matlock, and Bryant. Socialists in Rupert, Idaho, seated a sheriff and a county clerk in

Minidoka County. And while socialist candidates failed to win larger elections, they nonetheless posted strong showings. Idahoans elected Democrat Moses Alexander governor in 1914, but socialist detractors altered the vote count in labor-friendly counties, contaminating the actual socialist showing. In Bonner County, northern Idaho, Democrats and Alexander struggled in the face of stronger socialist support. Don Moore, editor of the *Northern Idaho News*, congratulated Governor Alexander on his victory but was apologetic that in Bonner County the socialists were "too strong for us." Moore noted the socialist strength in Idaho again in a letter to the Democratic state chairman, Joseph Pence. "The strength of the socialist party," he wrote, "has also been one of the things the democrats have had to fight against. They have been aggressive and have rounded up a great deal of the discontent that would have otherwise gone to the Democratic Party. Two years ago [1912] they surprised many people by their sudden [show] of strength in polling about 26 per cent of the vote." Indeed, election results showed few signs of declining support for Idaho's socialists.[26]

In Montana, too, electoral victories continued after 1912. In Butte, voters reelected Lewis Duncan in 1913 with a 601-vote plurality. Butte socialists, according to the *Commonwealth*, "made nearly a clean sweep" as the party this time elected five of nine aldermen. Duncan enthusiastically wired the *Appeal to Reason* to announce "this clinches Socialist supremacy in this city." More victories for Montana's socialists came in 1914. Statewide, socialists gained seventeen thousand votes over 1912 and elected three socialists to the state legislature. Also, socialist city government spread beyond Butte when Missoula socialists captured the city administration by a "safe majority."[27]

Despite indications of party strength, by 1915–1916 Pacific Northwest socialists detected signs of trouble. While the campaigns immediately following the 1912 successes offered encouragement and excitement, a number of later elections were disheartening. J. M. Salter, socialist commissioner of public works in Everett, failed in his 1915 reelection bid. Organizers blamed the defeat on "overconfidence." In Spokane, where socialists fielded thirty-six candidates in 1915, election results were also disappointing. None of the three socialist candidates for commissioner received more than five hundred of the sixty thousand possible votes.[28] The 1916 presidential election was another disappointment for the party. The first hint of its impending troubles came when Debs, the socialist nominee in the previous four elections, declined the fifth in order to run for Congress from Indiana's fifth district. Subsequently, Debs's previous running mate, Allan Benson, failed to live up to his party's post-1912 expectations. As the socialist presidential nominee in 1916, Benson received only 3.2 percent of the vote nationally and 5.3 percent in the Pacific Northwest. This disappointing showing compared poorly to 1912, when Debs received 6 percent of the vote nationally and 11.8 percent in the Northwest. Despite evidence of an active and methodical membership, Northwest presses blamed the party's 1916 stumble on a lack of organization. Post-election commentary in the *Northwest Worker,* for example, argued that the 1916 decline "only emphasizes the need for a strengthening of our movement." The paper also cast acerbic blame on the "great portion" of the working class composed of "dumb, sluggish, thick-headed brutes."

As socialist party organizers searched for answers to explain their defeats, even geography entered the issue. "Our party organization itself has been localized," critics charged, and "the different parts have largely lost touch with one another [and] the sense of nation-wide unity of the movement has been weakened." The increased focus on local issues and concerns, at the expense of broad regional platforms, argued some in the Pacific Northwest, helped explain disappointing elections. Socialists in North Yakima recommended a "closer relation to one another . . . [for] it has been a party dominated by the coast counties, and principally by the cities that hover along the Sound." Indeed, no SPW members from eastern Washington ever served on the state executive committee.[29]

By 1915–1916 many of the region's socialists had become apathetic about party involvement. From 1914 to 1915 the national party membership fell off by 14,201 members. Oregon and Idaho both reported declining memberships. In late 1916, the Idaho socialist party state secretary, C. F. Fields, received increasingly fewer reports from locals, including approximately thirty that were delinquent in dues. "Since 1912," he complained, "there has been practically no organization work done in the state." Despite the flurry of party activity during the time, leaders like Fields looked for scapegoats, and "organization" failures provided an easy target. While Washington was the Northwest's exception as one of only six states to show party growth from 1914 to 1915, even the robust SPW reported inactive locals, going so far as to remove eighteen from its roster, citing "long inactivity." Secretary Herman had reprimanded seventy-seven locals for their failure to report. "Do not let it happen again," he warned.[30]

Socialists in the Puget Sound region also saw a connection between disappointing campaign results and declining member activism. During the 1916 campaign, Everett socialists admitted, "We failed to recognize the necessity for the fullest organized effort." When the city hosted speakers such as George Kirkpatrick and Ryan Walker, the events were "poorly advertised" and drew low attendance. Member inactivity also caused the *Northwest Worker* to cancel its funding drive for a new mailing machine after the editors realized the "uselessness of trying to raise the money." Spokane socialists, similarly, admitted that their movement was now "sadly lacking in organization and solidarity." Party leaders in Montana recognized their organization remained "relatively weak" and faced a great deal of work fighting their "powerful capitalist enemies."[31] State socialists even struggled to fill complete party tickets. E. A. Sperber wrote from Hamilton that a full 1916 slate looked "rather doubtful," and accordingly, "our showing is liable to be poor." V. C. McCone, the Oregon state secretary, was equally frustrated. "Outside of Portland," he admitted, "there is no campaign at all." In April 1916 he learned that the state party planned only six meetings statewide. "Oregon sleeps on seemingly unconscious," he grumbled. Electoral stumbles clearly began to squelch socialists' formerly exuberant optimism.[32]

Coupled with fewer victories, fewer members and their declining enthusiasm characterized the ideological and personal differences between the party's earliest years and its post-1916 ennui. By 1912–1913, on the heels of the party's greatest political successes and as activists looked to a bright future, party factionalism began to boil over. Socialists watched the rising internal strife both nationally and in the Pacific Northwest, especially Washington. While prominent socialists such as *International Socialist Review* editor Frank Bohn proclaimed that the party was "absolutely indestructible," something was askew. In the same 1913 party overview Bohn also acknowledged "deep-seated forces of disruption" in the organization. He pointed to the SPW's split between reformists and radicals as evidence of the party's divisiveness. Party members disagreed over a wide range of issues, but most infighting centered on organizational and ideological questions. For some, state organizations were too lax in monitoring expenses or producing effective mailings, but these disputes were among the least significant. More and more, the most passionate revolutionary socialists failed to agree with the "gas and water" socialists most concerned with incremental reform. These philosophical debates had divided the party for years. When the party faced more troubles in 1917, socialist Henry Slobodin cited the "division between the revolutionists and constructivists" as the biggest problem.[33]

An especially sensitive ideological issue concerned the Industrial Workers of the World, which was particularly popular in the West. The IWW forced the region's socialists to reflect on the value of taking direct action and employing industrial violence as political approaches. Considerable debate occurred amongst "radical" and "moderate" northwest socialists on this IWW issue, particularly after the 1912 SPA convention. Big Bill Haywood shocked many conservatives when he told socialists at the meeting that "a little sabotage in the right place at the proper time . . . won't hurt you." Morris Hillquit and Victor Berger countered this position by amending the SPA constitution to allow the removal of any party member "who opposes political action or advocates crime." State committees received the referendum for a vote, and the results illustrated party divisions. Indicative of their radical leanings, Washington, Oregon, and Montana voted against the referendum, yet conservatives carried the day, passing it 23,495 to 10,944. Nationally, the SPA swung to the side of conservatives, particularly the "Hillquit-Berger axis," at the expense of party cohesiveness.[34]

The Pacific Northwest's socialists fought many of the same organizational and ideological battles the national organization faced. The Socialist Party of Oregon typified the philosophical disputes on the national stage. Oregon's socialists were continually "scrapping among themselves," observed state secretary C. W. Barzee in 1914. This "scrapping" mainly occurred between the state's radicals and moderates. In Portland, observed the *Portland Labor Press*, there were "two types of Socialists." On one side stood the city's "regular" members, as they were called, socialists who hoped to gain political power and legislate collectivism. The regulars faced revolutionary socialists who demanded the abolition of state government. In 1912 Portland's most radical socialists prevailed in a fight for "possession of the party machinery" and moved party headquarters from Portland to Salem. The regulars held separate and sporadic meetings in Portland. During the 1913 campaign, indicative of their conservative beliefs, Portland socialists called for the "social [public] ownership of public utilities." This internal dissention dominated Oregon party politics at the expense of propaganda outreach and electioneering.[35]

Idaho and Montana faced similar party wrangling. Idaho's socialists adopted a succinct 1914 state platform that the *International Socialist Review* deemed "the shortest, yet one of the most complete state platforms ever set forth by any political party." But adopting the platform proved arduous. Radicals and moderates debated the semantics of "immediate demands," arguing over the very political objectives that had divided them in the party's earliest years. Two years later the Idaho party was still preoccupied with infighting. In an open letter to state members,

O. H. Price, an organizer from Pocatello, urged the them to "put aside their grievances." "Scores of instances" of dissent, censures, and accusations, he observed, left Idaho "so torn with internal strife and dissention" that socialists could not expect much from upcoming elections. Again, internal strife consumed much time and energy.[36]

In Montana, factionalism also grew out of ideological struggles. Lewis Duncan, the state's preeminent socialist, claimed the "rupture in the party" began in 1912. At the time, although largely unfounded, Montana had been saddled with a reputation for being particularly pro-IWW. The result, in Duncan's words, meant that Montana, and especially Butte, "became a sort of Mecca for the I.W.W. pilgrims." Butte's rumored sympathies for "direct action, sabotage, and violence" attracted a number of "red" Wobblies to Butte, and shortly, into the city's socialist local. The IWW element quickly took control of the party and, according to Duncan, increased "disharmony and disruption" in the local. The new party leadership, whom Duncan labeled the "disruptionists," moved for the expulsion of Duncan and Butte's five socialist aldermen from the party. The showdown grew so severe that Montana's state executive committee held an emergency meeting in June of 1913 and reorganized the Butte local under a new charter to exclude IWW sympathizers.

Two years later Montana socialists remained at odds, in Butte and elsewhere. In 1915 Finnish organizer Henry Polsa wrote to state secretary A. F. Meissner regarding problems with two separate Finnish locals in the community of Red Lodge. Polsa's complaint came because the state committee granted a charter to more radical Red Lodge Finns with the understanding that "the so called radical (disrupters) [sic] was not to have a rival Finnish local." "I am powerless to change the matter," Meissner replied, because the state committee had authorized the "radical" Finns to exist. The secretary encouraged the divided Finns to "not waste all your efforts in fighting each other but in trying to devise ways and means of fighting the master class."[37] As Red Lodge socialists struggled to resolve their intra-party differences, Butte emerged as the epicenter for Montana's troubles, with the IWW presence creating serious consequences for the city and its socialists. While historians such as Richard Judd have called Butte's IWW troubles an "organizational crisis," the city was nothing short of a war zone during 1914 and 1915.

During the summer of 1914 tensions finally erupted between moderate members of the Butte Miner's Union (BMU) and their radical IWW counterparts. Demonstrations on June 13 and June 23 brought the two factions nose to nose. Violent confrontations culminated when the Butte Miners' Union Hall was dynamited. Following the destruction, pro-IWW forces established a new "Butte Mine Workers' Union." The following summer, socialists faced further violence. On June 15, 1915, a dynamite blast destroyed the Butte Socialist Publishing Company, home of the *Butte Socialist*. Socialists estimated the damages at twenty-five hundred dollars and blamed the explosion on "the dominant mining interests" of Butte. They quickly rebuilt the plant, but only after membership in the local fell by approximately 66 percent. The *Butte Socialist* folded that December. The paper succumbed, the party faithful claimed, to "the combined forces of industrial tyranny, commercialized vice, political bigotry and chicanery, business and commercial intrigue, religious intolerance, social cowardice and indifference, economic fear, and . . . working class ignorance."[38]

In July 1914, following the explosion that leveled the union hall, Mayor Duncan witnessed first-hand the city's working-class volatility. While in the city clerk's office on a Friday afternoon, Duncan received a visit from Erik Lantala, a Finnish socialist not only brooding over his ten dollar fine for assault but also demanding the deportation of a Finn rival, Frank Aaltonen. When Lantala named Aaltonen, Duncan nonchalantly asked, "What trouble can he make?" to which Lantala replied, "I show you." Pulling a knife, he charged the mayor. Duncan, who had taken to carrying a revolver because of the recent turmoil, could not get control of the gun. In the scuffle, Lantala stabbed him three times: in the head, the back, and inflicting the deepest cut into Duncan's shoulder. By all accounts, Alderman Henry Davis, along with Building Inspector Lewis Van Horne, rushed in, overpowered Lantala, and saved Duncan's life.[39]

Amidst this ferment, Governor Samuel Stewart declared martial law in Butte. He held the city's socialist leaders, particularly Mayor Duncan, responsible for the crisis. After a grand jury investigation found them guilty, on October 6, 1914, authorities removed Duncan and Democratic sheriff Tim Driscoll from office. The official charge against Duncan was "neglect and inefficiency in discharging the duties of office during the June troubles." Socialists called the "farcical" trial part of a capitalist conspiracy. The ousted mayor pledged to "fight on till either the capitalist system which enslaves my brothers and sisters is dead, or I am dead." The city council, meeting late on October 6, elected Clarence Smith mayor and Duncan, in attendance, could only act as spectator. He never again held public office.[40]

When, in 1915, opponents "overwhelmingly defeated" Butte's socialist administration, the former mayor had an explanation. "The spirit of the people of Butte," he telegraphed, "has been crushed by the brutal exercise of the tremendous economic and political power of the local Rockefeller interests." Yet Duncan's account failed to convince some local party members. Butte socialist Lowndes Maury submitted a scathing article to the *International Socialist Review* that offered a different version of Butte's stumble. Duncan, he said, only hoped to "create the impression that the defeat of the Socialist Party in Butte is due to external forces separate and distinct from the Socialist Party," he wrote. For Maury, Butte's socialists had assumed power as "men with working class tendencies and socialist ideas," but political power corrupted them and led them to enact "arbitrary and autocratic policies." Maury was not alone in his criticisms of Montana's party leadership. Another Montana socialist admitted, "My enthusiasm is gone," and complained that the "leaders who run the party are too liberal with the money."[41]

Party bickering and organizational challenges in Oregon, Idaho, and Montana paled in comparison to Washington's fac-

tionalism as the SPW's power struggle between Reds and Yellows
continued. The "diverse interests" among Washington's socialists divided the state between its "direct action-sabotage" and
"political actionist" wings. The state executive committee found
itself consumed by "attempts to settle party quarrels" and over-
run with the "obstructive activity" of "enemies of the administration." This fallout ultimately resulted in formal schisms and
intervention by the party's national leadership.[42]

The SPW's troubles spilled over about the time of the state's
1913 convention in Tacoma. Observers noted "personal dislikes,
slander, cupidity, and trickery" at the meeting. State secretary
Frans Bostrom admitted, "We cannot harmonize the factions of
the party." By the close of the convention on March 12, the state's
conservatives had officially left the SPW and established their
own moderate party. This action, witnesses quipped, made the
party's 1913 "session" look more like "secession." Some delegates
were uneasy about the division because the "capitalist press" was
quick to celebrate the SPW's "big split." Meanwhile, the newly
formed Yellow Party, centered in the Puget Sound region,
claimed approximately two thousand of the state's six thousand
socialists. Their chief target was the "IWW faction" allegedly out
either to "rule or ruin" the socialist movement in Washington.
The Yellows particularly resented the "anarchists, direct action-
ists, impossibilists, down-and-outers, free lovers, and worse," who
had taken over the SPW.[43]

Washington's "big split," as it became known, did not go unno-
ticed. In 1914 the SPA's national executive committee (NEC)
began investigating the SPW and its internal strife. In April 1914
a preliminary committee, composed of N. A. Richardson of California and S. W. Motley of Idaho, made an investigative visit to
Seattle and Everett. The national committee then selected them
to hold open meetings with Washington socialists and to meet
with secretary Bostrom. The investigators found that a group of
"extremists . . . now constitute the regularly recognized organization, locally denominated the 'Reds'; and though they constitute but a small minority of the state membership, they dominate

it to a degree out of all proportions to their numerical strength."
The committee reported these other findings on factionalism to
the NEC but, as ordered, made no recommendations.

From May 10 to 13, 1914, the SPA took up the "Washington
controversy" at its national convention, where the Washington
division was the "overshadowing issue." Based on Richardson
and Motley's report, the NEC handed down a series of instruc-
tions to the SPW. First, a committee of three Washington socialists would meet to "bring organic unity" to the SPW. Next, a
statewide convention would draft a new constitution and platform, based on "a full and unqualified acceptance of the
national platform and constitution of the Socialist party." Also,
SPW members could bring any disagreements over the language
of the new constitution to the NEC. If the SPW failed to comply
with the rulings of the NEC, the national body could revoke the
state party's charter.[44]

On June 18, 1914, in accordance with the NEC's wishes, the
SPW factions met in Seattle. This new "Unity Conference" witnessed four days of debate on the language and content of its
new state constitution. Based on the constitutions in California,
New York, and Pennsylvania, the new document temporarily
appeased the delegates. Dissenters, though, had little choice but
to accept it, as rejection of the new constitution was grounds for
expulsion. Outwardly, the SPW seemed united once again. A
"large working class majority" elected L. E. Katterfield, the former lyceum bureau director, as state secretary. Various locals sent
reports of new cohesiveness. In Spokane, Red and Yellow factions reorganized into "Local Spokane No.1." Similarly, locals in
Bremerton and South Bay, near Olympia, described united
locals.

Many in the SPW appeared eager to put party differences
behind them. Centralia's *Lewis County Clarion* typified this sentiment: "We believe too much written on the subject would have a
tendency to make division in the party. We have a strong, healthy
growth in the state and if we remain united it is only a question
of time when we will capture the state for socialism. We think it

unwise to discuss this question, and would ask our correspondents to discuss other subjects . . . of more general benefit to the members."[45] Even the state's socialist press made reconciliation efforts. The *Washington Socialist,* in Everett, reorganized in 1915 to capture a wider audience; it became the *Northwest Worker,* in order to "let the Reds of the Northwest draw closer together, through their common cause."[46]

Yet the issues of 1913–1914 were not altogether alleviated. As late as the 1918 convention, the SPW continued its internal wrangling over the old questions of philosophy. During the three-day meeting in Seattle, from March 9 to 11, interpretational debate marred the SPW's "chief work" on the party platform and constitution as radicals and moderates once again disputed party direction and specifically the question of whether to include immediate political demands. On the surface, party growth and the electoral successes of 1912 looked as though they would continue to build and increase as they always had. These years, however, again revealed ideological and political divisions that left socialists in the Pacific Northwest divided and susceptible, and they landed particularly defenseless against their greatest challenges: World War I and the approaching climate of paranoia and anti-radicalism.

6

"End War or War Will End You"
World War I and the Socialist Demise, 1916–1925

You workers must end war or war will end you.

Socialist Herald, 3 September 1915

WHILE socialist party factionalism and debates over the appropriateness of direct action, sabotage, and syndicalism slowly pulled the party apart, socialists faced a larger challenge. When war erupted in Europe, David Shannon has argued, "a new problem confronted American Socialists." Now, it seemed, anti-war agitation and dodging persecution for their "disloyalty" constituted most Pacific Northwest socialist activity.[1]

Socialist ideology had never fit with war and militarism. The Marxist interpretation of the war in Europe was clear: capitalism inevitably evolves into imperialism, as countries must expand beyond their boundaries; eventually, imperialism continues until capitalist nations confront each others' economic interests, the outcome of which is inevitably war. Socialists also decried the reality that workers provided the bulk of armies. "Every intelligent workingman and woman," announced the *International Socialist Review*, "is opposed to all capitalist wars." In addition to their opposition to capitalist wars, northwest socialists also criticized militarism generally. The SPW's 1912 platform, in fact, outlined formal objections to the Boy Scouts and the organization's militaristic lessons. In 1917 the SPW adopted resolutions against the compulsory military training that had been implemented in Washington's public high schools.[2]

Socialists, however, did not stand alone in their objections to the war. National organizations including the American Peace

Society, the American Union Against Militarism, the Women's Peace Party, the Emergency Peace Federation, and the Carnegie Endowment for Peace all voiced dissent. Even pacifistic and isolationist-leaning national political figures such as Woodrow Wilson, William Jennings Bryan, and Robert La Follette expressed their reservations about American involvement in European conflicts. Socialist objections, of course, differed, and centered on both a perceived capitalist conspiracy and the detrimental impact of war on workers. Without question, socialists were among some of the most unabashed and outspoken critics of U.S. involvement in the European war. Opponents of the war, including socialists, however, did not anticipate the kind of backlash their objections would bring. U.S. socialists, Shannon argued, knew neither "what is was to be a dissenter in a total war" nor "what degree of madness a war-enraged people is capable of." Indeed, socialists quickly realized, their Marxist objections held serious consequences for the party, as well as for specific activist individuals.[3]

Pacific Northwest socialists dedicated themselves to anti-war protest. They focused their demonstrations on the atrocities of war, the conscription of rank-and-file laborers, and the war's political implications. Before the United States became militarily involved, the region's socialists centered their attention on keeping the U.S. neutral. Even after German U-Boats sank the British liner *Lusitania* in 1915, regional socialists were confident that the United States would avoid war. "The destruction of the *Lusitania*," announced the *Washington Socialist*, "involving the death of over a hundred Americans, affords no just grounds for a declaration of war on Germany." Not all were so optimistic about the country's embrace of this perspective. "The sinking of the *Lusitania*," argued an Oregon socialist pamphlet, "gave the militarists and jingoes of this country the opportunity to demand an immediate declaration of war upon Germany."[4]

Two years after the *Lusitania* attack, socialists' worst fears were realized. President Wilson's famous call for war came on April 2, 1917; the formal resolution passed both houses of Congress on

April 6, despite the objections of prominent statesmen like William Jennings Bryan and Robert La Follette. In response to the impending military preparations, on April 7, 1917, the SPA held an emergency convention in St. Louis. Approximately two hundred delegates descended on the city's Planters Hotel as "war clouds grew thicker and thicker." Convention attendees adopted a "united, decisive, and determined position on the question of war," one that expressed the party's explicit anti-war commitment and reinforced its objections to looming conscription and strike-activity restrictions. Delegates drafted a pamphlet titled "Proclamation and War Program" and state leaders, including those in the Pacific Northwest, planned campaigns to distribute their position literature.[5]

Yet unanimity on the party's war position, the St. Louis meeting quickly demonstrated, did not prevail among socialists. At the convention, Kate Richards O'Hare chaired a new "War and Militarism" committee to hear the varied voices of delegates. Kate Sadler, of Washington State, was seated on the committee. Not surprisingly, the hearings reflected that a clear majority unabashedly opposed the war and were in favor of continuing their vocal resistance. Of the three formal opinions submitted to the committee, the first and most popular voiced clear opposition to capitalist wars and conscription. Three delegates, including Sadler, submitted a more moderate position that reiterated the majority opinion almost entirely, but which was in favor of muting their public disagreement on the issue. Finally, a small but significant minority resolved to support the war and make the necessary sacrifices the nation needed. Before the delegates took the first vote on the referendums, the convention excluded the middle position for its similarity to the majority one. During national balloting, socialists ultimately supported, by a nearly three-to-one margin, the majority opinion of opposition to the war.[6]

But socialist unity was not fully realized, and the St. Louis resolution opposing the war represented only superficial agreement on the issue. From the first anti-war resolutions, according to historians H. C. Peterson and Gilbert Fite, the war issue threatened

to "split the Socialist party wide open." As their European counterparts did, several popular and vocal American socialist intellectuals—Charles Edward Russell, John Spargo, Upton Sinclair,
and William English Wallace—supported the American war effort
and criticized the party's treasonous anti-war position throughout
1917. Several, including Spargo, Russell, and Sinclair, formally
defected from the party. Although their leaving did not dramatically alter party membership, it underscored beliefs that the party
was factionalized. In the Pacific Northwest, too, socialists both pro-
and anti-war surfaced. An article titled "Socialism and the War,"
printed in Everett's *Co-operative News,* observed that "the Socialists
of America have split into two factions. It is one of the most
remarkable political phenomenon of our history that at [a] time
when the Socialistic movement of many years seemed nearest
fruition, the Socialist[s] should fall out among themselves."
Nationally and regionally there were always exceptions, but
according to David Shannon, "an overwhelming majority of
Socialist Party members were strongly opposed to the war and
were committed to agitation against it." Across the country, socialists voiced their anger in anti-war speeches, demonstrations, and
propaganda. Adolph Germer, the SPA national secretary in 1917,
encouraged his comrades to "keep up the war on war. Don't relax
one moment in your agitation."[7]

   In the Pacific Northwest, as the nation stared war in the face, a
majority of the region's socialists protested openly through pamphlets, demonstrations, and speeches. In Stevens County, Washington, socialists demanded that the United States government
"use its utmost efforts to end this war at the earliest possible
moment." In Idaho, socialists voiced their concern directly to the
governor. W. A. Gresham and J. A. Standley from Pocatello wrote
to Governor Alexander regarding their group's recently adopted
war resolutions. "The Socialists of Pocatello," the chapter resolved,
"are unconditionally opposed to war as the greatest deterioration
of the human family known to mankind." The local urged "all
good citizens to join with us in protesting . . . the efforts to involve
the cream of our country into [*sic*] the harrows of war." Anti-war

pamphlets circulated throughout the region, some of them capturing limited- or non-English-reading socialists. In 1915 the
Swedish-Finnish Socialist Club of Portland, Oregon, published an
"anti-military" leaflet in both English and Swedish.

In accordance with directives from the SPA leadership, socialists flocked to public meetings and committed to marching and
speaking against the war. Washington's *Party Builder* rallied socialists to organize, telling them to "let the capitalist class and their
politicians know that if they plunge the Nation into war . . . the
working class will NOT enlist until all capitalists, politicians and
others . . . responsible for [it] are actually on the firing line." Anti-
war sentiments boiled over in the first months of 1917. As Congress was addressing the war measure, the *Seattle Union Record*
reported on April 7 that agitators there and in Spokane, among
other cities, were voicing their opposition to the war. In early 1917,
Spokane's socialists filled their hall for a "mass anti-war meeting."
The gathering hoped "to protest against the threatened war with
Germany, and all wars." George Kirkpatrick, author of the popular anti-war pamphlet "War, What For?" and the 1916 socialist vice
presidential candidate spoke at several packed northwest meetings. The *Washington Socialist* declared of him, there was "no one
better fitted to undertake a crusade against war."[8]

After American entry into World War I, socialists used vivid
descriptions of war and labor's involvement to rally working-class
opposition. "The workers of one country are misled to believing
that they have some advantage in slaying the workers of another
country," Eugene Debs contended in the *Northwest Worker*. "War
is Murder in Uniform," he declared later. "It is hell," the great
agitator continued, "and the profit-mongers for whom it exists
. . . are devilish." Reports of battle atrocities at places like Verdun,
France, reinforced war's viciousness. A French army captain,
reported the *Northwest Worker*, described seven thousand dead
bodies "heaped" along a seven hundred yard battlefront.[9]

Socialists claimed the conscripted laborers of the Pacific Northwest could face the same harsh reality. Even before the government instituted conscription, northwest socialists attacked the

proposition. Tacoma's *Truth* reminded workers of a 1909 Washington state law that gave the "overlords of capitalism" the "supreme power" to call to service all able-bodied men from age eighteen to forty-five. The paper rhetorically asked readers if they were aware they were "soldier[s] and must kill your fellow worker, when ordered." As unemployment reports counted hundreds of out-of-work laborers in Colfax, Walla Walla, and Ritzville, socialists took notice. "Start a war with Germany—no matter what for," quipped a *Northwest Worker* editorial, "This will settle the unemployment problem for some time." Socialists even decried the government's manipulation of language. In a piece titled "How to Fool the Public," the *Northwest Worker* exposed the omission of terms such as "draft" or "conscription" from mainstream papers by government order. Instead, journalists began using the more politically neutral phrase "selective service."[10]

Despite the objections of some socialists and others on the left, the military conscription law passed on May 18, 1917. Aside from broad socialist opposition, leftist critiques of the draft did not reflect national sentiments. According to Peterson and Fite, Americans in general did not generate a massive outpouring of opposition to conscription, instead "the vast majority" of citizens "accepted conscription in rather calm resignation," believing it an obligatory and patriotic duty to support and raise an army.[11]

While many Americans tolerated conscription, socialists continued their loud opposition to the new draft law—ultimately to their detriment. On June 3, 1917, the SPW adopted an anti-conscription resolution, opposing the draft as "contrary to the 13th amendment" which mandates no "slavery or involuntarily servitude" except in punishment of a crime. "Therefore we are opposed to conscription," SPW leaders wrote, and the state party refused to "sanction the mass murder of the worker in the interest of the capitalist class. We pledge ourselves to continued efforts for the repeal of the conscription law and pending such repeal will support all mass movements to that end." And they held true to their promise. In June 1917, approximately six hundred Butte protestors took to the streets in opposition to draft registration. Their demonstration met a quick end, however, when "patriotic citizens" and police broke up the march after shots rang out. The demonstrators were arrested en masse, and authorities declared martial law.[12]

The most dogmatic socialists viewed the rejection of capitalist wars and conscription as some of their most important work. The *Northwest Worker* targeted capitalism and the "militarist conspiracy" for imposing "upon the people of the United States compulsory military service." Pragmatic party organizers, however, also appeared to recognize the political worth of anti-war agitation. From the national office, secretary Germer praised the "fearless working class stand on the war," capitalizing on its political usefulness. "Thousands who were 'stung' by voting for Wilson because 'he kept us out of the war,'" he wrote, had "learned their lesson" and were poised to "join our ranks." Pacific Northwest socialists echoed this rhetoric. H. H. Stallard, an organizer from Yakima, believed that the war would spell "the death of the capitalist system," and that, ironically, "its own war was its slayer." The *Co-operative News* in Everett extended this theme of the capitalist class and its "brutal persecutions" and "pretentious patriots," calling capitalists "criminally incompetent." The paper claimed these factors, exposed by the war, fueled the socialist movement and weakened the "political prestige of the ruling class." "This is our opportunity," it proclaimed, and in the Northwest this "war against war" continued after the U.S. entered the conflict in April 1917. The socialist *Party Builder* encouraged activists to "keep up the agitation." When the paper learned that President Wilson was "annoyed" by these protests "flooding his office," the *Party Builder* urged its readers to "keep up the good work." "Worry him some more."[13]

Yet anti-war agitation also had its risks. The right to free expression had been tested in the free-speech fights of Seattle (1907) and Spokane (1909–1910), but mainstream repression of leftist political dissent now reached a fevered pitch. Fervent patriots increasingly labeled radicals, socialists, and anti-war advocates disloyal troublemakers. Following popular sentiment, the federal government initiated several anti-radical measures to halt anti-war politicizing. The Espionage Act of June 1917, the Trading with the Enemy Act of October 1917, and the Sedition Act of May 1918 all targeted radicals through restrictions on speech and expression. America's socialists immediately felt the sting of these measures.

For the socialist press, the Espionage and Trading with the Enemy Acts, authorizing postal officials to deny postage to disloyal publications, held dire consequences. By the middle of 1917 post offices regularly blocked distribution of the *International Socialist Review* and the *Appeal to Reason*. Later in the year authorities blacklisted approximately sixty socialist newspapers nationally.[14]

Socialists throughout the Northwest blasted these restrictive actions. A *Northwest Worker* headline challenged, "Government by the People?" accusing "President Wilson and a bunch of plutocratic parasites" for "telling us during the past few months that we are fighting a war for democracy, yet every move that the government has made has been in contradiction to democracy." The *Co-operative News* also attacked the inconsistency of Wilsonian rhetoric. "The slogan of those who are boosting for the war is 'Make the World safe for democracy,'" observed the paper. "Be not deceived . . . behind the mask the legend reads 'Make the world safe for plutocracy.'"[15]

Wartime hysteria propelled indictments and prosecution of radicals and socialists to new heights. In the Pacific Northwest, Schwantes observed that "wartime zealotry and a spirit of conformity" reigned throughout the war. Paranoia had taken hold; in Montana rumors spread of German plots to bomb Helena, to destroy the state wheat crop with toxic bees, and to sabotage flour sacks with ground glass. Governments and concerned citizens targeted northwest radicals and socialists for their "disloyal" speeches and literature. Alarmed, socialists observed the region's shift into a state of "hysteria." "Various parts of the country are going spy mad," remarked the *Northwest Worker*. "We are crying 'traitor' at each other; our post office is suppressing papers without trial or hearing; honest criticism of war policies is . . . called sedition . . . let us banish this war hysteria."[16]

In this government clamp down, socialist newspapers in the Pacific Northwest were among the main targets. The Idaho *Party Builder* faced restricted mailings, while in Everett the *Co-operative News* also felt the pinch of anti-radicalism. "These are difficult times," its headline warned, "there is no telling when the heavy hand of authority (official or unofficial) may fall on us." The *News* complained it was watched by the government "as by a flock of hawks." Authorities twice visited the party's offices to search and interview staff members for evidence of sedition. "It appears that the masters are consistently following a plan whereby active socialists throughout the country are to be disposed of one by one," the *News* brooded. The future was not bright for the region's radical press.[17]

Public concern over loyalty continually targeted national and regional anti-war socialists. In June 1918 Eugene Debs delivered his famed anti-war speech in Canton, Ohio, a scathing talk that stretched three hours, telling the audience they were slaves and "cannon fodder." He promptly faced conviction under the auspices of the Espionage Act and received a ten-year sentence. Congress twice refused Milwaukee's Victor Berger his rightful seat, and in 1920 the New York State Assembly unseated five socialists. Actions against outspoken socialists appeared with increasing regularity; persecution ranged from discrimination to violence. At first, socialist candidates' campaigns suffered sabotage. They cried foul in Washington State when officials omitted the name of a socialist party candidate for Congress, R. J. Olinger, from the ballot. The secretary of state, finally blaming clerical error, placed Olinger's name on the ballot. A similar "clerical mistake" occurred in 1918 when J. M. Salter, formerly Everett's socialist commissioner of public works and a current member of the SPW's state executive committee, filed with the secretary of state to run for Congress. The state ultimately refused Salter a place on the ballot and returned his filing fee.[18]

The persecution of socialists steadily shifted beyond name-calling and clerical slips as stories of arrests and indictments grew increasingly common. In mid-1917 and 1918 charges against socialists spread. Minnesota politicians Jacob Bentall and James Peterson served time in prison for their anti-conscription and anti-war actions. When Scott Nearing published an anti-war pamphlet, "The Great Madness," he faced indictment for disloyalty. Across the country, opposition to the war met with quick reaction from authorities.[19]

Northwest experiences typified the escalated persecution of anti-war socialists. Seattle authorities arrested four SPW members under the Sedition Act for distributing twenty thousand anti-war flyers. The seditious pamphlets were headlined: "No Conscription! No Involuntary Servitude! No Slavery!" Edward Hofstede, a lawyer from Orofino, Idaho, also experienced harassment. Although not a party member, Hofstede had expressed socialist sympathies and—citing the Thirteenth Amendment—he encouraged clients not to register for the draft. Authorities found him guilty of "counseling draft evasion." Police arrested Everett socialist Nils Osterberg in 1918 for espionage, but released him due to insufficient evidence. Finally, Frans Bostrom, the former SPW state secretary, had several confrontations with authorities. In November 1917 authorities jailed him for three hours for displaying a cartoon from *The Masses* in his office window. Members of the Everett Rotary Club reported him to the police, and authorities released him after he agreed to remove the offending cartoon. The next month Tacoma police arrested Bostrom again, for selling a pamphlet written by Daniel H. Wallace, called "Shanghaied Into the European War." After finding the pamphlet circulating among soldiers at Fort Lewis, authorities arrested Bostrom on charges of being "pro-German." Before his release, Bostrom told officials he was pro-war—because the war's shortcomings would facilitate a socialist republic.[20]

Anti-war demonstrations also provoked violent responses. The Northwest's most famous war-related murder occurred in 1917 in Butte, Montana, a city that came to typify the persecution of anti-war dissent. When IWW agitator Frank Little called American soldiers "uniformed scabs," Butte vigilantes forcibly took him from his home and hanged him from a nearby railroad trestle. Several Montana papers promptly applauded the lynching of Little as patriotic. The murder, however, served as a harbinger of Montana's anti-radicalism. By the next summer, state patriots established the Montana Loyalty League in July 1918 with a professed membership of sixty thousand. With its sizable prosocialist population, Butte remained the epicenter for the speech fight. William Dunne, publisher of the socialist Butte Bulletin, met repression of speech rights head on and resisted state authorities' attempts to shut down his paper. An electrician and former boxer turned labor advocate, Dunne lambasted Montana's big business and its "kept press." For the "red socialist's" dangerous and disloyal statements, the gerrymandered Montana Council of Defense convicted Dunne of sedition in 1919, a decision the state's supreme court did not overturn until 1920.[21]

Charges of disloyalty were also made against other socialist publishers and party leaders. Among the national leadership, Victor Berger, J. Lewis Engdahl, Irwin St. John Tucker, William F. Krause, and Adolph Germer faced indictments. Of the one hundred party leaders indicted under the Espionage Act by late 1917, eleven hailed from the Pacific Northwest. In April 1918, the SPW's state secretary, Emil Herman, was arrested for sedition after police confiscated approximately seven hundred pieces of "disloyal" literature and seven cases of correspondence, mailing lists, stickers, and receipt books from his office. A federal grand jury in Seattle charged Herman with seven counts of sedition, claiming that he had "willfully and feloniously attempted to cause insubordination, disloyalty, mutiny, and refusal of duty." The court found him guilty and sentenced him to ten years in federal prison. In Oregon, activist A. J. Partan faced similar persecution for distributing the pamphlet, "War—for What," which labeled patriotism a tool of "tyrant[s] and . . . the industrial ruling class."[22]

While wartime flag-wavers kept a watchful eye on socialists, the IWW was the special target of persecution. Beginning in 1917, Wobblies across the Pacific Northwest reported harassment. In Seattle, Spokane, and Great Falls and St. Maries, Idaho, authorities raided and closed IWW halls. In early 1918 Yakima authorities accused IWW members of conspiring to "aid the enemy" and plotting to poison the city's drinking water. Later that year, reminiscent of the fatal attack on Frank Little, Frank Myers of the IWW was dragged from his room and tarred and feathered.[23]

Idaho's 1917 criminal syndicalism law specifically targeted the IWW. Between 1917 and 1920, twenty states passed similar laws. The Idaho law primarily defined criminal syndicalism as disloyal speech, and restricted firearms sales. State attorney general A. H. Conner claimed the law "has worked very satisfactorily." "Without its aid," he said, "the I.W.W. situation could not have been so successfully handled; it has had a decidedly wholesome influence in the curbing of criminal radicalism, and there is no agitation for its appeal." In 1923, however, the American Civil Liberties Union protested in a letter to Idaho Governor C. C. Moore that the legislation "was passed in order to jail certain types of radicals against whom there was considerable popular feeling at the time." The governor remained firm on the limits of free speech, and in private correspondence made his reasoning for keeping the bill on the books clear: "I am not in favor of advocating anarchy."[24]

Such crackdowns on the IWW and criminal syndicalism hurt the socialists too because differences had steadily blurred between the two organizations. As both groups faced persecution during the Red Scare, the Socialist Party and the IWW found themselves curious bedfellows. Both objected to conscription and the war; the region's socialist press celebrated the IWW's vigilance in the face of indictments and other reprisals. The two organizations seemed to agree on the principles concerning industrial unionism and the emancipation of the working class. Even Debs echoed IWW rhetoric when he announced in Seattle his support for a "consolidation of all labor crafts and other organizations of the laboring man and woman into one great industrial union." Yet some party members hoped to distinguish themselves from their sabotage-promoting brethren. In Idaho, the Socialist Party and the IWW were "increasingly regarded as birds of a feather," noted Hugh Lovin. "The Idaho Socialist Party tried," he continued, "to little avail, to escape the anti-IWW animus."[25]

Other socialists and party presses, particularly Everett's *Co-operative News*, defended the IWW. An editorial on "the IWW spirit" dismissed the organization's reputation as "roughnecks, law breakers, trouble makers, and anarchists," instead, calling it one of "modern crusaders . . . permeated with the spirit of individual self sacrifice for the common good." Throughout the war, socialists reminded IWW critics, no convictions of Wobblies occurred for disloyalty or violence. And, pointing to the government's persecution of them, the *International Socialist Review* claimed in "The truth about the I.W.W.": "It is no fiction that they are being raided, lynched, and driven out, without due process of law."[26]

The region's socialists mounted their best efforts against the government's provocations. Rights to speech and justice, they asserted, were consistently compromised. The capitalists "who are in control . . . of the government of the United States," said the *Party Builder,* "have illegally abolished the first amendment to the Constitution, i.e., Free Speech and Free Press." Socialists rallied on behalf of accused comrades, such as in June 1917, when Seattle comrades gathered under the auspices of the "The International Workers' Defense League" to support Aaron Fislerman, R. A. Rice, Hulet Wells, and Sam Sadler, four SPW members arrested for circulating their anti-conscription pamphlets. Approximately fifteen hundred people attended the benefit, raising $106.82 for their legal defense fund. The SPW also established a fund for "dependents of our imprisoned comrades . . . who have dared to exercise their rights as American citizens" only to be "ruthlessly thrown in jail and given long terms in U.S. prisons." Most often, though, the socialists' predominant effort was in their official declarations of protest against restrictive federal legislation. In August 1918, Spokane "set the pace," responding to the three anti-war acts with the statement: "We most solemnly and earnestly protest against this flagrant violation of law and justice." The nation's socialists and leftists also continually demanded the repeal of the government's undemocratic regulations. After the war, in May 1919 the Worker's Defense Union of New York unanimously adopted a resolution condemning the Espionage Act. It claimed to have the support of the AFL and "Socialist Party branches," with a total membership of eight hundred thousand working men and women. But the objections of the Worker's Defense Union and others fell on deaf ears.[27]

Despite their maneuvering, socialists could stop neither the country's anti-radicalist sentiment nor the war. As David Shannon expressed it, "They did not know [how] to stop the bloodshed . . . there was little they could do." Radical writer Randolph Bourne recognized that "the war [would] go on whether it [was] popular or not." And, as the backlash demonstrated, socialists' resistance exacted a high price. The party's opposition to the war, historian Eric Foner observed, "laid the party open to . . . massive repression" and ultimately led to its demise.[28]

World War I ended on November 11, 1918, with the Allied powers' Armistice with Germany. After years of anti-war agitation and anti-radical backlash, socialists hoped finally to address other issues. In Everett's *Party Builder,* Eugene Debs asked, "The war is over . . . and now what?" He encouraged his comrades to move on, emphasizing there was "not the slightest cause for discouragement . . . we have lost nothing and gained much." He hoped the party would continue its activism and once again secure political victories. But if the paranoia of the Great War hindered the region's socialist party, the subsequent Red Scare all but finished it off. While the lines between the end of wartime persecution and the beginning of the Red Scare often blurred, the results were the same. After 1919 northwest socialists faced continued opposition and discrimination that brought widespread political ineffectiveness and party defections.[29]

After World War I, according to historian Kurt Wetzel, socialists, Wobblies, and "other political nonconformists" continued to face harassment. In Cincinnati mobs built a bonfire with socialist literature raided from the local hall, and in Philadelphia city officials forbade "radical meetings," taking firm aim at socialists. All potential revolutionists faced indictments and arrests, and nervous Northwesterners feared that revolutionists could be anywhere, including in Portland and Seattle. Two 1919 northwest events particularly contributed to Red Scare fears.[30]

While the post–World War I era included its share of national reactionalism, in the words of historian Jeremy Brecher, "nowhere did this radicalization go further than in Seattle." The post-war climate of tension escalated in the city in early 1919 when authorities arrested and tortured AFL activist Hulet Wells for his opposition to the war. His treatment, particularly in light of Russia's recent Bolshevik Revolution, radicalized more traditional portions of the Seattle labor movement and thousands, already angered by unfair wage scales, reportedly "flocked to" Seattle's unions. Beginning on January 21, 1919, thirty-five thousand shipyard workers walked off the job. This unprecedented waterfront strike eventually swelled to a broader general strike when Seattle's Central Labor Council pledged its support of the workers. While explicit socialist involvement in what became the Seattle General Strike of 1919 remains unclear, socialists would have sympathized with striking workers and may have been part of the approximately forty thousand "non-union" workers who also left their jobs. Regardless of whether socialists were directly involved, authorities called in both National Guardsmen and federal troops to crack down on the striking forces. Troops sacked the socialist party's Seattle headquarters, a labor group's printing office, and the IWW meeting hall.[31]

Seattle's five-day general strike took on national significance, setting off a tidal wave of labor unrest across the United States that eventually involved more than four million American workers and at times erupted into deadly violence. Later that year, for example, an armed confrontation between American Legionnaires and IWWs took place in Centralia, Washington, resulting in five deaths, including one World War I veteran and Wobbly, Wesley Everest. The "massacre" sent further shockwaves across the Pacific Northwest and many lawmakers abandoned their reservations about legislating against radicals. While the events of Seattle and Centralia received wide publicity, historian Hugh Lovin noted that the small but "persistent and innovative" socialist party of Idaho also provoked "some industrial unrest."

In the wake of the 1917 Bolshevik Revolution, northwest socialists, communists, and the IWW were all susceptible to attacks under the wave of anti-Bolshevism. Socialist Finns in Astoria, Oregon, were among those who felt the sting of post-war sentiments. Their socialist paper, the *Toveri*, announced that "radicalism was displacing disloyalty as the major threat to national security," aligning "aroused middle-class public opinion decisively against the Finnish Socialists." Astoria's new American Legion post organized an advertising boycott of the newspaper in 1919. The legionnaires also successfully lobbied the owner of the *Toveri*'s building to deny the Finns a lease renewal. In 1921, Enoch Bryan, the former president of Washington State College, in Pullman, declared Idaho "Reds" "the most active and dangerous foes of democracy." In Portland, socialists feared a "capitalist conspiracy," rumored to be a government "frame up" that aimed to persecute leading labor, IWW, and socialist activists. Socialists presumed that Albert Streiff, the state's SPA national committeeman, and Victor J. McCone, their state secretary, topped the government's "secret list."[32]

Within the spreading climate of Red Scare paranoia, socialist party activity slowed across the Northwest. Idaho's socialists "sought anonymity" and offered no candidates in the 1918, 1920, and 1922 local, state, and national elections. Idaho's socialist locals, according to secretary C. H. Cammans, were now "numerically weak and most of them without strong conviction for future success of our party in Idaho." In Washington, the SPW's new lower profile sparked rumors of the party's demise. The *Idaho Party Builder* refuted questions of the Washington organization's "break up." "The Socialist Party of Washington HAS NOT been 'broken up' nor 'disorganized,'" it declared. "We are NOT 'dead'—nor are we 'sleeping.'" Yet the SPW showed few signs of life and listed thirty-five delinquent locals and 633 delinquent members in May 1919.[33]

After the challenges of resisting World War I and the Red Scare, northwest socialists limped into the 1920s. As Schwantes was argued, World War I marked "the end of one era and the beginning of another" for the region's radicals. While America's concerns about radicalism had begun to wane, the weakened socialist party, according to Shannon, was "no longer potent enough to give nightmares to even the most apprehensive conservative." By the 1920s, a decade that included its share of political agitation, socialists rarely participated in the tumult.[34] Largely the victim of wartime backlash and Red Scare paranoia, the socialist moment was all but over.

Epilogue

DURING the mid-1920s the remnants of Pacific Northwest socialism moved ahead but often with disappointing results. Idaho
socialists once again formed locals in Pocatello, Twin Falls, Boise,
Nampa, and Caldwell. According to Hugh Lovin, however,
socialists were now "pesky but relatively harmless." The acting
party secretary for both Washington and Montana, Emil Herman, recorded twenty-three meetings over two months in 1923,
and an eighty-dollar treasury deficit for a virtually nonexistent
party. Even Seattle's once-powerful socialist organization sat dor-
mant until activists reorganized it in early 1931 with eight members.[1] The war and the persecution of radicals, according to
historian Hamilton Cravens, "wrecked" the Socialist Party of
Washington. By 1929 James Graham of Livingston, Montana,
gloomily noted that "for over ten years the Socialist Party has
made no progress in the west" and that, "as matters stand now,
our members are few." Oregon's party situation was similarly
bleak. In 1929 the state recorded only twenty members in good
standing. Modest reorganization efforts went on across the
region during the 1920s, but the party never regained the membership or activism it had once enjoyed.[2]

The conservative political climate of the 1920s also complicated the party's already weakened status. During and after
World War I, historian William Pratt has argued, many socialists
became "deradicalized" and searched for new political alternatives. Defections to other parties claimed countless members
during the decade; and combined with the loyalty crusades of
World War I and the Red Scare to end the Pacific Northwest
socialist movement. Persecution of socialists had already led
more conservative "reform socialists" to the Democratic Party

and the programs President Wilson proposed. As early as 1914 Oregon's socialists had begun observing these defections. According to the *Portland Labor Press*, Wilson was "making some loud promises" toward government ownership of certain essential services. Accordingly, some asserted that Wilson was "stealing the thunder of Socialism," and maybe party members as well. Later, at Montana's 1922 socialist convention, some delegates proposed fusion with state Democrats. Other delegates objected, including C. H. Brown of Whitefish, who believed that previously "useless attempt[s]" at unification had caused "all our failures in the political sense."[3]

More fervent socialists left to join the growing Communist Party of America (CPA). Established in 1919, it attracted many from the SPA's left wing, and within a few months, according to Schwantes, the "most committed revolutionaries" began subscribing to a "party line laid down in Moscow." The SPW had close ties to the communists and, as early as 1919, to the state organization affiliated with the Communist Labor Party (CLP). Editorials appeared in the *Party Builder* arguing that "the Socialist Party should be a closed chapter." One SPW member criticized the "politicians" within the party and demanded an alliance with "the only organization in existence which came into being in a legitimate way, and which truly represents the principles of Revolutionary Socialism— the Communist Labor Party." At an emergency convention the beleaguered SPW adopted resolutions for fusion with the Communist Party and the Communist Labor Party on behalf of "unity of all revolutionary Communist-Socialist organizations."[4] By mid-1920, the once exclusively socialist *Party Builder* reprinted the Manifesto of the Communist Labor Party of Washington and rejected motions to resume use of the name "the Socialist Party of Washington." In Oregon radicals also lost faith in the socialist party. By 1921, Astoria's Finnish *Toveri* was an exclusive organ of the Communist party. Like the Populists before them, socialists had learned the importance of party identity.[5]

In addition, two new parties attracted rural socialists during the 1920s. Former socialists in Idaho and Montana joined the

Non-Partisan League (NPL), established in North Dakota in 1915. The NPL gained much support as an insurgent political organization that appealed to farmers. The formation of Idaho's Non-Partisan League (INPL) in 1917 illustrated the line between the new party and the socialists. The NPL message of state ownership of farming implements, electrical systems, and credit banks attracted many socialists and their sympathizers. "Idaho Socialists flocked into the INPL," Lovin observed, and in Minidoka County, the 1918 county election included six of nine INPL candidates who were "known" socialists.[6]

In Oregon and Washington socialists searched for new political alternatives. By the 1920s the Farmer-Labor party symbolized cooperation between industrial and agricultural workers. During that decade, the Washington Farmer-Labor party secured the support of the Washington State Grange, the Washington Federation of Labor, and the SPW. With this broad support, most Farmer-Labor candidates finished second to victorious Republicans. While it was SPA policy "not to favor dual organizations," the decimated party had little choice; many prominent Washington socialists aligned with or joined the less threatening Farmer-Labor party. The surviving SPW also forged agreements with the Farmer-Labor leadership, promising in 1920 to support the Farmer-Labor ticket if its candidates did not campaign against Debs and agreed to "sufficient" representation of socialists within the party. These agreements, however, left the SPW politically ineffective. Eugene Debs, often the barometer of socialist success, received a scant 8,913 votes in Washington in 1920.[7]

For Pacific Northwest socialists, then, party decline was a gradual process. Its most optimistic years, from the 1912 elections to the solid achievements of 1916, brought steady growth, consistently outpacing socialist strengths in other regions of the country. Even so, party infighting and ideological debate grew increasingly troublesome after 1912, bringing internal uneasiness and even organizational schisms. Finally, the government measures against them for anti-war activities and the backlash during the Red Scare combined to deliver the final blows that destroyed the party. As elsewhere, northwest socialists could not surmount these crippling circumstances, and in the early 1920s most scattered to other political organizations. Though the Socialist Party would reorganize periodically throughout the twentieth century and beyond, offering up candidates and capturing a trifling share of votes, socialism never regained its significant third party status. Despite the party's ultimate demise, during the early twentieth century, Pacific Northwest socialists had pursued their cause with fervent commitment. As a third political party, they experienced extraordinary electoral success, making a significant imprint on regional politics, and leaving a unique legacy as an important center of American socialism.

Appendix A

Presidential Election Returns
in the Pacific Northwest, 1896–1924

Vote Totals (% of vote)

	1896			
	William McKinley (Republican)	William J. Bryan (Dem./Populist)	John M. Palmer (National Democrat)	Joshua Levering (Prohibition)
Idaho	6,324 (21.3)	23,135 (78.1)	0 (0)	172 (0.6)
Montana	10,509 (19.7)	42,628 (79.9)	0 (0)	193 (0.4)
Oregon	48,700 (50.0)	46,739 (48.0)	977 (1.0)	919 (0.9)
Washington	39,153 (41.8)	53,314 (57.0)	968 (1.0)	148 (0.2)
National Totals	7,108,480 (51.01)	6,511,495 (46.73)	133,435 (0.96)	125,072 (0.90)
Northwest Totals	104,686 (33.2)	165,816 (65.75)	1945 (0.5)	1,432 (0.53)

	1900			
	William McKinley (Republican)	William J. Bryan (Democrat)	John G. Wooley (Prohibition)	Eugene V. Debs (Socialist)
Idaho	27,198 (46.9)	29,484 (50.9)	857 (1.5)	0 (0)
Montana	25,409 (39.8)	37,311 (58.4)	306 (0.5)	711 (1.1)
Oregon	46,172 (55.5)	32,810 (39.4)	2,536 (3.1)	1,464 (1.8)
Washington	57,455 (53.4)	44,833 (41.7)	2,363 (2.2)	2,006 (1.9)
National Totals	7,218,039 (51.67)	6,358,345 (45.51)	209,004 (1.5)	86,936 (0.62)
Northwest Totals	156,234 (48.9)	144,438 (47.6)	6,062 (1.83)	4,181 (1.2)

	1904			
	Theodore Roosevelt (Republican)	Alton Parker (Democrat)	Eugene V. Debs (Socialist)	Silas C. Swallow (Prohibition)
Idaho	47,783 (65.8)	18,480 (25.5)	4,949 (6.8)	1,013 (1.4)
Montana	33,994 (53.5)	21,816 (34.3)	5,675 (8.9)	339 (0.5)
Oregon	60,309 (67.3)	17,327 (19.3)	7,479 (8.3)	3,795 (4.2)
Washington	101,540 (70.0)	28,098 (19.4)	10,023 (6.9))	3,229 (2.2)
National Totals	7,626,593 (56.41)	5,082,898 (37.60)	402,489 (2.98)	258,596 (1.91)
Northwest Totals	243,626 (64.15)	85,721 (24.63)	28,126 (7.73)	8,376 (2.08)

	1908			
	William H. Taft (Republican)	William J. Bryan (Democrat)	Eugene V. Debs (Socialist)	Eugene W. Chafin (Prohibition)
Idaho	52,621 (54.1)	36,162 (37.2)	6,400 (6.6)	1,986 (2.0)
Montana	32,471 (46.9)	29,511 (42.6)	5,920 (8.6)	838 (1.2)
Oregon	62,454 (56.5)	37,792 (34.2)	7,322 (6.6)	2,682 (2.4)
Washington	106,062 (57.8)	58,383 (31.8)	14,177 (7.7)	4,700 (2.6)
National Totals	7,676,258 (51.58)	6,406,801 (43.05)	420,380 (2.82)	252,821 (1.70)
Northwest Totals	253,608 (53.83)	161,848 (36.45)	33,819 (7.38)	10,206 (2.05)

	1912			
	Woodrow Wilson (Democrat)	Theodore Roosevelt (Progressive)	William H. Taft (Republican)	Eugene V. Debs (Socialist)
Idaho	33,921 (32.1)	25,527 (24.1)	32,810 (31.0)	11,960 (11.3)
Montana	28,129 (35.1)	22,709 (28.3)	18,575 (23.1)	10,811 (13.5)
Oregon	47,064 (34.3)	37,600 (27.4)	34,673 (25.3)	13,343 (9.7)
Washington	86,840 (26.9)	113,698 (35.2)	70,445 (21.8)	40,134 (12.4)
National Totals	6,293,152 (41.84)	4,119,207 (27.39)	3,486,333 (23.18)	900,369 (5.99)
Northwest Totals	195,954 (32.1)	199,534 (28.75)	156,503 (25.3)	76,248 (11.73)

	1916			
	Woodrow Wilson (Democrat)	Charles E. Hughes (Republican)	Allan L. Benson (Socialist)	J. Frank Hanly (Prohibition)
Idaho	70,054 (52.0)	55,368 (41.1)	8,066 (6.0)	1,127 (0.8)
Montana	101,104 (56.8)	66,933 (37.6)	9,634 (5.4)	0 (0)
Oregon	120,087 (45.9)	126,813 (48.5)	9,711 (3.7)	4,729 (1.8)
Washington	183,388 (48.1)	167,208 (43.9)	22,800 (6.0)	6,868 (1.8)
National Totals	9,126,300 (49.24)	8,546,789 (46.11)	589,924 (3.18)	221,030 (1.19)
Northwest Totals	474,633 (50.7)	416,322 (42.78)	50,211 (5.28)	12,724 (1.1)

	1920			
	Warren G. Harding (Republican)	James M. Cox (Democrat)	Parley Christensen (Farmer-Labor)	Eugene V. Debs (Socialist)
Idaho	88,975 (65.6)	46,579 (34.3)	0 (0)	38 (0)
Montana	109,680 (61.0)	57,746 (32.1)	12,283 (6.8)	0 (0)
Oregon	143,592 (60.2)	80,019 (33.6)	0 (0)	9,801 (4.1)
Washington	223,137 (56.0	84,298 (21.1)	77,246 (19.4)	8,913 (2.2)
National Totals	16,133,314 (60.3)	9,140,884 (34.17)	264,540 (0.99)	913,664 (3.42)
Northwest Totals	565,384 (60.7)	268,642 (30.28)	89,529 (6.55)	18,752 (1.58)

	Calvin Coolidge (Republican)	1924 John W. Davis (Democrat)	Robert La Follette (Progressive)	Herman Faris (Prohibition)
Idaho	72,084 (48.1)	24,217 (16.2)	53,664 (35.8)	0 (0)
Montana	74,246 (42.5)	33,867 (19.4)	65,985 (37.8)	0 (0)
Oregon	142,579 (51.0)	67,589 (24.2)	68,403 (24.5)	0 (0)
Washington	220,224 (52.3)	42,842 (10.2)	150,727 (35.8)	0 (0)
National Totals	15,717,553 (54.06)	8,383,169 (28.84)	4,814,050 (16.56)	54,833 (0.19)
Northwest Totals	509,133 (48.55)	168,515 (17.5)	338,779 (33.48)	0 (.0)

NOTE: Pacific Northwest totals are the sum of votes and the *average* percentages from Idaho, Montana, Oregon, and Washington.

Adapted from Goldfinger, *Presidential Elections since 1789*, 5th ed.

Appendix B

Party Platform of the Great Falls, Montana, Local, 1911

Adopted at the City Convention of the Socialist Party, at Great Falls, Mont., March 4, 1911

The Socialist Party in Municipal Convention assembled again adheres to the principles of Socialism as set forth in the National platform of 1908.

PROGRAM

As measures calculated to strengthen the working class for the realization of this ultimate aim, and to increase its power of resistance against capitalist oppression, we advocate and pledge ourselves and our elected officers to the following program.

IMMEDIATE DEMANDS

All person employed on municipal work shall be employed directly by the municipality, under an eight hour work day at the union wage scale and must be a member of a bona fide labor organization. Married men shall be given preference on all municipal works.

The immediate abolishment of the so-called peace agreement and to assist in protecting the rights of organized labor.

And to take such other measures with their power as will lessen the wide spread dissatisfaction of organized labor caused by the misrule and discrimination of the present administration.

Socialist Party Platform, Great Falls, Montana, Local, 1911. *Socialist Party of America Papers*, microfilm edition, Reel 99.

The municipality to furnish free water to widow women earning a living by laundry work.

The municipal ownership of the street railway, electric power, and gas plants.

The establishment of a municipal owned and controlled ice plant, coal yard, loan office, hospital, dance hall, sanitary department, and free employment office.

Free use of public buildings for public meetings, and absolute freedom of speech and assemblage.

INDUSTRIAL DEMANDS

The improvement of industrial conditions of the workers.

By assisting in securing to every worker a rest period of not less than one day each week.

By securing a more affective inspection of workshops and factories.

By forbidding the employment of children under sixteen years of age.

By the equalization of taxes.

Appendix C

Platform of the Socialist Party of Washington, 1912

Adopted at State Convention
Seattle, March 9, 10, 11, 12
Ratified by State Referendum "A"
Amended by State Referendum "C"

The Socialist Party of Washington, in conventions assembled, reaffirms its unfaltering loyalty to the principles of international Socialism, and the Socialist Party of the United States and presents the following as its platform:

In the struggle for freedom the interests of all modern workers are identical. The struggle is not only national, but international. It embraces the world, and will be carried to ultimate victory through intelligent class-consciousness political and industrial action.

Human labor creates machinery and applies it to the land to produce things necessary for human life. Whosoever has control of land and machinery controls human labor, and with it human life and liberty.

The working class own nothing but its labor power, and sells this for wages to the capitalist class.

The labor power applied to modern means of production and distribution, produces at least four times as much value as the working class receives in wages.

The capitalist class, unable to find a market either in this or foreign countries for the surplus product, are now closing the mines, mills and factories.

Platform of the Socialist Party of Washington, Ephemera, 1912, WSHS.

This, together with the constant invention of labor-saving machinery, throws men, women and children of the working class out of employment, causing untold misery and distress.

The lack and uncertainty of employment produces extreme poverty, which in its turn produces crime, insanity, prostitution of body and brain, suicides, drunkenness, disease and degradation.

The insecurity of a livelihood and consequent degenerating results are therefore directly due to the private ownership and control by the capitalist class of mine, factory, and land.

The remedy lies in the social ownership of these means of production and distribution, thereby giving all an equal opportunity to live and enjoy the product of their labor.

Humanity lives amid constant change. Laws, institutions and customs, once useful and popular, becomes oppressive, abusive, intolerable and dangerous to further progress of the race. It is at such a time that the race must find a new method, inaugurate a new system more in harmony with its needs. If any nation or community can not change for the better it is because it is either too ignorant or too terrorized by the ruling class. Tyranny rules from the top down, social democracy from the bottom up.

The socialist party is the only political party which stands for the overthrow of the present capitalist system of exploitation and the substitution of the social ownership of the source of food, clothing, shelter, and other necessities.

OUR ULTIMATE DEMAND

Our ultimate demand is the social ownership and democratic management of all the socially used means of production and distribution.

PROGRAM

As measures calculated to strengthen the working class in its fight for the realization of its ultimate aim, and increase its power of resistance against capitalist oppression; we advocate and pledge ourselves to the following program:

1. Collective ownership and management of all public utilities, and all industries that have become monopolized.
2. Abolition of private ownership of land and natural resources when used for exploitation and speculation.
3. Public employment of the unemployed at not less than prevailing union scale of wages and not more than eight hours per day.
4. We demand the enactment of a maximum eight-hour law to apply to both men and women employed in all capitalized industries.
5. We advocate initiative, referendum and recall to apply to all public officials, the petition not to exceed 10 per cent of the voters of the previous election.
6. Abolition of child labor under the age of 16 years.
7. The elimination of the injunction in labor disputes.
8. Abolition of all residential qualifications or other restrictions of voters. The abolition of all filing fees at primaries and other elections and repeal of all non-partisan laws. Abolition of property qualifications for jurors. We favor the election of a public defender as well as prosecutor together with the adoption of other means to insure the free administration of justice.
9. We favor a constitutional amendment abolishing the senate and we also demand that all cities be prohibited from enacting ordinances infringing on the right of free speech and free press.
10. We favor the establishment of a state board of health with full power for the inspection and condemnations of all unsanitary factories, tenements, etc., and the liberal appropriations for the use of the latest scientific methods of eliminating disease.
11. We demand the free use of all public buildings and property for public meetings including court houses, school houses, parks, etc. without discrimination, and we demand a liberal appropriation for promotion of social centers.

RESOLUTIONS

Resolved: That we, the Socialist party in convention assembled, do hereby recall to the minds of the working class all the arbitrary, cruel and inhuman methods used by the capitalist class in this class war, including the use of police power to suppress the freedom of speech, press and public assembly, as recently evidenced in several cities of this state, and as this abuse can only continue as long as we, the working class, remain divided, we here and now, urge the members of our class to devote their efforts towards greater solidarity, clearer class consciousness, and the necessity of united political action, and we hereby endorse the principle of revolutionary industrial unionism.

Resolved, That we, the Socialist party, hereby endorses all unified action of the workers and pledge ourselves to assist them by supplying speakers, money and other necessary support whenever possible, to the end that we may win our economic freedom and overthrow the capitalist system.

To the small farmer we say, we are opposed to the private ownership of land for the purpose of speculation and exploitation.

We are absolutely opposed to the Boy Scout movement, and the teaching of military drill with guns and other means of destruction of human life, to our school children.

Notes

Introduction

1. *Socialist Worker* (Tacoma, Wash.), 31 January 1914. Regional scholars have spent considerable time and energy defining the Pacific Northwest. I use "Pacific Northwest" throughout this study to describe Washington, Oregon, Idaho, and Montana collectively, not only because of the geographical cohesion the Columbia River Basin and Intermountain West provide but also because the states display a number of commonalities in their political, economic, and social climates. I also intermittently use "Northwest," in part for the sake of brevity and in part to denote the American Pacific Northwest. See Carlos Schwantes, *The Pacific Northwest: An Interpretive History* (Lincoln: University of Nebraska Press, 1996), 2–5.

2. William Leach, *Land of Desire: Merchants, Power, and the Rise of a New American Culture* (New York: Pantheon Books, 1993), 3; Alan Dawley, *Struggles for Justice: Social Responsibility and the Liberal State* (Cambridge, Mass.: Harvard University Press, 1991), 99, 135–36; Stephen Skowronek, *Building a New American State: The Expansion of National Administrative Capacities, 1877–1920* (Cambridge: Cambridge University Press, 1982), ix.

3. To Shannon, the Socialist Party remained a "fairly loose alliance of regional political groups." David Shannon, *The Socialist Party of America* (Chicago: Quadrangle Books, 1955), 7–8. Shannon also earlier asserted that America's socialists, because of regional, ideological, and other distinctions, were "as motley a group as any political party." Shannon, "The Socialist Party before the First World War: An Analysis," *Mississippi Valley Historical Review* 38 (September 1951): 280. In his study of Oklahoma socialists, Jim Bissett argued, "through these years of socialist relevance, the state of Oklahoma supported the most vigorous, ambitious, and fascinating socialist movement of all." Bissett, *Agrarian Socialism in America: Marx, Jefferson, and Jesus in the Oklahoma Countryside, 1904–1920* (Norman: University of Oklahoma Press, 1999), xiii.

4. Werner Sombart, *Warum Gibt es in den Vereingten Staaten keinen Sozialismus?* (Tuebingen, Germany, 1906); David Brody, "The Old Labor History

and the New: In Search of an American Working Class," *Labor History* 20 (Winter 1979): 111. See Morris Hillquit, *History of Socialism in the United States* (New York: Funk and Wagnalls, 1910; reprint, New York: Dover, 1971); Vernon L. Parrington, *The Beginnings of Critical Realism in America, 1860–1920* (New York: Harcourt, Brace, and Company, 1930); Aileen Kraditor, *The Radical Persuasion: 1890–1917* (Baton Rouge: Louisiana State University Press, 1981), 44. During the Progressive Era, Commons and the Wisconsin School stressed institutional and organizational history primarily, and political or biographical themes secondarily. These histories were most concerned with the ascendancy of unions, not with socialist politics or capitalist critiques. Leon Fink, "American Labor History," in *The New American History*, Eric Foner, ed. (Philadelphia: Temple University Press, 1990), 333–34; Fred E. Haynes, "The Significance of the Latest Third Party Movement," *Mississippi Valley Historical Review* 12 (September 1925): 177–86.

5. Daniel Boorstein, for example, stressed the "seamlessness" and "community" behind the "American way of life." D. H. Leon, "Whatever Happened to an American Socialist Party? A Critical Survey of the Spectrum of Interpretations," *American Quarterly* 23 (May 1971): 236, 254, 258. See Boorstein's *The Genius of American Politics* (Chicago: University of Chicago Press, 1953) and *The Decline of Radicalism* (New York: Random House, 1969). See also Louis Hartz, *The Liberal Tradition in America* (New York: Harcourt, Brace, and World, 1955); Ira Kipnis, *The American Socialist Movement, 1897–1912* (New York: Columbia University Press, 1952). See also Howard H. Quint, *The Forging of American Socialism* (Columbia: University of South Carolina Press, 1953), and Daniel Bell, "The Background and Development of Marxian Socialism in the United States," in Donald D. Egbert and Stow Persons, eds., *Socialism in American Life*, 2 vols. (Princeton: Princeton University Press, 1952). In addition to Weinstein, during the 1970s and 1980s a number of studies appeared on the demise of socialism. See John Laslett and Seymour Lipset, eds., *Failure of a Dream: Essays in the History of American Socialism* (Garden City, N.Y.: Anchor Press, 1974); Stephen Whitfield, "Autopsy Notes on American Socialism," *Reviews in American History* 3 (June 1975): 254–59; Erik Olssen, "The Case of the Socialist Party that Failed, or Further Reflections on an American Dream," *Labor History* 29 (Fall 1988): 416–49; and Eric Foner, "Why is there no Socialism in the United States?" *History Workshop* 17 (Spring 1984): 59–80; Richard Schneirov, "Editor's Introduction: The Socialist Party Revisited," *Journal of Gilded Age and Progressive Era* 2 (July 2003): 247.

6. Fink, "American Labor History," 333; Leon, "Whatever Happened," 258.

7. For more on the historiographical debate among labor historians, consult Brody, "The Old Labor History and the New," 111–26; Mari Jo Buhle and Paul Buhle, "The New Labor History at the Cultural Crossroads," *Journal of American History* 75 (June 1988): 151–57; and Ellen Fitzpatrick, "Rethinking the Intellectual Origins of American Labor History," *American Historical Review* 96 (April 1991): 422–28; Leon, "Whatever Happened," 242; Carlos Schwantes, "The History of Pacific Northwest Labor History," *Idaho Yesterdays* 28 (Winter 1985): 33.

8. See William G. Robbins, *Colony and Empire: The Capitalist Transformation of the American West* (Lawrence: University Press of Kansas, 1994), xiii; Brody, "The Old Labor History and the New," 121. For place-specific studies in the Pacific Northwest, see Jerry Calvert, *The Gibraltar: Socialism and Labor in Butte, Montana, 1895–1920* (Helena: Montana Historical Society Press, 1988); Jonathan Dembo, *Unions and Politics in Washington State, 1885–1935* (New York: Garland, 1983); Charles LeWarne, *Utopias on Puget Sound, 1885–1915* (Seattle: University of Washington Press, 1975); and Schwantes, *Radical Heritage*. For examples of regional socialist studies, see James R. Green, *Grass-Roots Socialism: Radical Movements in the Southwest, 1895–1943* (Baton Rouge: Louisiana State University Press, 1978); Donald Critchlow, ed., *Socialism in the Heartland: The Midwestern Experience, 1900–1925* (Notre Dame, Ind.: University of Notre Dame Press, 1986); Bruce M. Stave, *Socialism and the Cities* (Port Washington, N.Y.: Kennikat Press, 1975); Brad Paul, "Rebels of the New South: The Socialist Party in Dixie, 1892–1920" (University of Massachusetts, Ph.D. diss., 1999); Jason Mellard, "Lone Star Reds: The Socialist Party and Cotton Tenancy in Texas, 1901–1917" (Texas A&M University, M.A. thesis, 2000). Other centers of American socialism, such as Oklahoma, have been well covered by scholars. See James Green's *Grass-Roots Socialism*, Garin Burbank's *When Farmers Voted Red: The Gospel of Socialism in the Oklahoma Countryside, 1910–1924* (Greenwood Press, 1977), and John Thompson's *Closing the Frontier: Radical Response in Oklahoma, 1889–1923* (Norman: University of Oklahoma Press, 1986). Bissett, *Agrarian Socialism in America*, xiii. For specific city studies, see John T. Walker, "Socialism in Dayton, Ohio, 1912–1925: Its Membership, Organization, and Demise," *Labor History* 26 (Summer 1985): 384–404; Errol Wayne Stevens, "Labor and Socialism in an Indiana Mill Town, 1905–1921," *Labor History* 26 (Summer 1985): 353–83; and Douglas E. Booth, "Municipal Socialism and City Government Reform: The Milwaukee Experience, 1910–1940," *Journal of Urban History* 12 (November 1985): 51–74.

9. Brody, "The Old Labor History and the New," 122.

10. Bissett, *Agrarian Socialism in America*, xiii.

1. Fanning the "Flame of Revolution"

1. Richard Schneirov, Shelton Stromquist, and Nick Salvatore, *The Pullman Strike and the Crisis of the 1890s* (Urbana: University of Illinois Press, 1999), 6; T. J. Jackson Lears, *No Place of Grace: Antimodernism and the Transformation of American Culture, 1880–1920* (New York: Pantheon Books, 1981), xvi–xvii; William Leach, *Land of Desire: Merchants, Power, and the Rise of a New American Culture* (New York: Pantheon Books, 1993), 3.

2. Alan Dawley, *Struggles for Justice: Social Responsibility and the Liberal State* (Cambridge, Mass.: Harvard University Press, 1991), 1.

3. Schwantes, *The Pacific Northwest*, 261, 352; William G. Robbins, *Colony and Empire: The Capitalist Transformation of the American West* (Lawrence: University Press of Kansas, 1994), 85; Schneirov, "Editor's Introduction: The Socialist Party Revisited," 246.

4. Schwantes articulates the idea of the region as an economic hinterland in his regional text, *The Pacific Northwest*, 14–16. *American Federationist* 18 (October 1911): 816; Robert Wayne Smith, *The Coeur d'Alene Mining War of 1892: A Case Study of an Industrial Dispute* (Corvallis: Oregon State University Press, 1961), 2, 8; Michael Malone, Richard Roeder, and William Lang, *Montana: A History of Two Centuries* (Seattle: University of Washington Press, 1991), 207; Limerick quoted in Robbins, *Colony and Empire*, 84, 88; Cloice R. Howd, *Industrial Relations in the West Coast Lumber Industry* (Washington, D.C.: Washington Government Printing Office, 1924), 6; Dorothy O. Johansen, *Empire of the Columbia: A History of the Pacific Northwest*, 2d ed. (New York: Harper & Row, 1967), 317.

5. Gender in these expanding industries may have contributed to the shaping of Pacific Northwest radicalism as well. The region's work force was generally "male, manual, and mobile." Demographically, the late-nineteenth- and early-twentieth-century Northwest had a younger workforce, more of whose members were unmarried, than in the rest of the country. By the turn of the twentieth century several booming northwestern communities were decidedly male communities. The 1900 census revealed Butte, Montana, as nearly 60 percent male and Seattle as 64 percent. Male majorities certainly added to a "rough and tumble" frontier economy. This was particularly true because at the time Northwest urban environments such as Portland focused their attention on becoming "civilized communities." Carlos Schwantes, "Patterns of Radicalism on the Wageworkers' Frontier," *Idaho Yesterdays* 30 (Fall 1986): 25–26; Schwantes, *The Pacific Northwest*, 330. The fervent radicalism of the West and the "miners and lumberjacks of the Western mountains," according to historian David Shannon, were in step with the surrounding circumstances. "If many Western Socialists were

tough, hard-bitten, and primitive," he observed, "so were the conditions from which they came." Shannon, *The Socialist Party of America*, 39.

6. *Oregonian* (Portland, Ore.), 17 January 1895; Smith, *The Coeur d'Alene Mining War*, 14; Katherine G. Aiken, *Idaho's Bunker Hill: The Rise and Fall of a Great Mining Company, 1885–1981* (Norman: University of Oklahoma Press, 2005), xvii, 18; Frank Steunenberg, Annual Report (hereinafter *AR*), 5 January 1899, AR 2/4, Box 1, Idaho State Historical Society (hereinafter ISHS); Lukas, *Big Trouble*, 104–105.

7. Smith, *The Coeur d'Alene Mining War*, 15; see also Linda Carlson, *Company Towns of the Pacific Northwest* (Seattle: University of Washington Press, 2003); Leach, *Land of Desire*, 4–5, 11; Schwantes, "Patterns of Radicalism," 27; Robbins, *Colony and Empire*, 6.

8. *Spokesman-Review* (Spokane, Wash.), 23 and 26 February 1897.

9. Robbins, *Colony and Empire*, 74, 141–42; Donald Meinig, *The Great Columbia Plain: A Historical Geography, 1805–1910* (Seattle: University of Washington Press, 1995), 365; Schwantes, *The Pacific Northwest*, 329. Labor historian Melvyn Dubofsky articulated this viewpoint as well, arguing that the quick "shock of change" exacerbated social shifts and encouraged radicalism among late-nineteenth-century workers. See Dubofsky, *Hard Work: The Making of Labor History* (Urbana: University of Illinois Press, 2000) and *Industrialism and the American Worker, 1865–1920* (Wheeling, Ill.: Harlan Davidson, 1996).

10. Robbins, *Colony and Empire*, xiii; Robert R. Swartout, Jr., "From Kwangtung to the Big Sky: The Chinese Experience in Frontier Montana," in *Montana Legacy: Essays on History, People, Place*, Harry Fritz, Mary Murphy, and Robert R. Swartout, eds. (Helena: Montana Historical Society Press, 2002), 49–50, 58; Hugh France to Frank Steunenberg, 1 November 1899, AR 2/4, Box 2, ISHS; *American Federationist* 9 (March 1902): 125. For more on the Chinese and Japanese labor experience in the Northwest and related labor conflicts, see also Carlos Schwantes, "Protest in a Promised Land: Unemployment, Disinheritance, and the Origin of Labor Militancy in the Pacific Northwest, 1885–1886," *Western Historical Quarterly* 13 (October 1984): 373–90; and John Belshaw, *Colonization and Community: The Vancouver Island Coalfield and the Making of the British Columbian Working Class* (Montreal, Can.: McGill-Queen's University Press, 2002).

11. Lears, *No Place of Grace*, 29.

12. Schwantes, *The Pacific Northwest*, 317–18; Aiken, *Idaho's Bunker Hill*, 3, 10–11; Howd, *Industrial Relations*, 108.

13. Robbins, *Colony and Empire*, 91–92; Johansen, *Empire of the Columbia*, 360–61; Schwantes, *The Pacific Northwest*, 261; Jeremy Brecher, *Strike!*

(Cambridge, Mass.: South End Press, 1997), 87. Of the 20,000 out-of-work Montanans, 8,000 left the state searching for greener economic pastures. Dave Walter, "Hogan's Army," in *Montana Legacy*, 66–67.

14. Schneirov, et al., *The Pullman Strike*, 4; *Oregonian*, 15 January 1895; Walter, "Hogan's Army," 67–68, 73; The Seattle contingent numbered 900, the Tacoma army 700. Carlos Schwantes, *Coxey's Army: An American Odyssey* (Lincoln: University of Nebraska Press, 1985), 198, 232; Johansen, *Empire of the Columbia*, 364.

15. Johansen, *Empire of the Columbia*, 350; Aiken, *Idaho's Bunker Hill*, 21, 27, 30.

16. *American Federationist* 9 (March 1902): 125.

17. Sheldon Stromquist, "The Crisis of 1894 and the Legacies of Producerism," in Schneirov, et al., *The Pullman Strike*, 180; Foner, "Why is there No Socialism," 59; Schwantes, "Patterns of Radicalism," 28.

18. William Haywood and Frank Bohn, *Industrial Socialism* (Chicago: Charles H. Kerr & Co., 1911), 40; Schwantes, *The Pacific Northwest*, 336–37.

19. In 1886 more trade unions had joined the BMU to form the Silver Bow Trades and Labor Assembly. Malone et al., *Montana*, 207; Smith, *The Coeur d'Alene Mining War*, 14; Melvyn Dubofsky, *We Shall Be All: A History of the Industrial Workers of the World* (Urbana: University of Illinois Press, 2000), 19–21; *American Federationist* 8 (August 1901): 294.

20. Hugh France to Frank Steunenberg, 15 August 1899, AR 2/4, Box 2, ISHS.

21. *Oregonian*, 29 October 1896; *American Federationist* 8 (August 1901): 293.

22. *Oregonian*, 15 January 1895; *International Socialist Review* 1 (July 1900): 52, 2 (August 1901): 152.

23. *Oregonian*, 22 September 1896; *Spokesman-Review*, 21 and 23 February, 18 and 29 June 1897. Author's italics added at "have *no* classes."

24. Leach, *Land of Desire*, 6. The SLP had noteworthy members nationally. Among those who emerged as significant within the more successful Social Democratic Party (SDP) and Socialist Party of America (SPA) were Morris Hillquit, a local SLP leader in New York who warned against alienating unionist factions; Eugene Debs, president of the ARU; and Victor Berger of Milwaukee, and his independent SDP. Anthony Esposito, *The Ideology of the Socialist Party of America, 1901–1917* (New York: Garland Press, 1997), 16; Proceedings of the Ninth National Convention of the Socialist Labor Party, July 4 to July 10, 1896, Socialist Labor Party of America Papers (microfilm edition), Reel 35, State Historical Society of Wisconsin, Madison. J. Benoit, the Everett secretary, believed his duties included setting

monthly dues ($.25 per month), purchasing stationery, planning the first public meetings, and applying for a national charter. The Everett SLP section's charter was approved in 1898. A February 1, 1898, list of delinquent members reported nine delinquent members during the previous three months. Everett Section Minutes, 7 and 14 November 1897, 16 and 23 January 1898, Socialist Labor Party of America Papers, microfilm edition (Glen Rock, N.J.: Microfilming Corporation of America, 1975), Reel 95. The nominees were Thomas Young and Thomas Lawry for Supreme Court justices and Walter Walker and M. A. Hamilton for the U.S. House. Feeling alienated by fusion, Young and Walker defected from the Populist cause. Schwantes, *Radical Heritage*, 82.

25. Proceedings of the Tenth National Convention of the Socialist Labor Party, 2 June to 8 June 1900. Socialist Labor Party of American Papers, Reel 35.

26. Hillquit, *History of Socialism*, 231.

27. Edmond S. Meany, *History of the State of Washington* (New York: The Macmillan Company, 1910), 321; Charles LeWarne, *Utopias on Puget Sound, 1885–1915* (Seattle: University of Washington Press, 1975), 25–35, 52.

28. Meany, *Washington*, 321; Schwantes, "Patterns of Radicalism," 28. Colony members published Home's paper under a number of titles. First published as the *New Era* in June 1897, the paper functioned as the *Discontent* from March 11, 1898, to April 30, 1902. It was published as the *Demonstrator* from March 1903 to February 19, 1908, and finally as the *Agitator* from November 1910 to 1912. Cooperative Colonies File, WSHS. By WWI Home had approximately 500 residents. LeWarne, *Utopias*, 168, 173–74, 186, 193; Walter Goldwater, *Radical Periodicals in America, 1890–1950* (New Haven: Yale University Press, 1964), 11.

29. Eugene Debs accepted a post as an organizer in 1897, fresh off his radicalization in prison, a six-month sentence he served in 1895. Debs did little organizing and had a different vision than BCC leaders. He saw colonies like Equality as safe havens for the unemployed during economic crises, and he split with the BCC and eventually the later Social Democracy of America. LeWarne, *Utopias*, 60–61; Lukas, *Big Trouble*, 413–14.

30. Equality's founders and financiers were mostly eastern intellectuals and socialist activists. The colony received considerable funding and support from outside memberships and from members not living at Equality. BCC membership peaked at 3,558 in 1898. The colony's general assembly endlessly debated apparently insignificant questions, such as how the boards on the new printing building would be nailed. LeWarne, *Utopias*, 55, 63–66, 72–73, 110.

31. The result was an ideological split between pro-colonization factions that formed the SDA and politically minded socialists, led by Milwaukee's Victor Berger, who formed the SDP. Kipnis, *The American Socialist Movement*, 61; Esposito, *Ideology*, 31–32; LeWarne, *Utopias*, 134; *Spokesman-Review*, 22 and 26 June 1897.

32. *Spokesman-Review*, 16 and 24 June 1897. There were others who subscribed to ideas outlined in Bellamy's novel *Looking Backward*. SLP defectors also formed groups of the Bellamy Nationalists. The first club of this kind was organized in 1899 in Tacoma. Most of these clubs, according to Schwantes, "remained basically non-Marxian, middle-class study groups." Schwantes, *Radical Heritage*, 91. The "Back to Bellamy" movement also enjoyed success in Oregon. In 1890 Coquille City established a Bellamy Nationalist club and a number of others followed. Other Oregon towns that had Bellamy clubs included Corvallis, Astoria, Beavercreek, and Natal. Oregon's clubs, like Washington's, remained isolated, short-lived social groups. James J. Kopp, "Looking Backward at Edward Bellamy's Influence in Oregon, 1888–1936," *Oregon Historical Quarterly* 104 (Spring 2003): 70, 78, 80–81. Those he helped to migrate would be assessed a $.15 a month tax payable to the SDA. Quickly, 200 Detroit socialists denounced Debs's Washington colony idea as "communistic . . . and impossible of achievement." *Spokesman-Review*, 29 June 1897.

33. Established in Seattle in 1898, organizers named the association the Cooperative Brotherhood to avoid confusion with the colonization commission of the SDA, already incorporated in Kansas, called the Cooperative Commonwealth Company. Burley residents published the *Cooperator* until 1906. LeWarne, *Utopian Communities*, 138–42, 239; *Cooperator* (Olalla, Wash.), 19 and 26 December 1898, 10 April 1899. Cooperative Colonies File, WSHS.

34. Washington's socialist colonies also spurred labor radicalism and propaganda. LeWarne, *Utopian Communities*, 72, 238–39.

35. London, "Revolution,"113; Rally Flyer, 19 June 1901, WSHS.

36. The *Leader* only saw publication in 1895. Carlos Schwantes, "Labor-Reform Papers in Oregon, 1871–1976: A Checklist," *Pacific Northwest Quarterly* 74 (October 1983): 157–59.

37. Rally Flyer, 2 April 1901, WSHS. As early as 1897 SDA locals emerged in eastern Washington, when a local was organized in Palouse. LeWarne, *Utopian Communities*, 133; Terrence McGlynn, "Socialist Organizers in Montana," 21 April 1972, vertical file typescript, Montana Historical Society (hereinafter MHS); *Montana Standard*, 27 April 1969; William Butscher to J. D. Stevens, 29 August 1900, MSS 1187, Oregon Historical Society (here-

inafter OHS); Schwantes, *Radical Heritage*, 132; *Seattle Post-Intelligencer* (Seattle, WA), 7 October 1900. Similarly, the *Spokesman-Review* covered Debs's plans to tour Washington during the 1900 trip that included stops in Walla Walla, North Yakima, Spokane, Seattle, and Tacoma. *Spokesman-Review*, 13 February 1898, 19 April 1900.

38. Ballot, 1900, Pierce County (Tacoma), Ephemera, WSHS; *Oregonian*, 7 November 1900.

39. *Oregonian*, 22 October 1898.

40. Lukas, *Big Trouble*, 413–414; J. Hayes to J. D. Stevens, 3 December 1895, John Daniel Stevens Papers, MSS 1187, OHS; Rally flyer, 9 December 1900, WSHS.

41. Esposito, *Ideology*, 21. As the ARU President at the time, Debs also visited Seattle, Tacoma, and Portland. *Spokesman-Review*, 13 February 1898, 15 and 16 March 1895. Schwantes, *Radical Heritage*, 90; Proceedings of the Ninth National Convention of the Socialist Labor Party, 4 July to 10 July 1896. Socialist Labor Party of America Papers, Reel 35. Illustrative of the fluidity between Populists and socialists, by 1897 Washington's "middle-of-the-road" Populists supported, according to historian Thomas Riddle, "the unqualified collectivism of socialism and the unqualified individualism of laissez faire advocates such as William Graham Sumner." Thomas Wayne Riddle, "The Old Radicalism in America: John R. Rogers and the Populist Movement in Washington, 1891–1900" (Washington State University, Ph.D. diss., 1976), 204.

42. Populism achieved different levels of support in the Pacific Northwest. In Washington, Populist candidates continually won more support than elsewhere. Washington's Populist vote for Congress, which in 1892 was 19,165, reached 25,119 in 1894. Eastern Washington (with its ties to the silver mines of northern Idaho) and Oregon, however, experienced a decline in Populist support from 1892 to 1896. *Oregonian*, 18 September 1895, 7 and 2 November 1896.

43. *International Socialist Review* 2 (August 1901): 151; *Oregonian*, 22 October 1898.

44. Some Debs "supporters" also asked him to withdraw from the race because, even though it was not obvious how it would happen, the cooperative commonwealth would be "hastened by Bryan's election." *Seattle Post-Intelligencer*, 3 November 1900; *Oregonian*, 5 November and 3 October 1900.

45. *International Socialist Review* 1 (December 1900): 321; ibid., 2 (August 1901): 154.

46. Ibid., 1 (September 1900): 180–181; London, "Revolution," 99–100.

47. *International Socialist Review* 1 (September 1900): 182.

48. Ibid., 1 (March 1901): 534, 2 (August 1901): 151.

2. Building a "Typically American Party"

1. *International Socialist Review* 1 (December 1900): 321; ibid., 2 (August 1901): 151.

2. Hillquit, *History of Socialism*, 308; Shannon, *The Socialist Party of America*, 1, 3–4. According to Alan Dawley, Daniel DeLeon of the SLP was called "the pope" in response to his "self proclaimed infallibility on Marxist doctrine." He nevertheless found his organization quickly surpassed by the new SPA. Alan Dawley, *Struggles for Justice: Social Responsibility and the Liberal State* (Cambridge, Mass.: Harvard University Press, 1991), 99; Kipnis, *The American Socialist Movement*, 81; Dembo, *Unions and Politics*, 32–33.

3. *Seattle Post-Intelligencer* (Seattle, Wash.), 30 July 1901. Convention debate centered on the adoption of "immediate demands" for municipal reforms. The adopted planks included: (1) "the public ownership of all means of transportation and communication and all other public utilities, as well as all industries controlled by monopolies, trusts and combines"; (2) "the progressive reduction of the hours of labor and increase of wages"; (3) "state or national insurance of working people in case of accidents, lack of employment, sickness and want in old age"; and (4) "the inauguration of a system of public industries, public credit to be used for that purpose in order that the workers might secure the full product of their labor." *Seattle Post-Intelligencer*, 1 August 1901; Shannon, *The Socialist Party*, 4.

4. Terrence D. McGlynn, "Socialist Organizers in Montana," 21 April 1972, Typescript, Vertical File, "Socialism," MHS, 1. In 1904 state socialists named James D. Graham of Livingston their secretary. Terrence D. McGlynn, "Lewis J. Duncan: Butte's Socialist Mayor," 25 September 1982, Typescript, Vertical File, "Socialism" MHS, 3; *Liberator* (Portland, Ore.), 7 March 1903.

5. Dembo, *Unions and Politics*, 34, 46; Schwantes, *The Pacific Northwest*, 352.

6. *International Socialist Review* 4 (May 1904): 666; Terrence D. McGlynn, "Socialist Newspapers of Montana," 17 April 1971, Typescript, Vertical File, "Socialism," MHS, 1.

7. In 1905 Titus moved the *Socialist* from Seattle to Toledo, Ohio, believing Toledo was at the heart of American industry. He and the paper moved again in 1906, this time to Boise, Idaho, in part to witness the Frank Steunenberg murder trial, where authorities tried WFM leaders, Bill Haywood among them, for the governor's 1905 assassination. Titus moved the paper

back to Seattle in 1907. Schwantes, *Radical Heritage*, 96, 107, 169; Dembo, *Unions and Politics*, 39, 46, 54; Kipnis, *The American Socialist Movement*, 292.

8. Carlos Schwantes, "Labor-Reform Papers in Oregon, 1871–1976, a Checklist," *Pacific Northwest Quarterly* 74 (October 1983): 155, 158–59; *Liberator*, 30 May and 7 March 1903.

9. *Liberator*, 30 May and 4 April 1903; Kipnis, *The American Socialist Movement*, 123; Shannon, *The Socialist Party*, 39, italics author's.

10. Flyer, 17 February 1902, Vertical File, "Socialism," MHS; McGlynn, "Socialist Organizers in Montana," 2. Similarly, "The Parable of the Water Tank," taken from Bellamy's *Equality*, was distributed in Tacoma during the summer of 1901. Ephemera, WSHS. See also James J. Kopp, "Looking Backward at Edward Bellamy's Influence in Oregon, 1888–1936," *Oregon Historical Quarterly* 104 (Spring 2003): 62–95.

11. *International Socialist Review* 2 (May 1902): 774–75.

12. *International Socialist Review* 4 (April 1904): 633; Schwantes, *Radical Heritage*, 107; Lukas, *Big Trouble*, 414. Marilyn P. Watkins, *Rural Democracy: Family Farmers and Politics in Western Washington, 1890–1925* (Ithaca, N.Y.: Cornell University Press, 1995), 113–14, 122.

13. Leach, *Land of Desire*, 12; John P. Enyeart, "Revolution or Evolution: The Socialist Party, Western Workers, and Law in the Progressive Era," *Journal of Gilded Age and Progressive Era* 2 (October 2003): 377–78; Dawley, *Struggles for Justice*, 100; *International Socialist Review* 1 (March 1901): 524.

14. More specifically, socialist leaders had "Suggested Lines of Socialist Municipal Activity" from party leaders that addressed (1) "Public Education" (manual training in all grades, night schools for adults, and "teaching of economics and history with evolution of industry as base"); (2) "Care of Children" (free text books, meals, clothing, and medical service); (3) "Equipment" (adequately sized schools, playgrounds, museums, and libraries); (4) "Suggested industries for Public Ownership" for streetcars, franchises, electric and gas lighting, telephones, bakeries, ice-houses, coal and wood yards; (5) "Working Class Government" (police not used in interest of employers against strikers, free legal advice); (6) "General Measures for Public Relief" (works for unemployed, free medical service, homes for aged & invalid, pensions for all public employees, free public crematory); (7) Public Health: (public disinfection after contagious disease, publicly owned & administered baths, drug stores, laboratories, etc.); (8) "Child Employment," demanded "no child under 18 permitted to work in any gainful occupations" in occupations such as selling papers and blacking shoes; (9) "Taxation": Progressive income tax when possible and taxation of ground rent; and (10) "Miscellaneous" aims including the erection of

"Labor Temple" by the local municipality as a headquarters, meeting place, and educational center for laborers of the city. Socialists also typically called for the "publication of a municipal bulletin, containing complete news of city activity." *International Socialist Review* 3 (December 1902): 329–31.

15. *Liberator*, 4 April 1903. Idaho's socialist candidates in the 1904 election were: John A. Davis, representative in Congress; Augustus M. Slater, governor; Louis N. B. Anderson, lieutenant governor; William D. Candee, secretary of state; George W. Herrington, state auditor; James E. Miller, state treasurer; David W. Smith, attorney general; O. Chalmus Smith, inspector of mines; John C. Elder, justice of the supreme court. "Abstracts of the Votes Cast in the Several Counties of the State of Idaho: General Election of 4 November 1902," AR 2/5, Governor Frank Hunt Papers, ISHS.

16. Titus and Oldman, in tune with municipal strategies, campaigned on a platform of universal kindergartens, an increase in the number and salary of teachers, tenure for teachers, and more union workers in education. The vote tally reported 689 for Titus, 729 for Oldman, and 2,108 and 2,190 for two Republican candidates. Dembo, *Unions and Politics*, 34–35; *Seattle Post-Intelligencer*, 1 and 7 November 1904. The rivalry between the SPW and the remnants of the SLP was not unusual. Many SPA/SPW members at the turn of the 20th century embraced "Immediate Demands" (direct legislation and municipal ownership) as a political tactic, while SLP purists dismissed immediate demands as "nonsense" and lacking revolutionary spirit. The rivalry was not friendly. As early as 1898, F. J. Dean, the SLP organizer for Washington, labeled members of the Social Democracy of America "damd [*sic*] asses." Schwantes, *Radical Heritage*, 104–105.

17. Sproule received 3,131 votes in the race. Jerry Calvert, "The Rise and Fall of Socialism in a Company Town, 1902–1905," *Montana The Magazine of Western History* 36 (Autumn 1986): 4–7, 9–10, 12–13; Malone et al., *Montana*, 267; McGlynn, "Lewis J. Duncan," 3; Enyeart, "Revolution or Evolution," 397.

18. Carolyn Goldinger, ed. *Presidential Elections since 1789*, 5th ed. (Washington, D.C.: Congressional Quarterly, 1991), 119–20; *Oregonian*, 1 and 15 November 1904. Leaving hope for higher returns to come in, socialists added: "It should in all fairness be noted that nearly every state complains of fraud in the count of Socialist ballots." *International Socialist Review* 1 (September 1900): 182; ibid., 5 (December 1904): 343–44.

19. *Oregonian*, 10 November 1904; *International Socialist Review* 5 (December 1904): 340.

20. *International Socialist Review* 3 (November 1902): 264; *Liberator*, 7 March 1903; Shannon, *The Socialist Party*, 37.

21. Dembo, *Unions and Politics*, 33; Schwantes, *Radical Heritage*, 104 (italics author's). Mischaracterizations and rivalries existed between socialists in different regions. "The leaders and intellectuals of the eastern movement," David Shannon explained, "tended to regard as 'wild men' the relatively unread, generally more radical Westerners." Simultaneously, "the New Yorkers liked to think of themselves as the core and most important element of the party" and downplayed radicalization in the West. Shannon, "The Socialist Party before the First World War," 281; Shannon, *The Socialist Party*, 42.

22. Schwantes, *Radical Heritage*, 105; *International Socialist Review* 3 (October 1902): 226; *Seattle Post-Intelligencer*, 1 August 1901.

23. The national constitution outlined the monthly obligations for state organizations in Article XII, Section 5 read: "The state committees shall make monthly reports to the national secretary concerning their membership, financial condition and general standing of the party." Section 6 mandated, "The state committees shall pay to the national committee every month a sum equal to 5 cents for every member in good standing within their respective territories." *International Socialist Review* 4 (May 1904): 677, 661; ibid., 3 (October 1902): 224–26.

24. *Liberator*, 4 April 1903. The Northwest's representatives at the convention were E. B. Ault (Idaho), C. C. McHugh, W. G. O'Mally, J. H. Walsh, and John J. Hirt (Montana), Irene M. Smith (Oregon), and O. Lund and Hermon F. Titus (Washington). *International Socialist Review* 4 (May 1904): 686–87. Washington alone may have been allotted eleven delegate slots. See Schwantes, *Radical Heritage*, 169.

25. Schwantes, *Radical Heritage*, 104.

26. Washington's socialists did not tolerate party intermingling. When Erwin C. Chase of Bothell accepted the Republican nomination for justice of the peace he was expelled for this action. "Minutes of the Full State Committee Meeting," Seattle, 1 January 1905, MSS 1513: "Politics & Misc." Box 18, Folder 12, OHS. The division between Washington's conservative and radical socialists did not typify the national SPA. In the national organization, conservative forces dominated the leadership, whereas in Washington, conservative members and "Yellows" in the SPW were the minority. As Dembo argued, "The Red-Yellow conflict took precedence over all other issues in the SPW." Dembo, *Unions and Politics*, 35–37, 39, 46; Schwantes, *The Pacific Northwest*, 352.

27. Shannon, *The Socialist Party*, 7; *International Socialist Review* 2 (May 1902): 776; American socialists, interestingly, did not obsess about such egregious "concentrated ownership." "To the contrary," Dawley continued, "they

believed they would one day reap the harvest of socialized production unwittingly being sown by the giant trusts." Dawley, *Struggles for Justice*, 100.

28. Dawley, *Struggles for Justice*, 84; *International Socialist Review* 4 (May 1904): 669.

29. Shannon, "The Socialist Party before the First World War," 288; *International Socialist Review* 4 (May 1904): 669; London, "Revolution,"100. As Dubofsky also explained, socialists' common beliefs were almost all they had politically. "Like the Republicans and Democrats," he wrote, "the Socialists had their regional and ideological differences. But unlike Republicans and Democrats, socialists usually lacked the glue of patronage; they had to maintain their coalition on the basis of shared values, not the spoils of office." Dubofsky, *Industrialism and the American Worker*, 113–14.

30. *American Federationist* 10 (April 1903): 260.

31. *International Socialist Review* 3 (November 1902): 264, 257. In June 1902 the Western Labor Union, in confederation with the Western Federation of Miners and United Association of Hotel and Restaurant Employees, met in Denver. "The principal topic of discussion at all three conventions," Morris Hillquit recalled, "was the relation of the organizations represented by them to the Socialist Party." The Western Labor Union and the WFM embraced "independent political action, . . . the Socialist Party as the representative of the working class in the field of politics, . . . and the platform of the party." Hillquit, *History of Socialism*, 311–12; Lukas, *Big Trouble*, 46; Shannon, "The Socialist Party before the First World War," 284; Schwantes, *Radical Heritage*, 105.

32. Gompers acknowledged both sides and their recognition of labor's plight, but was weary of socialism's ideology. In an address titled "Trade Unionism versus Socialism" delivered at the 1904 AFL convention, Gompers explained the similarities and differences: "Our friends, the socialists, always when with us have an excellent conception of the trouble in our industrial life. They say, as we say, and as every intelligent man or woman says, that there are miseries which surround us. We recognize the poverty, we know the sweatshop, we can play on every string of the harp, and touch the tenderest chords of human sympathy; but while we recognize the evil and would apply the remedy, our socialist friends would look to the promised land, and wait for 'the sweet by and by.' Their statements as to economic ills are right, their conclusions and their philosophy are all askew." *American Federationist* 10 (April 1903): 260; ibid., 11 (January 1904): 44–45.

33. Dembo, *Unions and Politics*, 45; *International Socialist Review* 4 (April 1904): 633.

34. *American Federationist* 10 (April 1903): 260.

3. "Friends and Enemies"

1. London, "Revolution," 113. Idaho's socialist candidates in 1906 were: Thomas F. Kelley, governor; John Chenowath, lieutenant governor; Joseph F. Hutchinson, secretary of state; James Smith, treasurer; Morgan P. Tifford, auditor; Louis E. Workman, attorney general; Grace E. Workman, superintendent of public instruction; Charles Trimble, mine inspector; Hermon F. Titus, supreme court justice. *Oregonian* (Portland, Ore.), 29 October 1906. Oregon's socialist candidates in 1906 were: J. D. Stevens and A. G. Simola, senators; W. W. Myers, congressman; C. W. Barzee, governor; R. C. Brown, secretary of state; G. R. Cook, state treasurer; M. W. Robbins, supreme court justice; J. E. Hosmer, superintendent of public instruction; J. C. Cooper, state printer; W. S. Richards, labor commissioner. Abstract of Votes, 25 June 1906, Ephemera, OHS. The state party nominated these candidates at a March 1906 convention in Portland. R. C. Brown to John Daniel Stevens, 19 March 1906, MSS 1187: John Daniel Stevens Papers, 1847–1932, OHS. In Seattle, too, socialists made impressive showings in losing efforts. A party member up for superior court judge, Richard Winsor, received 1,942 votes, the highest ever for a socialist candidate to that point. *Seattle Post-Intelligencer* (Seattle, Wash.), 9 November 1906.

2. Stephen Skowronek, *Building a New American State: The Expansion of National Administrative Capacities, 1877–1920* (Cambridge: Cambridge University Press, 1982), 165. Link and McCormick argued that socialists maintained this third party role until 1912 and the emergence of the Progressive party. Arthur Link and Richard McCormick, *Progressivism* (Wheeling, Ill.: Harlan Davidson, 1983), 41; Stephen Diner, *A Very Different Age: Americans of the Progressive Era* (New York: Hill and Wang, 1998), 68; *Oregonian*, 7 November 1908.

3. The party had approximately 8,000 active locals in 1908. Nick Salvatore, *Eugene V. Debs: Citizen and Socialist* (Urbana: University of Illinois Press, 1982), 220–21; *International Socialist Review* 9 (October 1908): 309. Other estimates count 58,000 members in the SPA by 1908. Link and McCormick, *Progressivism*, 40; Ira Kipnis, *The American Socialist Movement*, 211. The *Spokesman-Review* printed a large picture of Eugene Debs; the caption described his 1908 "whirlwind campaign." *Spokesman-Review*, 3 November 1908.

4. *International Socialist Review* 9 (October 1908): 310–13; Malone et al., *Montana*, 267.

5. *International Socialist Review* 9 (January 1909): 534; *Oregonian*, 6 and 7 November 1908. Debs claimed that a number of disgruntled radical Democrats voted socialist in 1904, in protest to the nomination of Alton

Parker. In 1908, he contended, those voters returned to the Democrats to support William Jennings Bryan once again. Debs is quoted in the *Spokesman-Review,* 6 November 1908. For complete election results, consult Appendix A in this volume. These shifting political allegiances were especially common in the West. See Paul Kleppner, "Politics without Parties: The Western States, 1900–1984," in *The Twentieth Century West,* Gerald Nash and Richard W. Etulain, eds. (Albuquerque: University of New Mexico Press, 1989): 296–317.

6. Kipnis, *The American Socialist Movement,* 213; *International Socialist Review* 9 (January 1909): 533; Goldinger, *Presidential Elections,*120–21.

7. *International Socialist Review* 7 (June 1907): 751.

8. The party reorganized in 1909 with Everett bookstore owner Frans Bostrom as the acting state chairman and he relocated the SPW offices to Everett. Titus and a number of his supporters unsuccessfully protested the constitutionality of the "Everett convention," and many left the SPW to form the United Wage Workers' Party. Schwantes, *Radical Heritage* 171–76; Terry Willis, "The Black Hole of Seattle: The Socialist Free Speech Movement, 1906–1907," *Pacific Northwest Quarterly* 91 (Summer 2000): 126; Dembo, *Unions and Politics,* 66.

9. Jerry Calvert, *The Gibraltar,* 33–34; Terrence D. McGlynn, "Lewis J. Duncan: Butte's Socialist Mayor," 25 September 1982, Typescript, Vertical File, "Socialism," MHS, 4, and "Socialist Papers of Montana: Personnel and Problems," 17 April 1971, Typescript, Vertical File, "Socialism," MHS, 3, 5, 7–8. Delegates from Billings, Bozeman, Butte, Dell, Dillon, Fridley, Great Falls, Helena, Laurel, Lewistown, Phillipsburg, Rollins, Roundup, and Stockett signed the final condemnation of Hazlett and Graham at the party's 1910 convention in Butte. "To the Comrades, friends, and sympathizers of the Socialist Party of Montana," it read, "We the undersigned, members of the state committee of the Socialist Party of Montana, having carefully and deliberately considered the evidence of the different parties to the controversy over the *Montana News,* submit to you the following statement: That James D. Graham has, for the past two years, deliberately practiced deception upon the comrades of Montana; that he has maligned and vilified every comrade who stood in the way of the fulfillment of his ambition, that he deliberately did everything in his power to prevent the success of the *Montana News* while it was under the management of Stoner, Tipton, and Harrack in the Fall of 1908, that in conjunction with Ida Crouch Hazlett he planned to get possession, for their own benefit, of the *Montana News* plant which represents the hard-earned money of the socialists of the North-West; and that when the party officers undertook to thwart his plans,

he used and still continues to use every means at his command to oppose them and to cripple, financially, and to retard the growth of the socialists party of Montana. Ample proof of all these charges has been shown to us in letters over the signatures of James D. Graham and Ida Crouch Hazlett. In short, his whole conduct, since the beginning of the controversy, is more becoming a Tammany ward-heeler than a comrade of the socialist party." Montana Socialist Party Convention Minutes, 3 August 1910, MF 425, Socialist Party of Montana Records, 1899–1950, Folder 100, MHS.

10. *International Socialist Review* 6 (May 1906): 643. Anti-socialist sentiment seemed on the rise nationally. President Theodore Roosevelt labeled socialists "free lovers" in a 20 March 1909 issue of *Outlook*. *Appeal to Reason* (Girard, Kan.), 24 April 1909; *Oregonian*, 7 October 1905. The *Appeal* responded to Hanford because, as the paper argued, he "conveniently ignored the capitalist despotism which already rules every department of our government and keeps the working class in subjection." *Appeal to Reason*, 16 October 1909, 20 November 1909; *Seattle Post-Intelligencer*, 23 October 1906; *Spokesman-Review*, 6 November 1908; *International Socialist Review* 10 (May 1910): 1048.

11. *Appeal to Reason*, 16 January and 13 November 1909; Salvatore, *Eugene V. Debs*, 242.

12. *Appeal to Reason*, 20 November 1909. The Northwest also remained active in national socialist affairs. The region sent six delegates to the 1910 Socialist Congress. The delegates were: T. J. Coonrod (Idaho), C. L. Cannon and Tom J. Lewis (Oregon), George W. McDermmott (Montana), and E. D. Cory and W. H. Waynick (Washington). *International Socialist Review* 10 (June 1910): 1138. By 1910 socialists might have benefited from heightened American reformism. During 1910–1911, historian George Mowry observed that Progressive reform shifted from a "rebellion" to a "revolution." Mowry, *The California Progressives* (Berkeley: University of California Press, 1951), 105–134; National Socialist Party Weekly Bulletin, 17 September 1910, Microfilm (hereinafter MF) 425: Socialist Party of Montana Records, 1899–1950, Folder 103, MHS.

13. Lewis J. Duncan to L. B. Chesner, 24 September 1910, MF 425, Folder 33, MHS. The party's national office stipulated, "Any number of persons, not less than five, may organize a local." Montana's six new locals were: Columbia Falls, Fortime, Libby, Missoula, Monarch, and Mondak. Charter Applications, 15 October, 4 November, 22 October, 15 November, and 26 September 1910, MF 425, Folders 12, 21, 39, 43, 44, and 45, MHS; Lewis J. Duncan to F. C. Hall, 1 March 1911, MF 425, Folder 43, MHS. Between July 1910 and March 1911 the state party nearly doubled its paid membership from 445 to 921. By early 1911 the state party added approximately 100

members per month. "Tabulated Reports of the Local or Branches in the State of Montana," MF 425, Folder 105, MHS; Johanne Rae to Socialist Party of Montana State Convention, 3 August 1910, MF 425, Folder 23, MHS; Calvert, *The Gibraltar*, 34.

14. The number of subscribers and the national subscription rank, listed by state, were: Idaho, 1,774 (36th); Oregon, 6,661 (16th); Montana, 4,118 (22nd); Washington, 11,811 (9th); *Appeal to Reason*, 30 January 1909. The October figures were: Idaho, 1,919 (37th); Oregon, 7,507 (16th); Montana, 3,805 (26th); Washington, 13,909 (8th). *Appeal to Reason*, 22 January 1910, 2 October 1909; Schwantes, "Labor-Reform Papers in Oregon," 159; McGlynn, "Socialist Papers of Montana," 2–3.

15. *Appeal to Reason*, 30 April and 2 July 1910, 11 December 1909, 26 March 1910; *International Socialist Review* 10 (September 1909): 280.

16. Debs visited 31 western cities. Organizers particularly appreciated their fundraising value as each meeting raised between $25 and $400 for the respective locals. *Appeal to Reason*, 5 November 1910. Some of Debs's specific speaking dates included: Great Falls, October 13; Butte, October 15; Moscow, Idaho, October 17; Spokane, October 19; Everett, October 20; Seattle, October 21; Portland, October 22; Salem, October 24; Boise, Idaho, November 1; and Pocatello, Idaho, November 2. *Appeal to Reason*, 25 June and 1 October 1910.

17. Returns indicated significant increases over 1908 in a number of counties and precincts. Washington reported 1,893 more votes, Montana 1,555, and Idaho 169. *Appeal to Reason*, 19 November 1910. The 1910 socialist ticket in Washington was: W. W. Smith, congress; and W. E. Richardson, E. J. Brown, Samuel Sadler, A. H. Barth, and Horace Cupples, supreme court judges. *Seattle Times*, 1 November 1910, italics added. The newspaper reported this because in Kitsap County four of the socialist candidates for supreme court judge—Brown, Richardson, Sadler, and Barth—finished second to the Republican candidates but ran well ahead of nonpartisan candidates. *Seattle Post-Intelligencer*, 10 and 11 November 1910.

18. *Oregonian*, 10 November 1910; *Seattle Post-Intelligencer*, 9 November 1910; *Seattle Times*, 9 November 1910; A. E. Melander to Lewis J. Duncan, 16 November 1910, MF 425, Folder 45, MHS.

19. *Appeal to Reason*, 12 November 1910; Salvatore, *Eugene V. Debs*, 242.

20. Dembo, *Unions and Politics*, 62. The Wobblies and the AFL fought for support, often with a fair amount of hostility, until WWI. Seattle's AFL organ, the *Union Record*, labeled the IWW the "Industrious Wreckers of the Workers." Schwantes, *Radical Heritage*, 154, 184; Erik Olssen, "The Case of the Socialist Party that Failed, or Further Reflections on an American Dream," *Labor History* 29 (Fall 1988): 435–36.

21. *American Federationist* 13 (October 1906): 823.

22. Olssen, "The Case of the Socialist Party," 436; *Oregonian*, 5 and 3 November 1906.

23. *American Federationist* 15 (May 1908): 341–42; *Oregonian*, 2 and 4 November 1908.

24. Kipnis, *The American Socialist Movement*, 212. Gompers claimed the train contained "all the luxurious accessories which modern transport can accomplish." The SPA countered with a published report of all individual donations that paid the $23,000 in rail costs. *American Federationist* 15 (September 1908): 736–37.

25. *Appeal to Reason*, 27 February 1909, 30 April 1910, 23 January 1909. In various northwest communities cooperation existed between more conservative socialists and trade unionists. Will Daly, president of the Oregon State Federation of Labor, welcomed a significant socialist contingency to a 1909 Portland labor rally. Daly believed the socialist presence within the state federation represented "a growing conviction among the people that the old parties should be abandoned and that all should unite in a movement for real freedom in the United States." Socialists in Miles City, Montana, had similar ties to local trade unions. Local leaders reported close connections to the International Association of Machinists and the Miles City Trades and Labor Council. Robert D. Johnston, "The Myth of the Harmonious City: Will Daly, Lora Little, and the Hidden Face of Progressive-Era Portland," *Oregon Historical Quarterly* 99 (Fall 1998): 254; Charter Application, 5 July 1910, MF 425, Folder 42, MHS.

26. *Seattle Times*, 13 November 1910. These socialist demands came in the wake of similar endorsements from trade unions. The United Mine Workers announced at their 1909 convention their "unanimous commitment" to socialism. Socialists called the declaration a "great surprise," but recognized the move as "extremely significant and marks an epoch in the Socialist movement of the United States." The United Mine Workers of America, according to the resolution text, "recognize and declare for the necessity of the public ownership and operation and the democratic management of all those means of production and exchange that are collectively used." This statement reinforced socialist principles that believed in government ownership and regulation of industries such as public utilities to ensure fairness for all. *Appeal to Reason*, 6 February 1909; *Oregonian*, 5 November 1908.

27. Dubofsky, *We Shall Be All*, 81; Greg Hall, *Harvest Wobblies: The Industrial Workers of the World and Agricultural Laborers in the American West, 1905–1930* (Corvallis: Oregon State University Press, 2001), 6.

28. Salvatore, *Eugene V. Debs*, 206, 208, 244–45; Dubofsky, *Industrialism and the American Worker*, 117. Although prominent socialists like Debs and

the *International Socialist Review*'s Algie Simons defended the IWW, according to Dubofsky "most Socialists preferred to remain within and support the AFL." Many socialists worried that IWW adherents would weaken the socialist presence in the AFL, an organization some still hoped to take over. Dubofsky, *We Shall Be All*, 95–96. Debs's endorsement upset many within the AFL, no one more than Samuel Gompers. Gompers later reminded workers how Debs "threw himself, body, boots, and breeches," toward the IWW, and "advocated the destruction of every trade and labor union, including the American Federation of Labor." *American Federationist* 15 (September 1908): 739.

29. Hall, *Harvest Wobblies*, 85; Dubofsky, *We Shall Be All*, 82–84, 112–13. During their association the IWW and the socialist party used delicate phraseology in both their endorsements and distancing. When the Charles Kerr publishing house in Chicago produced a pamphlet on industrial unionism, the traditionally socialist company (its publications included the *International Socialist Review*) added a special "publisher's note" to qualify any pamphlet statements. While the publishers recognized that "the principle of industrial unionism must be adopted in the near future," they remained cautious. "Our publication of this booklet," the note read, "is not to be taken as an endorsement of any particular organization; our object is simply to put valuable information within the reach of as many workers as possible." William E. Trautmann, "Publisher's Note," *Industrial Unionism* (Chicago: Charles H. Kerr & Company, 1909). Dubofsky, *Industrialism and the American Worker*, 117; Robert Tyler, "I.W.W. in the Pacific N.W.: Rebels of the Woods," *Oregon Historical Quarterly* 55 (March 1954): 6. The socialist *Appeal to Reason* typified shifting attitudes toward the IWW. At first the newspaper and its editor, Fred Warren, accepted the IWW. But the socialist paper grew increasingly resentful as the IWW radicalized, and, socialists believed, took members from their political base. Shannon, *The Socialist Party*, 32–33.

30. Some members split over the IWW-socialist relationship, particularly at individual locals. Nick Salvatore noted that "what worried these Socialists was not the revolutionary rhetoric of the IWW—that, they felt, would have little sustaining appeal to American workers—but rather the very real organizational threat the industrial union presented to the AFL and to the party." At the time, the approximately 27,000 members of the WFM were already organized and many were uncomfortable with the SPA's political approach and hated the AFL. Salvatore, *Eugene V. Debs*, 209; Tyler, "I.W.W. in the Pacific N.W.," 29; Schwantes, *The Pacific Northwest*, 339; Schwantes, *Radical Heritage*, 151, 184–85.

31. Tyler, "I.W.W. in the Pacific N.W.," 5; *Spokesman-Review*, 31 December 1905; an identical report of the night's events appeared in: *Oregonian*, 31

December 1905; Shannon, *The Socialist Party*, 31. Orchard's legal name was Albert Horsley. He worked as a union terrorist, was involved in the 1899 Bunker Hill blast, and claimed Haywood and Pettibone had promised him hundreds of dollars and a ranch in return for the Steunenberg murder. Lukas, *Big Trouble*, 250, 557.

32. Shannon, *The Socialist Party*, 31. During appeals, only one Supreme Court justice, Joseph McKenna, objected to the transfer. Dubofsky, *We Shall Be All*, 100; Schwantes, *Radical Heritage*, 170; *International Socialist Review* 7 (May 1907): 686.

33. Colorado socialists went so far as to nominate Haywood, in a Boise jail cell at the time, as their 1906 socialist gubernatorial candidate. Dubofsky, *Hard Work*, 87; *American Federationist* 14 (September 1907): 673. Titus returned the *Socialist* to Seattle in late 1906. Schwantes, *Radical Heritage*, 169–170. The *Appeal to Reason* also closely followed the trial and authorities indicted the *Appeal's* editor, Fred Warren, for his "scurrilous, defamatory, and threatening" articles. He was sentenced to six months in jail and charged a $5,000 fine. Shannon, *The Socialist Party*, 31. During the trial, in addition to distributing the *Socialist*, the defense also handed out to residents the WFM's *Miners' Magazine*, the *Idaho Unionist*, and the *Appeal to Reason*. Lukas, *Big Trouble*, 419, 422, 429.

34. According to *Review* editor Algie Simons, the accused were socialists and "tireless, incorruptible, uncompromising, intelligent champions of working-class interests." The Butte comrade also called the Boise events "reflections of the great struggle going on throughout the country." *International Socialist Review* 6 (May 1906): 647; ibid., 7 (June 1907): 750; ibid., 7 (May 1907): 686–87.

35. *American Federationist* 14 (September 1907): 672; *Appeal to Reason*, 12 June 1909.

36. For more on the Northwest's free-speech fights and their use as an IWW tactic, see Dubofsky, *We Shall Be All*, 173–97. Titus served one full day of a forty-day sentence. Other prominent socialists jailed during the Seattle fight were: Emil Herman, Hulet Wells, and Oregon socialist party state secretary Tom Sladden. Willis, "The Black Hole," 124–25, 128–29. The eight arrested socialists were: E. J. Brown, Hermon Titus, J. A. McKorkle, H. A. Adams, T. C. Winswell, C. Seuit, D. L. Kercher, and A. Wagenknecht. Fifteen more arrests occurred on November 2. *Seattle Post-Intelligencer*, 4 November 1906; Tyler, "I.W.W. in the Pacific N.W.," 32.

37. Schwantes, *The Pacific Northwest*, 139; *International Socialist Review* 9 (March 1909): 832–33; ibid., 10 (December 1909): 484, 487.

38. Schwantes, *The Pacific Northwest*, 339–40; *Appeal to Reason*, 1 January 1910.

39. Flynn also participated in the Missoula free-speech fight during October 1909. Authorities arrested her during IWW attempts to hold an open-air meeting in the city's "business section." Flynn told police that the IWW could not be stopped even if ten men were jailed each day. During the next week Wobblies kept up their agitation in Missoula and IWWs flocked there, particularly from Spokane. Finally, the Wobblies claimed a "complete victory" and "privilege of the streets." During her trial Flynn was "in a maternal condition," and critics argued that a proposed six-month sentence "would mean punishment of the innocent, even if she is guilty." Flynn received a ninety-day jail sentence. *Appeal to Reason*, 20 November, 11 and 18 December 1909, 1 January 1910; *International Socialist Review* 10 (November 1909): 466–67; ibid., 10 (January 1910): 611, 613.

40. *International Socialist Review* 10 (February 1910): 765, 761; ibid., 10 (December 1909): 483, 488; ibid., 10 (January 1910): 643. In another example of fund raising, Flynn traveled to British Columbia to solicit funds for Spokane defendants. *Appeal to Reason*, 11 December 1909, 12 February and 29 January 1910.

41. *International Socialist Review* 10 (April 1910): 948; ibid., 10 (January 1910): 642; *Appeal to Reason*, 5 and 19 March 1910; Schwantes, *The Pacific Northwest*, 339–41.

42. *Appeal to Reason*, 2 April 1910.

4. "Socialist Victories and Splendid Gains"

1. Goldinger, *Presidential Elections,*122; Shannon, *The Socialist Party of America*, 39; Schwantes, *The Pacific Northwest*, 352.

2. Idaho's socialist vote increased from 624 in 1908 to 5,342 in 1910. Similarly, Oregon reported an increase from 7,440 socialist votes in 1908 to 8,059 in 1910. Later issues reported Montana's socialist vote had remained stable from 1904 to 1908, with approximately 5,000 socialist votes in 1910. Washington's socialist vote, like Idaho and Oregon, also showed steady increase, from 14,182 in 1908 to 15,994 in 1910. *Appeal to Reason*, 28 January and 25 March 1911.

3. *Appeal to Reason*, 23 March 1912. This northwestern local success and gradualist approach—that is, focusing energy on local elections and moderate platforms—remains especially telling, particularly as the prevailing interpretation has contended that the gradualist embrace of moderated electoral strategies hindered party success. Ira Kipnis and Anthony Esposito, among others, have driven this interpretation. Enyeart, "Revolution or Evolution," 377–78.

4. *Socialist Voice* (Seattle, Wash.), 18 March 1911; *Appeal to Reason*, 18 March 1911; socialist party officials, and presumably some of Spokane's most radical socialists, asked Coates to resign. Coates refused the request,

claiming he served the people of Spokane and not a faction of the socialist party. *Portland Labor Press* (Portland, Ore.), 22 June 1911. "Growth of Socialist vote" quote appears in *Appeal to Reason*, 28 September 1912.

5. In Coeur d'Alene, reports indicated no socialist votes in the elections of 1908 or 1910, but 766 votes in the 1911 elections. *Appeal to Reason*, 18 November and 22 April 1911, 2 March 1912, 15 April 1911; The *New York World* to James H. Hawley, November 24, 1911, AR 2/9, Box 12, ISHS.

6. *Socialist Voice*, 11 March 1911. Emphasis on the campaign's "clean" nature reflected the 1911–1912 Seattle mayoral race, a recall of Mayor Hiram Gill. He faced a number of accusations by Progressive crusaders hoping to clean up city government. Gill's alleged faults as mayor included "gross incompetence," and some called his continued tenure "a menace to the business enterprises and moral welfare of said city." Republican George Dilling defeated Gill in the election. Mansel G. Blackford, "Reform Politics in Seattle during the Progressive Era, 1902–1916," *Pacific Northwest Quarterly* 59 (October 1968): 180–81; *Appeal to Reason*, 25 February, 12 August, and 22 April 1911.

7. *Socialist Voice*, 15 April 1911. Duncan's plurality was, in his words, "nearly 2,000." More precise figures, published in the *Appeal to Reason*, placed Duncan ahead of Democrat J. J. Quinn by 1,834 votes. Lewis J. Duncan to James Pearson, 10 May 1911, Small Collection (hereinafter SC) 2175, Folder 6, MHS; Enyeart, "Revolution or Evolution," 397–98; *Appeal to Reason*, 15 April 1911.

8. Lewis J. Duncan to Hiram Pratt, 20 May 1911, Duncan to H. A. Barton, 12 May 1911, Duncan to Carl D. Thompson, 19 May 1911, SC 2175, Folders 4 and 6, MHS.

9. Duncan defended the victorious Butte election as "a strictly working class victory," but admitted, "1,200 of my vote represented Republicans and Democrats who had nothing better to vote for than a socialist." R. F. Hoxie to Duncan, 12 June 1911, Duncan to R. F. Hoxie, 16 June 1911, Duncan to James Pearson, 10 May 1911, SC 2175, Folders 4, 6, and 7, MHS. Some in the AFL echoed this sentiment. John Morrison, writing in the *American Federationist*, claimed, "In the socialist vote recently cast, it is safe to say that not over 5 per cent of them are believers in the Socialistic theory of government, but [*sic*] is purely a negative vote as a protest against things as they are." *American Federationist* 19 (April 1912): 304.

10. Basin Local Socialist Party of Montana to Lewis J. Duncan, 23 May 1911, SC 2175, Folder 1, MHS; Duncan to A. G. Hinckley, 28 July 1911, SC 2175, Folder 8, MHS.

11. Duncan responded to Moore days later, noting, "We are doing all that we can to give an exemplification of municipal government according to

Socialist principles and up to this time our efforts seem to be very well received by the citizens generally." A. E. House to Duncan, 6 May 1911, H. E. Hudson to Duncan, 9 July and 3 August 1911, Duncan to Samuel Jenkins, 9 August 1913, Charles H. Moore to Duncan, May 13, 1911, Duncan to Charles H. Moore, 17 May 1911, SC 2175, Folders 3, 4, 6, and 10, MHS.

12. Duncan retained a sense of humor with his correspondence duties, taking the time to send a note to Lewis Duncan of Chattanooga, Tennessee, quipping, "You have a good name. Stay with it." James Pearson to Duncan, 5 May 1911, George Kirkpatrick to Duncan, 12 May 1911, Duncan to Lewis S. Duncan, 23 May 1911, SC 2175, Folders 3, 4, and 6, MHS.

13. Duncan to R. F. Hoxie, 16 June 1911, SC 2175, Folder 7, MHS; *Appeal to Reason*, 19 August 1911.

14. F. A. Livin to Duncan, 19 February 1914, SC 2175, Folder 1, MHS; Harry Fritchman to Duncan, 31 May 1911, ibid.; Duncan to Anna Maley, 14 July 1911, SC 2175, Folder 8, MHS.

15. O. R. Smith to Duncan, 24 July 1913; Robert G. Hiden to Duncan, 17 June 1911; W. M. Doyle to Duncan, 13 June 1911; J. Mahlon Barnes to Duncan, 3 July 1911, SC 2175, Folders 1–4, MHS.

16. The positions gained included 145 constables, 56 mayors, 55 justices of the peace, 40 school board members, and 39 village presidents. Anthony Esposito, *The Ideology of the Socialist Party of America, 1901–1917* (New York: Garland Publishing, 1997), 159; Richard W. Judd, *Socialist Cities: Municipal Politics and the Grass Roots of American Socialism* (Albany: State University of New York Press, 1989), 73. Washington socialists also elected mayors in Edmonds and Tukwila in 1911 and in Burlington and Hillyard in 1913. Dembo, *Unions and Politics*, 87. Tukwila's socialist mayor, J. Guntert, made an emphatic plea for socialism in the *Appeal to Reason*. "Become a socialist yourself and help to make this a better world to live in," he wrote; "you owe it not only to yourself but to your children." *Appeal to Reason*, 7 September 1912; see, for example, Schwantes, *The Pacific Northwest*, 352, which argues that socialist candidates "seldom influenced election results."

17. State party officials typically regarded the standing of locals and members in terms of paid dues (usually in the form of dues stamps). *Official Bulletin of the Socialist Party of Washington for the Month of July, 1912*, reprinted in the *Commonwealth* (Everett, Wash.), 23 August 1912. The state party displayed considerable growth from membership totals for late 1911 into early 1912. The state office reported on January 15, 1912, only 105 paid-up locals and 2,433 members in good standing. Official Bulletin of the Socialist Party of Washington for the Month of December 1911, reprinted in the *Commonwealth*, 19 January 1912.

18. *Commonwealth*, 9 February 1912. The weekly socialist newspaper in Everett operated under a number of different titles from 1911 to 1918. The paper began as *Commonwealth* (26 January 1911–9 April 1914) and evolved into the official paper of the Socialist Party of Washington. Because of the weekly's relationship to the state party organization it became *The Washington Socialist* (16 April 1914–24 June 1915). As readership expanded the title was changed to *The Northwest Worker* (1 July 1915–27 September 1917). Finally, it became *The Co-operative News* (25 October 1917–20 June 1918). The four state secretaries in April 1912 were as follows: Idaho, I. F. Stewart (of Nampa); Montana, Alma M. Kriger (Butte); Oregon, Charles H. Otten (Portland); Washington, Frans Bostrom (Everett). *International Socialist Review* 12 (April 1912): 680.

19. *Commonwealth*, 19 July 1912. This renewed hopefulness, especially in Seattle, arose because in previous election cycles Seattle socialists did not have the help of a socialist weekly or pamphlet distribution. The *Socialist Voice* reported a "splendid response" to its first months of publication and anticipated doubling or tripling its circulation. *Socialist Voice*, 11 March 1911; *Portland Labor Press*, 12 January 1911.

20. *Commonwealth*, 9 August 1912; *Socialist Voice*, 4 and 11 March 1911.

21. The three new locals in Helena, Hoffman, and Washoe were indicative of other charters requested during the period. W. J. Beans to C. E. Day, 16 February 1912, Socialist Party of Montana Records, 1899–1950; Duncan to F. C. Hall, 1 March 1911, MF 425, Folders 1, 29, 32, 43, and 64, MHS.

22. Socialists elected to the Butte Miner's Association were: George Curry, president; John Driscoll, vice president; Joe Little, recording secretary; M. J. Cleary, secretary-treasurer; Max Marvin, assistant secretary-treasurer; Charles Actis, warden; Manus Duggan, conductor; William Powell, Frank Auxier, and John Koich, finance committee. The *International Socialist Review* called the victory an important step toward what "socialists are striving for—when the miners own the mines." *International Socialist Review* 12 (February 1912): 520, 12 (June 1912): 885.

23. *Appeal to Reason*, 2 March 1912.

24. *International Socialist Review* 12 (May 1912): 792.

25. Oregon's socialist strength was confined to Portland. The *American Federationist* observed at the time that "Oregon is overwhelmingly Republican." Further, the *Portland Labor Press* had a circulation of 7,500, and outside Portland city limits union activity remained limited. *American Federationist* 18 (January 1911): 53–54; *International Socialist Review* 12 (March 1912): 606. In early 1912 the *Portland Labor Press* estimated 5,000 unemployed. *Portland Labor Press*, 4 April 1912.

26. The Butte section of the Western Federation of Miners, founded in 1893, remained crucial to labor organization in the city. Bohn gave Butte Local No. 1 of the WFM a favorable review. While some elements of the WFM were "not composed of angels" but always "clear as to the purpose of the organization and the interest of their class," he observed, Butte seemed the exception. Comparing his 1905 and 1912 visits to Butte, Bohn praised the Butte local for not having lost "its old time spirit." *International Socialist Review* 13 (August 1912): 123–28. Duncan respectfully declined a 1912 request by the WFM to hold its convention in Butte. Duncan and other city leaders who were not members of the WFM hoped to avoid influencing the organization's proceedings. Duncan to W. S. Snyder, 25 July 1911, Duncan to Carl D. Thompson, 19 May 1911, SC 2175, Folders 6 and 8, MHS; *International Socialist Review* 13 (November 1912): 425.

27. *International Socialist Review* 13 (September 1912): 263–64; ibid., 13 (November 1912): 425.

28. *Appeal to Reason*, 20 April 1912, 7 October 1911, 5 October 1912; *Portland Labor Press*, 2 May 1912.

29. Reprinted in *Appeal to Reason*, 23 March 1912; *Portland Labor Press*, 25 May 1911.

30. The national membership fluctuated during 1912 with 121,862 members in January and 135,436 by April. Interestingly, the train tickets issued were for Pullman cars, the very mode of transportation Debs promised never to use after the famous strike in 1894. Shannon, *The Socialist Party*, 71; Eric Chester, *Socialists and the Ballot Box: A Historical Analysis* (New York: Praeger, 1985), 35.

31. The support for Haywood in Montana, Oregon, and Washington perhaps indicates the empathy some northwest socialists felt toward more radical approaches. The SPA-member votes for Haywood in each state were as follows: Montana (436–245), Oregon (323–321), Washington (768–528). The expulsion of Haywood was the only time the party ever enforced the constitutional clause on sabotage. Shannon, *The Socialist Party*, 73, 77–78.

32. The four state secretaries in April 1912, with their city of residence noted, were: Idaho, T. J. Coonrod (Emmett); Montana, Lewis J. Duncan (Butte); Oregon, Charles H. Otten (Portland); Washington, Frans Bostrom (Everett). *Appeal to Reason*, 25 March 1911. See Appendix C in this volume, "Party Platform, Socialist Party of Washington, 1912," Ephemera, WSHS; *International Socialist Review* 12 (May 1912): 775. The socialist candidates for Washington state offices in 1912 were: Anna Maley, governor; A. H. Barth, lieutenant governor; Frans Bostrom, secretary of state; Bruce Rogers, attorney general; J. E. Arnett, state auditor; Minnie

Parks, state treasurer; Frances C. Sylvester, superintendent of public instruction; H. G. Cuples, land commissioner; Alfred Wagenknecht and M. E. Giles, congressmen. *Commonwealth,* 23 August 1912.

33. This ratio of members to Washington population was the best in the country, 50 percent better than California and 100 percent better than all other states. *International Socialist Review* 12 (May 1912): 775.

34. Calvert, *The Gibraltar,* 43. See also Appendix B in this volume, "Socialist Party Platform, Great Falls, Montana, Local, 1911." In January 1911 the number of dues-paying members reported to the Montana state secretary was 744. By January 1912 the membership increased to 2,013. *International Socialist Review* 12 (May 1912): 785–86; ibid., 13 (November 1912): 442.

35. *International Socialist Review* 13 (December 1912): 506. In early 1912, Roundup, Montana, another small community, also saw success with the election of an alderman. *Appeal to Reason,* 6 April 1912; William Raoul to W. J. Beans, 25 February 1912, MF 425, Folder 72, MHS.

36. Duncan to Archer Rollins, 1 March 1912, MF 425, Folder 55, MHS. The Socialist Party of Montana reported in March 1911 the following figures: 605 paid members (counted by dues stamps), 921 total members, 98 newly admitted members, 77 meetings held, and 25 active locals. "Tabulated Reports of the Local or Branches in the State of Montana," March 1911, MF 425, Folder 105, MHS.

37. Twin Falls socialists referred to a mass mailing campaign to current party members by the central party urging greater activism. Yet the local deemed this type of mailing "unnecessary" and with no "possibility of adequate returns." In all, the 20,000 mailings cost the national office approximately $600. The national office responded in the pages of the *International Socialist Review,* citing clerical errors, and the party recognized that "much waste" could be reduced in the future. A response came from the national secretary of the National Socialist Lyceum Bureau, L. E. Katterfield, who noted, "In Twin Falls these letters seemed particularly appropriate, since we received reports that some members not only opposed taking up the proposition [the mailing campaign], but knocked it after the local had accepted it." *International Socialist Review* 12 (May 1912): 791–92.

38. *International Socialist Review* 13 (July 1912): 85; *Portland Labor Press,* 21 December 1911.

39. *Appeal to Reason,* 23 March 1912. The newly established Washington newspapers of 1911–1913 were: Everett, *Northwest Worker,* 1911; Kelso, *Socialist News,* 1911; Centralia, *Lewis County Clarion,* 1912; Seattle, *Herald,* 1912; Tacoma, *Truth,* 1912; Aberdeen, *New Era,* 1913. Dembo, *Unions and Politics,* 87.

40. Duncan to James Pearson, 10 May 1911, SC 2175, Folder 6, MHS; *Appeal to Reason*, 4 February 1911. The *Butte Socialist* enjoyed a statewide circulation. Many of the 15,000 copies printed every two weeks were distributed to Montana's various contributing locals. Duncan to Edwin S. Dew, 14 July 1911, SC 2175, Folder 8, MHS; Prospectus of Butte Socialist Publishing Company, Inc., Socialist Party of America Papers, Reel 99; Duncan to L. J. Andrews, 6 September 1913, SC 2175, Folder 10, MHS.

41. Before ceasing operation the *Inland Echo* was published under the name *Inland Empire*. Gustav Carlson Interview, 17 July 1976, ISHS; *Appeal to Reason*, 26 August 1911, 3 February 1912; *International Socialist Review* 12 (March 1912): 606; Schwantes, "Labor-Reform Papers," 160.

42. *Portland Labor Press*, 14 December 1911, 4 August 1913, 21 December 1911. Astoria's Finnish socialists established the *Toveri* in 1907 and produced it until 1931. By 1912–1913 *Toveri*'s editor Santeri Nuorteva also wrestled with the relationship between political socialism and logging and mining interests sympathetic to the IWW. P. G. Hummasti has ably profiled Astoria Finns and their socialist publication, the *Toveri*, in his 1996 article, "Ethnicity and Radicalism: The Finns of Astoria and the *Toveri*, 1890–1930," *Oregon Historical Quarterly* 96 (Winter 1995–1996): 362–63, 370–71. In Oregon, C. W. Barzee edited his own left-wing labor journal, *Alliance*, produced in Milwaukie from 1912 to 1915 and claimed it had a circulation of 2,000. The Medford, Oregon, newspaper, unnamed by the *Portland Labor Press* in 1911, is likely the precursor to the1913 *Saturday Review*, a strictly socialist paper based in the city. Also, the *Times* of Portland was published from 1911 to 1912. Schwantes, "Labor-Reform Papers," 159–60.

43. J. F. Mabie to William Fuller, 1 March 1912, MF 425, Folder 25, MHS. Havre topped the list for the *Appeal*'s subscription orders in September 1912 with a staggering order of 400. *Appeal to Reason*, 7 September 1912. Price was a member of the Seattle First Ward of the socialist party and the IWW. He spoke to crowds twice a week. Price sold regional and national publications. His cart offered copies of: *Appeal to Reason, California Social Democrat, Chicago Daily Socialist, Commonwealth, Coming Nation, Hope, International Socialist Review, Milwaukee Leader, National Rip Saw, New York Sunday Call,* and *Progressive Woman. International Socialist Review* 13 (July 1912): 83.

44. The Socialist Party of America employed an organized and thorough lecture circuit for socialist speakers and propaganda. Called the Socialist Lyceum Course, locals throughout the country (divided into twelve regional districts in January 1913) could host speakers in their areas. All arrangements, including contracts with locals, travel, speaking venues, and ticket sales were planned months before a speaking engagement. Idaho,

Oregon, and Washington comprised the 9th district of the course, while Montana was grouped with other Rocky Mountain West states—Wyoming, Colorado, Utah, Arizona, and New Mexico—comprising the 8th district. Organizers drew district lines based on distribution of party membership. *International Socialist Review* 13 (September 1912): 259.

45. *Appeal to Reason*, 31 August 1912. An August 31, 1912, issue of the *Anaconda Standard*, cited by Calvert, described the speech: "The reception given Debs was in the nature of an ovation. He spoke entirely without notes. With little exception, his talk was a plea for the workers to unite as a class." Calvert, *The Gibraltar*, 43. It was not Debs's first visit to Everett. The candidate remarked that "fifteen or more years had passed" since his last visit, and he had since "noted with great satisfaction the spirit of socialist sentiment" in Everett. *Commonwealth*, 6 September, 16 August, and 8 October 1912.

46. The rally was held at the Gypsy Smith auditorium in Portland. Debs predicted in his speech that Oregon would be one of the first to be "swept into the socialist ranks." *International Socialist Review* 13 (October 1912): 372; *Portland Labor Press*, 5 September 1912.

47. *Commonwealth*, 6 and 27 September 1912.

48. While in Montana, Wilson stopped in Miles City, Lewistown, Butte, Kalispell, Columbia Falls, and Missoula. He then visited Wallace, Burke, and Moscow, Idaho. Warren's appearances and dates were: Butte, October 6; Great Falls, October 7; Spokane, October 9; North Yakima, October 11; Everett and Seattle, October 13; Portland, October 14; Baker (Ore.), October 16; Boise, October 17; Salem, October 21; and Roseburg (Ore.), October 22. *Commonwealth*, 27 September 1912; *Appeal to Reason*, 6 and 20 May 1911, 5 and 26 October 1912; *Portland Labor Press*, 17 October 1912.

49. *Portland Labor Press*, 17 October 1912.

50. Several prominent Progressive politicians emerged during this period, including, from Oregon, Jonathan Bourne, Jr., U.S. senator (1907–1913), George E. Chamberlin, U.S. senator (1909–1921), and Oswald West, governor (1911–1915); from Washington, Marion Hay, governor (1909–1913); and Idaho, William E. Borah, U.S. senator (1907–1940). Schwantes, *The Pacific Northwest*, 347, 349–350. Progressive-socialist intermingling typified the national stage. Wisconsin socialist Victor Berger and his brand of "scientific socialism," observed historian Ira Kipnis, resembled the "good government" and "antimonopoly" rhetoric of middle-class Progressives. Kipnis, *The American Socialist Movement*, 47; *Portland Labor Press*, 8 June 1911, 4 July 1912; *Commonwealth*, 19 July 1912; Seymour Lipset and Gary Marks, *"It Didn't Happen Here": Why Socialism Failed in the United States*

(New York: W.W. Norton and Company, 2000), 267; *Appeal to Reason*, 5 October 1912.

51. *Commonwealth*, 12 July 1912; See also Ann-Marie Syzmanski, *Pathways to Prohibition: Radicals, Moderates, and Social Movements Outcomes* (Durham, N.C.: Duke University Press, 2003). A drinking culture thrived in Montana's working-class communities. In 1914 Butte's Silver Bow County had three breweries and over 250 saloons. Montana's temperance movement gained strength and in 1916 the citizens voted for statewide prohibition. The proposal passed easily with 58 percent of the vote. Butte's Silver Bow County was one of only three to oppose the referendum, with 58 percent of its residents voting against dry laws. According to historian Mary Murphy, "Silver Bow County's vote against Prohibition was hardly surprising. Butte was the largest city in the state, and drinking was an integral part of its male-dominated, immigrant culture." Mary Murphy, *Mining Cultures: Men, Women, and Leisure in Butte, 1914–1941* (Urbana: University of Illinois Press, 1997), 44; *Socialist Voice*, 18 March 1911. Socialist positions on temperance seemed to conflict with working-class drink culture, particularly given the socialist electoral success in brewing centers such as Milwaukee, Wisconsin. There are few studies on the relationship between labor, politics, and alcohol. In his study of Worcester, Massachusetts, historian Roy Rosenzweig recognized that "the drink question . . . spawned a bewildering array of positions," and that "the saloon and the temperance movement thus became intense battlegrounds buffeted by the powerful and complex forces of class, gender, and ethnicity." Roy Rosenzweig, *Eight Hours for What We Will: Workers and Leisure in an Industrial City, 1870–1920* (Cambridge: Cambridge University Press, 1983), 60, 116–17.

52. In 1871 Henry George explained in *Our Land and Land Policy* that "land belongs equally to all [and] should be shared among all." Later economists and social radicals simplified George's philosophy as "the single tax," a ground rent tax on landowners as a means of equally distributing land wealth. Government, proponents argued, could assess the single tax on land's unimproved value, rather than its selling price. Returning the value of owned lands to the people, "single taxers" asserted, would decrease economic disproportion. Kenneth C. Wenzer, *An Anthology of Henry George's Thought*, vol. 1 (Rochester, N.Y.: University of Rochester Press, 1997), 3; Robert Wiebe, *The Search for Order, 1877–1920* (New York: Hill and Wang, 1967), 137; *Appeal to Reason*, 24 August 1912; *Portland Labor Press*, 23 November and 9 February 1911. Oregon had a history of single-tax proponents. During the 1890s legislator William S. U'Ren encouraged initiatives for a single tax in Oregon. Steven Cord, *Henry George, Dreamer or*

Realist? (Philadelphia: University of Pennsylvania Press, 1965), 81; *Oregon Socialist Party Bulletin*, 15 August 1912; Lawrence M. Lipin, "'Cast Aside the Automobile Enthusiast': Class Conflict, Tax Policy, and the Preservation of Nature in Progressive-Era Oregon," *Oregon Historical Quarterly* 107 (Summer 2006): 168; *Socialist Party of America Papers*, Reel 110.

53. *Appeal to Reason*, 19 August 1911; Calvert, *The Gibraltar*, 49. Butte's socialists proceeded with statewide prostitution reforms. In 1917 Montana Attorney General Sam Ford ordered the statewide closure of all brothels and red-light districts. Prostitutes, however, moved to regular hotels to find work. Murphy, *Mining Cultures*, 78–79; Duncan to Charles E. Taylor, 7 August 1911, SC 2175, Folder 9, MHS; *Commonwealth*, 12 and 19 July 1912.

54. Schwantes, *The Pacific Northwest*, 163–65; *Appeal to Reason*, 16 November 1912. The vote in Montana on female suffrage was close: 41,302 to 37,588. The most opposition for the Montana amendment came from more established mining and agricultural areas. Malone et al., *Montana*, 264; *Portland Labor Press*, 5 September 1912; *Oregon Socialist Party Bulletin*, August 15, 1912, *Socialist Party of America Papers*; *Socialist Voice*, 11 March 1911.

55. *Appeal to Reason*, 10 August 1912. This involvement of socialist women in the Northwest was in some ways an anomaly; see, for example, Sally Miller, "Other Socialists: Native Born and Immigrant Women in the Socialist Party of America, 1901–1917," *Labor History* 24 (Winter 1983), 84–102; see Mari Jo Buhle, *Women and American Socialism, 1870–1920* (Urbana: University of Illinois Press, 1981); *International Socialist Review* 13 (November 1912): 425.

56. Keith Murray, "Issue and Personalities of Pacific Northwest Politics, 1889–1950," *Pacific Northwest Quarterly* 41 (July 1950): 223; see also Tyler, "I.W.W. in the Pacific N.W.," 3–44, and Greg Hall, *Harvest Wobblies: The Industrial Workers of the World and Agricultural Laborers in the American West, 1905–1930* (Corvallis: Oregon State University Press, 2001); *Portland Labor Press*, 4 April 1912; Enyeart, "Revolution or Evolution," 392; Duncan to William Thurston Brown, 29 May 1911, Duncan to Ida Ericsson, 16 June 1911, SC 2175, Folder 7, MHS.

57. Gompers further detailed the sweeping call for socialist revolution versus his affinity for the specific wage strike: "The ultimate object of syndicalism as a movement is the social revolution through an all-encompassing general strike of the working classes." Samuel Gompers, "Syndicalism, 'Partyism,' and Unionism," *American Federationist* 19 (May 1912): 361, 363, 370; *Portland Labor Press*, 5 September 1912, 24 August 1911. According to Melvyn Dubofsky, the AFL saw its "tenuous hegemony over the nation's

working class" threatened by this socialist/radical threat. Dubofsky, *Industrialism and the American Worker*, 110, 114; Enyeart, "Revolution or Evolution," 384.

58. Peter Collins of the Brotherhood of Electrical Workers claimed, "The greatest enemy of trade unionism is socialism" because socialists preached only "the doctrine of class hatred." *Portland Labor Press*, 28 March, 29 August, and 29 February 1912.

59. *Portland Labor Press*, 23 May 1912; Platform of the Socialist Party of Washington, 1912, Ephemera, WSHS.

60. Pamphlets and books such as this one were typically purchased at party offices or through the mail via advertisements in journals such as the *International Socialist Review*. *Socialist Voice*, 4 March 1911; Platform of the Socialist Party of Washington, 1912, Ephemera, WSHS.

61. *International Socialist Review* 13 (December 1912): 461; *Appeal to Reason*, 16 November 1912; Shannon, *The Socialist Party*, 39. The official vote tally for Debs exceeded the *Appeal's* estimate: Idaho: 11,960, Montana: 10,811, Washington: 40,134. Oregon turned in a disappointing 13,343 votes. Goldinger, *Presidential Elections*, 122. The success of Debs was indicative of western trends. As historians Seymour Lipset and Gary Marks have observed, in 1912 the socialist party's "greatest strength came from agrarian and mining states in the west and Midwest with predominately native-born electorates." The states in 1912 that mustered at least 10 percent of the vote for socialism included Arizona, California, Idaho, Montana, Nevada, Oklahoma, and Washington. Lipset and Marks, *"It Didn't Happen Here,"* 140.

62. Taft garnered 18.8 percent of the Silver Bow County vote while Roosevelt managed 15.1 percent. Vote totals for state and municipal offices showed an identical trend. Calvert, *The Gibraltar*, 46. *International Socialist Review* 13 (January 1913): 570–71, 13 (December 1912): 462; *Appeal to Reason*, 23 and 30 November 1912; Malone et al., *Montana*, 267; residents of Laclede, Idaho, elected a justice of the peace and constable in 1912. For more on Idaho's political history and third party candidates see Robert Blank, *Regional Diversity of Political Values: Idaho Political Culture* (Washington, D.C.: University Press of America, 1978).

63. *Appeal to Reason*, 16 and 30 November 1912; *International Socialist Review* 13 (January 1913): 572.

64. Nick Salvatore, *Eugene V. Debs: Citizen and Socialist* (Urbana: University of Illinois Press, 1982), 265; Jim Bissett, *Agrarian Socialism in America: Marx, Jefferson, and Jesus in the Oklahoma Countryside, 1904–1920* (Norman: University of Oklahoma Press, 1999), 122; *International Socialist Review* 13

(January 1913): 574; *Appeal to Reason*, 23 and 30 November 1912; Dembo, *Unions and Politics*, 87.

65. *Appeal to Reason*, 16 November 1912.

5. From "Socialist Supremacy" to "Disharmony and Disruption"

1. See William C. Pratt, "Socialism on the Northern Plains, 1900–1924," *South Dakota History* 18 (Spring/Summer 1988):18.

2. *Washington Socialist* (Everett, Wash.), 22 April 1914; *Commonwealth*, 21 March 1913. A 1916 SPW roster listed 181 locals, 2,997 members in good standing, and 244 new members. *Party Builder* (Everett, Wash.), 20 March 1916. Proportional to population, Washington's socialist membership was second only to Oklahoma's. *Northwest Worker*, 27 January 1916, 18 May 1916. Oklahoma was one of the movement's pacesetters. See Donald Critchlow, ed., *Socialism in the Heartland: The Midwestern Experience, 1900– 1925* (Notre Dame, Ind.: University of Notre Dame Press, 1986), 1. In 1914 the Socialist Party of Oregon had 35 locals and 652 members. *Oregon Socialist Party Bulletin* (Salem, Ore.), 15 September 1914; *International Socialist Review* 17 (October 1916): 250–51.

3. *Lewis County Clarion* (Centralia, Wash.), 26 March 1913; *Commonwealth*, 3 January 1913, 31 January 1913; *Socialist Worker*, 31 January 1914; *Socialist Herald*, 24 December 1915; *Northwest Worker*, 8 June 1916.

4. Bostrom's order for literature was the largest in the country. *International Socialist Review* 14 (November 1913): 316; ibid., 13 (March 1913): 699; ibid., 14 (February 1914): 509.

5. *Commonwealth*, 21 August 1913; *Washington Socialist*, 24 December 1914.

6. However, on the notion of an inclusive SPA, Miller also argued that the party did little practically to see that these inclusive attitudes came to light. In fact, she argues, "party policies and practices . . . suggests a different scenario." Sally Miller, "For White Men Only: The Socialist Party of America and Issues of Gender, Ethnicity and Race," *Journal of Gilded Age and Progressive Era* 2 (July 2003): 283–85.

7. Marilyn Watkins, *Rural Democracy: Family Farmers and Politics in Western Washington, 1890–1925* (Ithaca, N.Y.: Cornell University Press, 1995), 11; *Commonwealth*, 3 July 1913; *Socialist Herald*, 11 June 1915. Some of the social events reportedly netted "as much as $33.55." *Lewis County Clarion*, 26 March 1913; *Butte Socialist* (Butte, Mont.), 4 April 1915; *Flathead County Socialist* (Kalispell, Mont.), 15 September 1914; *Oregon Socialist Party Bulletin*, 15 September 1914; *Commonwealth*, 13 December 1912.

8. Richard Schneirov, "Editor's Introduction: The Socialist Party Revisited," *Journal of Gilded Age and Progressive Era* 2 (July 2003): 246; Enyeart,

"Revolution or Evolution," 391. Sally Miller has suggested that neglect of "significant socialist activity among many immigrant groups" can be partially explained by the limited language skills of many American historians. My own research in the Northwest, however, outside of some German and Finnish locals, uncovered few foreign language sources and hence little evidence of wide foreign-born activity. Miller, "For White Men Only," 290–93. By 1917, according to David Shannon, foreign federations comprised over one-third of the party's national membership. Shannon, *The Socialist Party of America*, 44.

9. Shannon, *The Socialist Party of America*, 44; Miller "For White Men Only," 291–92.

10. P. G. Hummasti, "Ethnicity and Radicalism," 362–68; Schwantes, "Labor-Reform Papers," 160.

11. The respective dues reductions for northwest Finns were Oregon: 50 percent; Idaho: 25 percent; Montana: 12.5 percent; Washington: 65 percent. Herman Louko to State Organizations of the Socialist Party, 12 October 1910, MF 425, Folder 86, MHS; Charter Application, 3 May 1911, MF 425, Folder 29, MHS; Watkins, *Rural Democracy*, 117–18; National Finnish Translator-Secretary's Financial Report of Party Dues, 31 December 1910, MF 425, Folder 86, MHS; see also George Hummasti, "Working-Class *Herrat*: The Role of Leadership in Finnish-American Socialist Movements in the Pacific Northwest," in *Finnish Diaspora II: The United States*, ed. Michael G. Karni (Toronto: Multicultural History Society of Ontario, 1981).

12. The other northwestern states ranked well: Oregon, 9,585 (16th); Montana, 7,108 (19th); Idaho, 5,696 (23rd). *Appeal to Reason*, 29 March 1913. The editor of the *International Socialist Review*, Charles Kerr, claimed that, considering population proportions, Butte circulated more literature on scientific socialism than any other area in the country. *International Socialist Review* 16 (January 1916): 442; ibid., 13 (May 1913): 829; ibid., 16 (June 1916): 763; ibid., 17 (August 1916): 119.

13. Schneirov, "The Socialist Party Revisited," 246; Anon., "Well! Well! Well! What in Thunder do you Socialists Want Anyhow?," MSS 1513: "Politics & Misc.," Box 18, Folder 12, OHS; *Northwest Worker*, 17 February 1916. Washington socialists claimed to have distributed 46,592 Benson flyers in a single week approaching the election. *Northwest Worker*, 14 September 1916, 24 August 1916, 21 September 1916.

14. *Northwest Worker*, 27 April 1916, 7 October 1915; *Portland Labor Press*, 13 October 1913.

15. *Washington Socialist*, 28 May 1914; *Northwest Worker*, 28 October 1915, June 1916, 3 February 1916; Schwantes, *Radical Heritage*, 211; *Co-operative*

News (Everett, Wash.), 28 February 1918. *International Socialist Review* 18 (January 1918): 380; ibid., 14 (August 1913): 121; ibid.,14 (November 1913): 317; ibid., 14 (March 1914): 568.

16. *Butte Socialist,* 4 April 1915; *International Socialist Review* 18 (February 1918): 423. Missoula and Kalispell also had socialist papers in 1914, the *Missoula Socialist* and *Flathead County Socialist,* respectively, Terrence D. McGlynn, "Socialist Newspapers of Montana," 17 April 1971, Typescript, Vertical File, "Socialism," MHS, 4; Verlaine McDonald, "'A Paper of, by, and for the People'—*The Producers News* and the Farmers' Movement in Northeastern Montana," *Montana, the Magazine of Western History* 48 (Winter 1998): 19–20; Everett's *Northwest Worker* deemed the paper "established." *Northwest Worker,* 11 January 1917.

17. Schwantes, "Labor-Reform Papers," 160–61; *Washington Socialist,* 1 April and 18 March 1915; *Portland Labor Press,* 4 August 1913, 12 January 1914.

18. *Northwest Worker,* 7 October 1915. Organizers could request and offer a series of five SPA-sponsored educational lectures. The national office selected Lyceum lecturers specifically, depending on the needs of different states and drawn from a pool of sixty speakers. In late March and early April 1913 five speakers came to Everett's Liberty Hall. Lecturers and their topics were: E. W. Perrin, "The Socialist Challenge"; N. A. Richardson, "What is Socialism"; Luella Twinning, "The Class Conflict"; Mary Geffs, "What Socialists Want"; and Robert Knight, "The Socialist Movement." *Commonwealth,* 21 March and 31 January 1913.

19. In 1913 Debs visited Spokane, Republic, Colville, Cheney, Wilbur, Colfax, Pomeroy, Pasco, Sunnyside, Eatonville, Seattle, Tacoma, Sumas, Burlington, and Wilkeson. *Appeal to Reason,* 6 September 1913; *Washington Socialist,* 28 January 1914, 21 January and 4 February 1915; *Seattle Post-Intelligencer,* 25 January 1915.

20. *International Socialist Review* 13 (April 1913): 771; ibid., 13 (May 1913): 829. Seidel spoke to approximately 500 people at Chehalis that summer. *Washington Socialist,* 14 May and 4 June 1914. Prominent northwest socialists, conversely, ventured to engagements in the east. During the 1913 election cycle Lewis Duncan embarked on a political tour that took him to Chicago, Ohio, and New York to help socialist campaigns. Lewis J. Duncan to Murray E. King, 30 September 1913, SC 2175, Lewis J. Duncan Papers, 1911–1914, Folder 10, MHS.

21. At the time there was only one socialist congressman, Victor Berger of Wisconsin. *Socialist Herald,* 2 July 1915. The state's leadership conducted lecture tours throughout Washington. Emil Herman, Mrs. G. H. Lockwood,

and L. E. Katterfield all had numerous speaking engagements in 1916. *Party Builder,* 20 March 1916; Walker reported capacity crowds at Payette, Caldwell, and Nampa, Idaho, meetings. *Northwest Worker,* 10 February, 2 and 16 March, 20 April, and 14 September 1916.

22. *Appeal to Reason,* 9 August 1913; *Northern Idaho News* (Sandpoint, Id.), 13 December 1914; *International Socialist Review* 14 (July 1913): 59; MF 425: Socialist Party of Montana Records, 1899–1950, Folder 30, MHS; *Portland Labor Press,* 29 December 1913; *Commonwealth,* 22 January 1914.

23. The 1916 socialist ticket in Washington included: L. E. Katterfield, governor; Katherine Hodgins, lieutenant governor; Bruce Rogers, senator; E. B. Tryon, R. J. Olinger, W. E. Ferguson, Walter Price, and John Powers congressmen (1st–5th districts, respectively); James Grant, secretary of state; Mary Stevenson, state treasurer; E. E. Owsley, state auditor; M. J. Schwartz, attorney general; F. I. McKay, state insurance commissioner; Frank Court, commissioner of public lands; Frances Sylvester, state superintendent of public instruction; Kazis Krauczunas and Peter Busby, supreme court judges. *Northwest Worker,* 21 September, 13 April, 21 and 14 September, and 18 May 1916.

24. *Appeal to Reason,* 18 October 1913; *Portland Labor Press,* 24 February 1913; *Butte Socialist,* 1 April 1915.

25. *Washington Socialist,* 9 July, 13 and 20 August, 3 September, and 31 December 1914. Salter's allegiance to workers was clear because, before settling in Everett, he had worked in lumber, mining, and construction camps in Montana, Idaho, eastern Washington, and Oregon. *Northwest Worker,* 30 and 2 September, 8 July, and 28 October 1915; Party Memorandum, 1915, SPA Papers, Reel 95. In 1916 the state Supreme Court declared Bowman's unemployment law unconstitutional. *Northwest Worker,* 3 February 1916.

26. *Commonwealth,* 9 April 1914; *Washington Socialist,* 11 March 1915. The Minnidoka County socialist sheriff was D. H. Gregory and its socialist county clerk was Charles Burgher. *Appeal to Reason,* 28 November 1914; Don C. D. Moore to Moses Alexander, 5 November 1914, AR 2.0011, Governor Moses Alexander Papers, Box 2, Folder 4, ISHS; Moore to Joseph Pence, 3 December 1914, AR 2.0011, Box 2, Folder 4, ISHS; In 1912 the socialist ticket for eight state offices in 1912 received 8,250 votes for an average of 1,031 votes each. The 1914 socialist ticket for the same eight offices received 8,829 votes for an average of 1,103. *Northern Idaho News,* 13 December 1914.

27. *Commonwealth,* 11 April 1913, 9 April 1914. Duncan's reelection did not surprise the *Appeal's* editors. His reforms, the paper claimed, "so

pleased the people that they re-elected a Socialist administration by increased majorities, against a combination of the old parties." *Appeal to Reason*, 11 April and 18 October 1913, 11 April 1914; *Northwest Worker*, 28 October 1915. The two socialist state legislators were elected to the house from Silver Bow County and another was elected to the senate from Mineral County. Socialists in Billings elected Adam A. Skirving and John Lundberg to the school board in 1915. *Washington Socialist*, 12 November 1914, 29 April 1915.

28. In 1914, across the Northwest, the most successful congressional races showed a decrease in the socialist vote from 1912 forward. The following results show the decline from 1912 to 1914. Idaho, 11,960 to 7,888 (Senate); Montana, 10,885 to 9,430 (House); Oregon, 13,343 to 10,666 (Senate); Washington, 40,134 to 30,234 (Senate). *International Socialist Review* 15 (February 1915): 486; G. W. Carr, a socialist city councilman in Everett, also lost his seat in April 1912. Socialists pointed to a restructuring of the city government as the reason for his dismissal. *Northwest Worker*, 11 November, 23 September, and 21 October 1915. Samuel Andrews, C. H. Bungay, and A. B. Ferguson were Spokane's three socialist commissioner candidates. They received 492, 439, and 217 votes, respectively. *Northwest Worker*, 18 November 1915.

29. Goldinger, *Presidential Elections*, 122–23; *Northwest Worker*, 25 May 1916, 1 February and 4 January 1917, 23 March 1916.

30. Idaho's socialists, with no party newspaper at the time, were slow to receive results of the 1916 election. "The election is over," they reported, "and we are now trying to figure out the results. Had we had an Idaho paper we would have had our comrades ready to send in the news of the elections . . . so far we have received no returns worth of mention." By early 1917 the SPW had thirty-three fewer locals than in December 1915. In March 1917 Fields received local reports from only fourteen locals, which he called "very discouraging." *Northwest Worker*, 27 January and September 1916, 11 January 1917, 7 December 1916, 4 January 1917, 23 November 1916, 1 March and 3 May 1917.

31. *Northwest Worker*, 13 April and 8 June 1916, 18 November 1915; Lewis J. Duncan to L. J. Andrews, 6 September 1913, SC 2175, Folder 10, MHS. George Kirkpatrick urged Bozeman organizer Evart Riddle to do "some systematic work in the matter of propaganda, and in building up the movement in Bozeman." George R. Kirkpatrick to Evart Riddell, 5 August 1925, SC 1263, Evart Riddle Papers, 1924–1926, MHS.

32. E. A. Sperber to Albert M. Meissner, 25 April 1916, Socialist Party of Montana Records, Folder 24, MHS. In 1916 the Socialist Party of Montana

was able to run numerous candidates for federal and state offices. One of their nominees included Lewis J. Duncan for governor. Albert Meissner to A. M. Alderson, 7 August 1916, Socialist Party of Montana Records, Folder 75, MHS; *Northwest Worker*, 25 May 1916.

33. Party disruption had organizational consequences, too. Bohn claimed that a 25 percent decrease in membership and a 75 percent decrease in party "activity" were due to party squabbling. Slobodin summarized the continued positions of radicals and moderates. Constructivists, he wrote, believed "change will come sometimes, but only by slow imperceptible degrees, a step at a time, and by legal means." Conversely, revolutionists felt "that the Socialist party will be the means of emancipating the working class . . . always by education and organization. Sometimes by force." *International Socialist Review* 14 (October 1913): 236; ibid., 17 (March 1917): 541.

34. Shannon, "The Socialist Party before the First World War," 286. Haywood and many of his supporters left the party after the referendum vote diffusing much of the SPA's most radical element. The result was a drop in party membership as well, and the average monthly membership for 1913 was a disappointing 95,401. Shannon, *The Socialist Party of America*, 77–79.

35. E. L. Cannon, a radical and the state secretary for Oregon, addressed the convictions of moderates regarding state ownership: "Here in Oregon we have quite a number of Socialists who seem to think that government ownership is about the next thing we want. It is true some entertain this opinion because they think government ownership is inevitable. But, of course, granting it is inevitable, that does not make it part of the Socialist program—or rather a part of what many of us think the Socialist program should be." *International Socialist Review* 14 (March 1914): 570; ibid., 16 (February 1916): 503; *Portland Labor Press*, 19 January 1914, 31 May 1913; *Northwest Worker*, 20 April 1916.

36. *International Socialist Review* 15 (September 1914): 184; *Northwest Worker*, 24 August 1916.

37. Lewis J. Duncan to V. R. Schmittroth, 8 October 1913, SC 2175, Folder 10, MHS; "Mayor Duncan's Statement to the Socialist Party and Press of America," 21 July 1913, SPA Papers, Reel 99; Henry Polsa to A. F. Meissner, 14 May 1915; Meissner to Polsa, 18 May 1915, MF 425, Folder 54, MHS.

38. Judd, *Socialist Cities*, 62; Malone et al., *Montana*, 273; McGlynn, "The Social Democratic Party in Montana, 1899–1914," 19 April 1969, Typescript, MHS, 21; Calvert, *The Gibraltar*, 100; *Northwest Worker*, 1 July and 30 December 1915.

39. *Anaconda* (Mont.) *Standard*, 4 July 1914; *Butte* (Mont.) *Daily Post*, 4 July 1914.

40. Duncan ran again for Butte mayor in 1916 and received only 1,612 votes, or 16 percent of the vote. According to historian Jerry Calvert, "The Socialist era in Montana politics was over." Calvert, *The Gibraltar*, 100; *International Socialist Review* 15 (February 1915): 473; ibid., 17 (October 1914), 223–28. The IWW's William Haywood tracked the Butte troubles in the pages of the *International Socialist Review* periodically through late 1914 and early 1915. See *International Socialist Review* 15 (August 1914); ibid.,15 (October 1914) and 15 (February 1915); *Anaconda Standard*, 7 October 1914.

41. *International Socialist Review* 15 (May 1915): 684–85; ibid., 16 (April 1916): 635.

42. W. S. Charles to Lewis J. Duncan, 16 June 1913, SC 2175, Folder 1, MHS; *Commonwealth*, 21 March 1913.

43. Flyer, 18 January 1914, SPA Papers, Reel 111; *International Socialist Review* 13 (May 1913): 818, 836; Schwantes, *Radical Heritage*, 210; W. H. Kingery to Carl D. Thompson, 24 July 1913, SPA Papers, Reel 111. Anna Maley, one of the first editors of the *Commonwealth* and a socialist candidate for governor in 1912, criticized the SPW's Reds in a 1913 letter. The "so-called 'red' group," she wrote, had "run things in such an autocratic and high-handed manner as to cause a serious rupture with the membership of the state." *Lewis County Clarion*, 9 April 1913; "Reasons for Division in Socialist Party of Washington," 1914, SPA Papers, Reel 111.

44. "Report of Committee on Investigation of Party Differences in the State of Washington," 10 May 1914, SPA Papers, Reel 111; *Washington Socialist*, 18 and 4 June 1914.

45. *Washington Socialist*, 11 June, 2 July, and 24 December 1914; *International Socialist Review* 15 (December 1914): 379; *Lewis County Clarion*, 16 April 1913.

46. *Washington Socialist*, 18 March 1915. The paper changed its title and audience in July 1915. The first issue of the *Northwest Worker* read: "Owing to the extension of our activities in the states of Idaho and Oregon and for other reasons, the *Washington Socialist* board of directors unanimously decided to change the name of the paper to the *Northwest Worker*." *Northwest Worker*, 1 July 1915; *Co-operative News*, 14 March 1918.

6. "End War or War Will End You"

1. Shannon, *The Socialist Party of America*, 80.

2. Ibid., 81–82; *International Socialist Review* 15 (November 1914): 309; *International Socialist Review* 15 (March 1915): 561; "Platform of the Socialist

Party of Washington, 1912, Ephemera," WSHS. The idea of mandatory military training in high schools, SPW state committee contended, promoted militarism and class distinctions, furnished strike breakers for times of protest, and would "Russianize" America. *Party Builder*, 20 February 1917.

3. Clemens P. Work, *Darkest Before Dawn: Sedition and Free Speech in the American West* (Albuquerque: University of New Mexico Press, 2005), 49; Shannon, *The Socialist Party*, 87, 98; David Kennedy, *Over Here: The First World War and American Society* (New York: Oxford University Press, 1980), 26.

4. *Washington Socialist*, 13 May 1915; "The American Socialists and the War," Pamphlet, 1917, MSS 1513, Box 18, Folder 12, OHS.

5. H. C. Peterson and Gilbert Fite, *Opponents of War, 1917–1918* (Seattle: University of Washington Press, 1957), 4–5, 8. This was the SPA's sixth national convention. Delegates from Washington, Idaho, and Montana all sat on committees. *Northwest Worker*, 5 and 12 April, 10 May 1917; Kennedy, *Over Here*, 26; Shannon, *The Socialist Party*, 93–94.

6. Shannon, *The Socialist Party*, 95, 97.

7. Peterson and Fite, *Opponents of War*, 10; Shannon, *The Socialist Party*, 99, 101–104; Kennedy, *Over Here*, 27; "The American Socialists and the War"; *Co-operative News*, 18 April 1918; Socialist Party Bulletin, March 1917, SPA Papers, Reel 130.

8. W. A. Gresham and J. A. Standley to Moses Alexander, 8 February 1917, AR 2.0011, Box 16, Folder 7, ISHS. For more on socialist agitation in Idaho during WWI see Hugh T. Lovin, "The Red Scare in Idaho, 1916–1918," *Idaho Yesterdays* 17 (Fall 1973): 2–13, and "Idaho and the 'Reds,' 1919–1926," *Pacific Northwest Quarterly* 69 (July 1978): 107–15; *International Socialist Review* 16 (October 1915): 252; *Party Builder*, 20 February 1917; Peterson and Fite, *Opponents of War*, 3. Spokane's mainstream newspapers covered the event, and as socialists complained, "the big newspapers discredited, misrepresented and belittled the meeting." *Northwest Worker*, 22 February 1917. Kirkpatrick spoke in Everett in February 1915. The *Everett Morning Tribune* and *Everett Evening Herald* reported the visit. He returned to Everett in March 1916. *Washington Socialist*, 10 September 1914, 25 February 1915; *Northwest Worker*, 3 February 1916. "War—What For?" sold 50,000 copies from 1911 to 1913. *Lewis County Clarion* (Centralia, Wash.), 9 April 1913.

9. *Northwest Worker*, 5 August 1915, 20 January and 1 June 1916.

10. *Truth* (Tacoma, Wash.), 28 June 1913; *Northwest Worker*, 9 September 1915, 17 May 1917.

11. Peterson and Fite, *Opponents of War*, 23.

12. *Northwest Worker*, 7 June 1917; Peterson and Fite, *Opponents of War*, 28.

13. *Northwest Worker*, 15 February 1917; Socialist Party Bulletin, March 1917, SPA Papers, Reel 130; H. H. Stallard, *World Problems*, Mini-Book, Yakima, Washington, February 1920, WSHS, 96; *Co-operative News*, 28 February 1918; *Party Builder*, 20 March 1917.

14. Ronald Schaffer, *American in the Great War: The Rise of the Welfare State* (Oxford: Oxford University Press, 1991), 13–15. According to the *Co-operative News*, a paper that itself saw increased censorship, "The blacklist includes everything from small, sporadic monthlies or weeklies to daily papers having half a million circulation." The *News* also noted that the blacklisted papers included both English and non-English publications. *Co-operative News*, 22 November 1917.

15. *Northwest Worker*, 14 June 1917; *Co-operative News*, 20 December 1917.

16. Schwantes, *The Pacific Northwest*, 354; Work, *Darkest Before Dawn*, 133–34; *Northwest Worker*, 13 January 1916, 9 August 1917.

17. Lovin, "The Red Scare in Idaho," 9. The *Co-operative News*'s last issue appeared on June 20, 1918. *Co-operative News*, 13 and 20 June 1918. In 1918, H. W. Watts, a British national elected in 1915 as the *Northwest Worker's / Co-operative News*'s editor, was deported in 1918. Officials deemed Watts an "undesirable alien" and an anarchist for his opposition to the war and conscription. *Co-operative News*, 28 February 1918.

18. Work, *Darkest Before Dawn*, 239, 246–47. Anti-radicalism and anti-socialism were not necessarily new phenomena in the Northwest. In 1913 "a rabid anti-Socialist administration" demoted Andrew Sorenson of Portland from sergeant to telephone operator for being an "avowed Socialist." *Appeal to Reason*, 9 August 1913. In the same year William Nolffsmith, the secretary-treasurer for a Washington, D.C., paper titled the *Home Defender*, wrote to Idaho governor John Haines for help "in our fight against Revolutionary Socialism." The *Home Defender*'s motto was "a national newspaper opposed to revolutionary socialism." William Nolffsmith to John Haines, 29 March 1913, AR 2/10, Governor John Haines Papers, Box 6, ISHS. The Northwest also experienced a number of armed conflicts, particularly in urban areas, between socialists, laborers, and IWWs and local authorities. See Dennis Hoffman and Vincent J. Webb, "Police Response to Labor Radicalism in Portland and Seattle, 1913–19," *Oregon Historical Quarterly* 87 (Winter 1986): 341–66; *Northwest Worker*, 26 October 1916; *Party Builder*, 20 August 1918.

19. Peterson and Fite, *Opponents of War*, 184.

20. The four arrested were King County socialist secretary Aaron Fislerman, businessman R. A. Rice, Hulet Wells, and Sam Sadler. Authorities

released them on $5,000 bail and the four awaited a federal grand jury decision. *Northwest Worker,* 7 June 1917, 24 May 1917; Lovin, "The Red Scare in Idaho," 9; *Co-operative News,* 2 May 1918, 15 November and 13 December 1917.

21. Federal troops responded to Butte's 1917 strikes. Northwest lumber strikes that threatened wartime production of planes and ships were also subject to forcible federal management of work sites. Schaffer, *American in the Great War,* 24–25, 36–37. Sixty-eight thousand mourners turned out for Little's funeral procession, driven, according to the *International Socialist Review,* by their "determination to call a halt on such murderous tyranny." *International Socialist Review* 17 (September 1917): 135; Kurt Wetzel, "The Defeat of Bill Dunne: An Episode in the Montana Red Scare," *Pacific Northwest Quarterly* 64 (January 1973): 12–13; Work, *Darkest Before Dawn,* 139, 159, 213–14.

22. Those indicted in the Pacific Northwest were Charles Bennett and Peter Green (Portland), Alton Soper (Astoria), Peter Kerkenon (Butte), J. T. Doran (Tacoma), J. A. MacDonald and Harry Lloyd (Seattle), and Don Sheridan, James Rowan, William Moran, and H. Huhphrey (Spokane). *International Socialist Review* 18 (November-December 1917): 270; Peterson and Fite, *Opponents of War,* 185, 331. Herman stayed active while awaiting trail. He attempted to travel to Chicago for an SPA secretaries meeting but U.S. marshals apprehended him August 6 in Havre, Montana. The *Party Builder* told socialists to "protest strongly against the injustice and persecution in this land." Also while in custody Herman was a candidate for the state legislature from Snohomish County. *Party Builder,* 20 August 1918, 20 April 1918; *Co-operative News,* 9 May and 13 June 1918; Schwantes, *The Pacific Northwest,* 354.

23. Violent confrontations between the IWW and local authorities were not new. When Everett citizen deputies confronted 250 IWW members on November 5, 1916, violence left seven dead and 50 injured. The IWW hosted a mass demonstration in Seattle where "approximately 5,000 participated." The meeting adopted resolutions demanding a federal investigation into the denial of free speech and lawlessness in Everett. Socialist locals wrote to the *Northwest Worker* and pledged monies for the IWW defense fund. *Northwest Worker,* 23 November 1916; *International Socialist Review* 18 (October 1917): 208; ibid., 18 (January 1918): 314; the socialist *Co-operative News* labeled Myers's attackers a "degenerate mob" and claimed that he was assaulted "in the name of patriotism." The mob told him he was going to get "the same treatment as Frank Little," and left him out in the cold overnight. *Co-operative News,* 14 February and 4 April 1918.

24. The Idaho bill passed in February 1917 after anti-IWW rhetoric from state lawmakers. Robert C. Sims, "Idaho's Criminal Syndicalism Act: One State's Response to Radical Labor," *Labor History* 15 (Fall 1974): 511–12, 522; *Northwest Worker*, 15 March 1917; A. H. Conner to C. C. Moore, 3 February 1923, Harry Ward and Roger Baldwin to Moore, 26 January 1923, AR 2/13: Governor C. C. Moore Papers, Box 1, ISHS.

25. Debs spoke 24 January 1915, at Seattle's Dreamland Pavilion. *Seattle-Post Intelligencer*, 25 January 1915; Lovin, "The Red Scare in Idaho," 8.

26. *Co-operative News*, 10 January and 6 June 1918. The Northwest was a central IWW battleground. "The two outstanding centers of [the] present conflict, so far as the I.W.W. is concerned," wrote the *International Socialist Review*, "are the forests of Washington, Oregon, and Idaho, and the copper mines of Montana." *International Socialist Review* 18 (January 1918): 332.

27. *Party Builder*, 20 June 1919, 20 August 1918; *Northwest Worker*, 28 and 14 June 1917. It became increasingly common for socialists to advertise events and publications under obscure names. Everett's socialists advertised a social sponsored by the "Everett Co-operative Society," rather than the socialist party. Newspapers followed suit. The *Northwest Worker* became the *Co-operative News* in 1917, presumably to skirt persecution by discriminatory postmasters. The *Socialist* abandoned its revolutionary motto for the more sanguine "In things essential, unity—In things doubtful, liberty, in all things, fraternity." *Co-operative News*, 15 November 1917.

28. Shannon, *The Socialist Party*, 85; Randolph Bourne, *War and the Intellectuals, 1915–1919*, Carl Resek, ed. (New York: Harper and Row, 1964), 41; Foner, "Why is there no Socialism," 72.

29. *Party Builder*, 20 December 1918.

30. Wetzel, "The Defeat of Bill Dunne," 12; Peterson and Fite, *Opponents of War*, 289; Schwantes, *The Pacific Northwest*, 374.

31. Brecher admits that, despite the backlash and as evidence suggests, socialists played "little role" in the General Strike. Brecher, *Strike!* 119–20, 126–28.

32. Dubofsky, *Industrialism and the American Worker*, 146; Lovin, "Idaho and the 'Reds,'" 107, 109; Schwantes, *The Pacific Northwest*, 360; P. G. Hummasti, "Ethnicity and Radicalism," 378; *Northwest Worker*, 17 May 1917.

33. Lovin, "Idaho and the 'Reds,'" 114; C. H. Cammans to Socialist Party of Idaho membership, 1 December 1928, SPA Papers, Reel 95; *Party Builder*, 20 October and 20 June 1919.

34. Schwantes, *Radical Heritage*, 212; Shannon, *The Socialist Party*, 125; James Weinstein, "Radicalism in the Midst of Normalcy," *Journal of American History* 52 (March 1966): 773.

Epilogue

1. Hugh T. Lovin, "Idaho and the 'Reds,' 1919–1926," *Pacific Northwest Quarterly* 69 (July 1978): 112, 115; SPW / Socialist Party of Montana Report, 27 October 1923, *Socialist Party of America Papers*, microfilm edition (hereinafter SPA Papers), (Glen Rock, N.J.: Microfilming Corporation of America, 1975), Reel 99; Charter Application, Seattle, Washington, 21 January 1931, SPA Papers, Reel 111.

2. Hamilton Cravens, "The Emergence of the Farmer-Labor Party in Washington Politics, 1919–1920," *Pacific Northwest Quarterly* 57 (October 1966): 154; James D. Graham to Socialist Party of Montana membership,1929, SPA Papers, Reel 99. Delegates to Montana's 1922 convention attempted to reorganize and nominate candidates for the 1922 election.Yet the Socialist Party of Montana had to start from the beginning. At the 1922 meeting state socialists passed motions to "organize the Socialist Party of Montana, and ask for a charter from the National Office." Socialist Party of Montana Convention Minutes, 30 September 1922, SC 1272, Montana, Ex. Rec. *Mills V. Stewart* Records, MHS. Party Report, Socialist Party of Oregon, 31 December 1928, SPA Papers, Reel 110. Oregon's party organization completely started over. S. R. McAlpine was made acting secretary and announced, "We are now making an attempt to increase our membership and to establish Locals throughout the state." S. R. McAlpine to Socialist Party of Oregon, 9 March 1929, SPA Papers, Reel 110. A month later seven members were added to Portland's local and socialists deemed this activity "Not so bad for a starter!" *Weekly Press News*, 20 April 1929, SPA Papers, Reel 130. By 1931 the *Social Vanguard*, the official organ of the socialist party's "Northwest Division," detailed reports from only a few field offices. Reports came from Bonner's Ferry, Coeur d'Alene, Sandpoint, and Hayden Lake, Idaho; Troy, Montana; and Reardan, Walla Walla, Pasco, Newport, Wilbur, Yakima, and Cheney, Washington. *Social Vanguard* (Spokane, Wash.), 4 July 1931.

3. William C. Pratt, "Rural Radicalism on the Northern Plains, 1912–1950," *Montana, the Magazine of Western History* 42 (Winter 1992): 44–45; Schwantes, *Radical Heritage*, 213–14; Shannon, *The Socialist Party of America*, 77–78; *Portland Labor Press*, 12 January 1914; Socialist Party of Montana Convention Minutes, 30 September 1922, SC 1272, MHS.

4. The splintered radicalism of the early 1920s was typical. "The revolutionary movement in America," socialists in 1919 criticized, "is now divided into several necessarily ineffectual organizations." *Party Builder*, 20 October and 20 November 1919. Accordingly, the different agendas of the country's most revolutionary reformers defected to various groups such as the Com-

munist party, and even to the SPA's old rivals, the Socialist Labor Party. Schwantes, *Radical Heritage*, 213–14. In Washington, SLP candidates joined SPA, Farmer-Labor, and Prohibition candidates as third party options. Pierce County Ballot, November 2, 1920, Ephemera, WSHS.

5. Communist party doctrine did not dramatically differ from socialist rhetoric. The CLP's manifesto affirmed its allegiance to the principles of "International Socialism." The document also echoed socialist strategies: "When elected to public office our members shall use such positions in every way possible, to hasten the abolition of Capitalism and to advance the cause of the Workers, and our endeavors shall not cease until our end is achieved and the Co-operative Commonwealth is firmly established in our land." *Party Builder*, 20 July 1920; P. G. Hummasti, "Ethnicity and Radicalism," 380.

6. The NPL arose in Idaho and Montana, although not with the same success North Dakota experienced. Charles "Red Flag" Taylor and the radicals of Sheridan, County, Montana, were the most active Montanans in the NPL. Pratt, "Rural Radicalism," 44–45. Yakima, Washington, socialists printed the NPL's original platform; the document included demands for hail-damage insurance provided by the state, state-run telephone systems, and equal taxation of utility companies. Schwantes, *Radical Heritage*, 215; H. H. Stallard, *World Problems*, Mini-Book, Yakima, Washington, February 1920, WSHS, 84–85; Hugh Lovin, "The Red Scare in Idaho," 11–12.

7. "In many states," James Weinstein has argued, "the achievements of the farmer-labor movement in these years far outstripped that of the old Socialist party at the height of its vitality, indicating that there existed a potential for radical politics on a much greater scale than that achieved by the party of Debs in the prewar period." Weinstein, "Radicalism in the Midst of Normalcy," 790. Political alliances between agriculturalists and industrialists had occurred previously. The SPA courted farmers for years, and in the Northwest broad cooperation was common. In 1917 the Oregon State Federation of Labor teamed with the state grange and farmer's union for a new legislative program. The alliance called for a consolidation of labor-oriented government positions, opposed an anti-picketing bill then before the Oregon legislature, and rejected any changes to the eight-hour day. *Northwest Worker*, 22 February 1917. Washington socialists made a poor showing in the 1920 presidential race and finished fourth behind the Republican (with 233,137 votes), Democrat (84,298), and Farmer-Labor (77,246) candidates. Cravens, "The Emergence of the Farmer-Labor Party," 148, 154, 157.

Bibliography

Archival Collections

Idaho State Historical Society, Boise
 AR 2/3, William J. McConnell Papers, 1893–1896
 AR 2/4, Frank Steunenberg Papers, 1897–1900
 AR 2/5, Frank Hunt Papers, 1901–1902
 AR 2/6, John T. Morrison Papers, 1903–1904
 AR 2/7, Frank R. Gooding Papers, 1905–1908
 AR 2/8, James H. Brady Papers, 1909–1910
 AR 2/9, James H. Hawley Papers, 1903–1915
 AR 2/10, John M. Haines Papers, 1913–1914
 AR 2/12, David William Davis Papers, 1919–1923
 AR 2/13, Charles Calvin Moore Papers, 1919–1927
 AR 2.0011, Moses Alexander Papers
 OH 145, Roy M. Watson Interview
 OH 228, Gustav Carlson Interview
Montana Historical Society, Helena
 SC 1263, Evart L. Riddle Papers, 1924–1926
 SC 1272, Montana, Ex Rel. Mills vs. Stewart Records, 1922
 SC 1888, Melinda Alexander Papers, 1901–1918
 SC 2135, Three Forks Socialist Party Records, 1914–1915
 SC 2175, Lewis J. Duncan Papers, 1911–1914
 MF 425, Socialist Party of Montana Papers, 1899–1950
Oregon Historical Society, Portland
 MSS 1513, Politics and Political Parties
 MSS 1187, John Daniel Stevens Papers, 1847–1932
 MSS 1505, Labor
Socialist Labor Party of America Papers
 Reel 35, National Convention Records, 1877–1900
 Reel 39, Everett, Washington Section Minutes, 1897–1898
Socialist Party of America Papers
 Series III, State and Local Files, 1897–1962
 Series V, Printed Matter, 1897–1964
Washington State Historical Society, Tacoma
 Ephemera Files, Socialism
 Cooperative Colonies Collection

Newspapers and Journals

Anaconda Standard (Anaconda, Mont.)
American Federationist (Washington, D.C.)
Appeal to Reason (Girard, Kan.)
Butte Daily Post (Butte, Mont.)
Butte Miner (Butte, Mont.)
Butte Socialist (Butte, Mont.)
Commonwealth (Everett, Wash.)
Co-Operative News (Everett, Wash.)
Cooperator (Olalla, Wash.)
Flathead County Socialist (Kalispell, Mont.)
International Socialist Review (Chicago, Ill.)
Lewis County Clarion (Centralia, Wash.)
Liberator (Portland, Ore.)
Northern Idaho News (Sandpoint, Id.)
Northwest Worker (Everett, Wash.)
Oregonian (Portland, Ore.)
Oregon Labor Press (Portland, Ore.)
Oregon Socialist Party Bulletin (Salem, Ore.)
Party Builder (Everett, Wash.)
Portland Labor Press (Portland, Ore.)
Seattle Post-Intelligencer (Seattle, Wash.)
Seattle Times (Seattle, Wash.)
Socialist: The Workingman's Paper (Seattle, Wash.)
Socialist Herald / The Herald (Seattle, Wash.)
Socialist News (Kelso, Wash.)
Socialist Voice (Seattle, Wash.)
Socialist Worker (Tacoma, Wash.)
Socialist World (Seattle, Wash.)
Spokesman-Review (Spokane, Wash.)
Truth (Tacoma, Wash.)
Union Record (Seattle, Wash.)
Washington Socialist (Everett, Wash.)

Books

Aiken, Katherine G. *Idaho's Bunker Hill: The Rise and Fall of a Great Mining Company, 1885–1981*. Norman: University of Oklahoma Press, 2005.

Belshaw, John Douglas. *Colonization and Community: The Vancouver Island Coalfield and the Making of the British Columbian Working Class.* Montreal: McGill-Queen's University Press, 2002.

Bissett, Jim. *Agrarian Socialism in America: Marx, Jefferson, and Jesus in the Oklahoma Countryside, 1904–1920.* Norman: University of Oklahoma Press, 1999.

Blank, Robert. *Regional Diversity of Political Values: Idaho Political Culture.* Washington, D.C.: University Press of America, 1978.

Brecher, Jeremy. *Strike!* Cambridge, Mass.: South End Press, 1997.

Buhle, Mary Jo. *Women and American Socialism, 1870–1920.* Urbana: University of Illinois Press, 1981.

Calvert, Jerry. *The Gibraltar: Socialism and Labor in Butte, Montana, 1895–1920.* Helena: Montana Historical Society Press, 1988.

Cherny, Robert. *American Politics in the Gilded Age, 1868–1900.* Wheeling, Ill.: Harlan Davidson, 1997.

Chester, Eric. *Socialists and the Ballot Box: A Historical Analysis.* New York: Praeger, 1985.

Critchlow, Donald. *Socialism in the Heartland: The Midwestern Experience, 1900–1925.* Notre Dame, Ind.: University of Notre Dame Press, 1986.

Dawley, Alan. *Struggles for Justice: Social Responsibility and the Liberal State.* Cambridge, Mass.: Harvard University Press, 1991.

Dembo, Jonathan. *Unions and Politics in Washington State, 1885–1935.* New York: Garland Publishing, 1983.

Diner, Stephen. *A Very Different Age: Americans of the Progressive Era.* New York: Hill and Wang, 1998.

Dubofsky, Melvyn. *Hard Work: The Making of Labor History.* Urbana: University of Illinois Press, 2000.

———. *Industrialism and the American Worker, 1865–1920.* Wheeling, Ill.: Harlan Davidson, 1996.

———. *We Shall Be All: A History of the Industrial Workers of the World.* 2d ed. Chicago: Quadrangle Books, 1988.

Edwards, Rebecca. *New Spirits: Americans in the Gilded Age, 1865–1905.* New York: Oxford University Press, 2006.

Egbert, Donald D., and Stow Persons, eds. *Socialism in American Life.* 2 vols. Princeton: Princeton University Press, 1952.

Emmons, David. *The Butte Irish: Class and Ethnicity in an American Mining Town, 1875–1925.* Urbana: University of Illinois Press, 1989.

Esposito, Anthony. *The Ideology of the Socialist Party of America, 1901–1917.* New York: Garland Publishing, 1997.

Fitrakis, Robert. *The Idea of Democratic Socialism in America and the Decline of the Socialist Party.* New York: Garland, 1993.

Frank, Dana. *Purchasing Power: Consumer Organizing, Gender, and the Seattle Labor Movement, 1919–1929.* New York: Cambridge University Press, 1994.

Friedheim, Robert L. *The Seattle General Strike.* Seattle: University of Washington Press, 1964.

Graham, John, ed. *"Yours for the Revolution": The Appeal to Reason, 1895–1922.* Lincoln: University of Nebraska Press, 1990.

Green, James. *Grass-Roots Socialism: Radical Movements in the Southwest, 1895–1943.* Baton Rouge: Louisiana State University Press, 1978.

Hall, Greg. *Harvest Wobblies: The Industrial Workers of the World and Agricultural Laborers in the American West, 1905–1930.* Corvallis: Oregon State University Press, 2001.

Hillquit, Morris. *History of Socialism in the United States.* New York: Funk and Wagnalls, 1910; reprint, New York: Dover, 1971.

Hummasti, P. G. *Finnish Radicals in Astoria, Oregon, 1904–1940: A Study in Immigrant Socialism.* New York: Arno Press, 1979.

Johnson, Oakley. *Marxism in United States History before the Russian Revolution, 1876–1917.* New York: Humanities Press, 1974.

Johnston, Robert. *The Radical Middle Class: Populist Democracy and the Question of Democracy in Progressive Era Portland, Oregon.* Princeton: Princeton University Press, 2003.

Judd, Richard. *Socialist Cities: Municipal Politics and the Grass Roots of American Socialism.* Albany: State University of New York Press, 1989.

Kennedy, David. *Over Here: The First World War and American Society.* New York: Oxford University Press, 1980.

Kipnis, Ira. *The American Socialist Movement, 1897–1912.* New York: Columbia University Press, 1952.

Kraditor, Aileen. *The Radical Persuasion: 1890–1917.* Baton Rouge: Louisiana State University Press, 1981.

Laslett, John. *Labor and the Left: A Study of Socialist and Radical Influences in the American Labor Movement, 1881–1924.* New York: Basic Books, 1970.

Leach, William. *Land of Desire: Merchants, Power, and the Rise of a New American Culture.* New York: Pantheon Books, 1993.

Lears, T. J. Jackson. *No Place of Grace: Antimodernism and the Transformation of American Culture, 1880–1920.* New York: Pantheon Books, 1981.

LeWarne, Charles. *Utopias on Puget Sound, 1885–1915.* Seattle: University of Washington Press, 1975.

Link, Arthur, and Richard McCormick. *Progressivism.* Wheeling, Ill.: Harlan Davidson, 1983.

Lipset, Seymour, and John Laslett. *Failure of a Dream?* Berkeley: University of California Press, 1984.

Lipset, Seymour, and Gary Marks. *"It Didn't Happen Here": Why Socialism Failed in the United States.* New York: W. W. Norton, 2000.

Lukas, J. Anthony. *Big Trouble: A Murder in a Small Western Town Sets Off a Struggle for the Soul of America.* New York: Simon & Schuster, 1997.

Malone, Michael. *The Battle for Butte: Mining and Politics on the Northern Frontier, 1864–1904.* Helena: Montana Historical Society Press, 1995.

Mercier, Laurie. *Anaconda: Labor, Community, and Culture in Montana's Smelter City.* Urbana: University of Illinois Press, 2001.

Mowry, George. *The California Progressives.* Berkeley: University of California Press, 1951.

Murphy, Mary. *Mining Cultures: Men, Women, and Leisure in Butte, 1914–1941.* Urbana: University of Illinois Press, 1997.

Peterson, H. C., and Gilbert Fite. *Opponents of War, 1917–1918.* Seattle: University of Washington Press, 1957.

Quint, Howard. *The Forging of American Socialism: Origins of the Modern Movement.* Columbia: University of South Carolina Press, 1952.

Robbins, William G. *Colony and Empire: The Capitalist Transformation of the American West.* Lawrence: University Press of Kansas, 1994.

Rosenzweig, Roy. *Eight Hours for What We Will: Workers and Leisure in an Industrial City, 1870–1920.* Cambridge: Cambridge University Press, 1983.

Salvatore, Nick. *Eugene V. Debs: Citizen and Socialist.* Urbana: University of Illinois Press, 1982.

Schwantes, Carlos. *The Pacific Northwest, An Interpretive History.* Lincoln: University of Nebraska Press, 1996.

————. *Radical Heritage: Labor, Socialism, and Reform in Washington and British Columbia, 1885–1917.* Moscow: University of Idaho Press, 1979.

Shannon, David. *The Socialist Party of America: A History.* Chicago: Quadrangle Books, 1955.

Skowronek, Stephen. *Building a New American State: The Expansion of National Administrative Capacities, 1877–1920.* Cambridge: Cambridge University Press, 1982.

Tyler, Robert. *Rebels of the Woods: The I.W.W. in the Pacific Northwest.* Eugene: University of Oregon Press, 1967.

Valelly, Richard M. *Radicalism in the States: The Minnesota Farmer-Labor Party and the American Political Economy.* Chicago: University of Chicago Press, 1989.

Watkins, Marilyn P. *Rural Democracy: Family Farmers and Politics in Western Washington, 1890–1925.* Ithaca, N.Y.: Cornell University Press, 1995.

Weinstein, James. *The Decline of Socialism in America, 1912–1925.* New York: Monthly Review Press, 1967.

Wiebe, Robert. *The Search for Order, 1877–1920.* New York: Hill and Wang, 1967.

Work, Clemens P. *Darkest Before Dawn: Sedition and Free Speech in the American West.* Albuquerque: University of New Mexico Press, 2005.

Young, Marguerite. *Harp Song for a Radical: The Life and Times of Eugene Victor Debs.* New York: Alfred A. Knopf, 1999.

Journal Articles and Book Chapters

Alexander, Thomas G., and Jessie L. Embry. "Toward a Twentieth Century Synthesis: The Historiography of Utah and Idaho." *Pacific Historical Review* 50 (November 1981): 475–98.

Berwanger, Eugene. "The Absurd and the Spectacular: The Historiography of the Plains-Mountain States—Colorado, Montana, Wyoming." *Pacific Historical Review* 50 (November 1981): 445–74.

Blackford, Mansel G. "Reform Politics in Seattle during the Progressive Era, 1902–1916." *Pacific Northwest Quarterly* 59 (October 1968): 177–85.

Brody, David. "The Old Labor History and the New: In Search of an American Working Class." *Labor History* 20 (Winter 1979): 111–26.

Brommel, Bernard. "Eugene V. Debs: Blue-Denim Spokesman." *North Dakota Quarterly* 41 (Spring 1973): 12–28.

Calvert, Jerry. "The Rise and Fall of Socialism in a Company Town, 1902–1905." *Montana, the Magazine of Western History* 36 (Autumn 1986): 2–13.

Cravens, Hamilton. "The Emergence of the Farmer-Labor Party in Washington Politics, 1919–1920." *Pacific Northwest Quarterly* 57 (October 1966): 148–57.

Dubofsky, Melvyn. "The Origins of Western Working Class Radicalism, 1890–1905." *Labor History* 7 (Spring 1966): 131–54.

Enyeart, John P. "Revolution or Evolution: The Socialist Party, Western Workers, and Law in the Progressive Era." *Journal of Gilded Age and Progressive Era* 2 (October 2003): 377–403.

Foner, Eric. "Why Is There No Socialism in the United States?" *History Workshop* 17 (Spring 1984): 59–80.

Haynes, Fred E. "The Significance of the Latest Third Party Movement." *Mississippi Valley Historical Review* 12 (September 1925): 177–86.

Hoffman, Dennis, and Vincent J. Webb. "Police Response to Labor Radicalism in Portland and Seattle, 1913–19." *Oregon Historical Quarterly* 87 (Winter 1986): 341–66.

Hummasti, P. G. "Ethnicity and Radicalism: The Finns of Astoria and the *Toveri*, 1890–1930." *Oregon Historical Quarterly* 96 (Winter 1995–1996): 362–93.

Johnston, Robert D. "The Myth of the Harmonious City: Will Daly, Lora Little, and the Hidden Face of Progressive-Era Portland." *Oregon Historical Quarterly* 99 (Fall 1998): 248–97.

Kleppner, Paul. "Politics without Parties: The Western States, 1900–1984." In *The Twentieth Century West*, edited by Gerald Nash and Richard W. Etulain, 296–317. Albuquerque: University of New Mexico Press, 1989.

Laslett, John. "Why Is There Not More of a Socialist Movement in the United States?" *Reviews in American History* 5 (June 1977): 262–68.

Leon, D. H. "Whatever Happened to an American Socialist Party? A Critical Survey of the Spectrum of Interpretations." *American Quarterly* 23 (May 1971): 236–58.

LeWarne, Charles. "The Reverend William Ellery Copeland: A Christian Socialist in the Northwest." *Pacific Northwest Quarterly* 81 (January 1990): 2–10.

Lipin, Lawrence M. "'Cast Aside the Automobile Enthusiast': Class Conflict, Tax Policy, and the Preservation of Nature in Progressive-Era Oregon." *Oregon Historical Quarterly* 107 (Summer 2006): 166–95.

Lovin, Hugh T. "Idaho and the 'Reds,' 1919–1926." *Pacific Northwest Quarterly* 69 (July 1978): 107–15.

———. "The Red Scare in Idaho, 1916–1918." *Idaho Yesterdays* 17 (Fall 1973): 2–13.

Markowitz, Norman. "Socialism and American Development." *Reviews in American History* 2 (March 1974): 107–15.

McDonald, Verlaine. "'A Paper of, by, and for the People'—*The Producers News* and the Farmers' Movement in Northeastern Montana." *Montana, The Magazine of Western History* 48 (Winter 1998): 18–33.

Miller, Sally. "For White Men Only: The Socialist Party of America and Issues of Gender, Ethnicity and Race." *Journal of Gilded Age and Progressive Era* 2 (July 2003): 283–303.

Moore, R. Laurence. "Insiders and Outsiders in American Historical Narrative and American History." *American Historical Review* 87 (April 1982): 390–412.

Murray, Keith. "Issue and Personalities of Pacific Northwest Politics, 1889–1950." *Pacific Northwest Quarterly* 41 (July 1950): 213–33.

Olssen, Erik. "The Case of the Socialist Party that Failed, or Further Reflections on an American Dream." *Labor History* 29 (Fall 1988): 416–49.

Pratt, William C. "Rural Radicalism on the Northern Plains, 1912–1950." *Montana, The Magazine of Western History* 42 (Winter 1992): 43–55.

———. "Socialism on the Northern Plains, 1900–1924." *South Dakota History* 18 (Spring / Summer 1988), 1–35.

Richards, Kent. "In Search of the Pacific Northwest: The Historiography of Oregon and Washington." *Pacific Historical Review* 50 (November 1981): 415–44.

Schneirov, Richard. "Editor's Introduction: The Socialist Party Revisited." *Journal of Gilded Age and Progressive Era* 2 (July 2003): 245–53.

Schwantes, Carlos. "Free Love and Free Speech on the Pacific Northwest Frontier." *Oregon Historical Quarterly* 82 (Fall 1981): 271–93.

————. "The History of Pacific Northwest Labor History." *Idaho Yesterdays* 28 (Winter 1985): 23–33.

————. "Labor-Reform Papers in Oregon, 1871–1976, A Checklist." *Pacific Northwest Quarterly* 74 (October 1983): 154–66.

————. "Patterns of Radicalism on the Wageworkers' Frontier." *Idaho Yesterdays* 30 (Fall 1986): 25–30.

————. "Protest in a Promised Land: Unemployment, Disinheritance, and the Origin of Labor Militancy in the Pacific Northwest, 1885–1886." *Western Historical Quarterly* 13 (October 1984): 373–90.

Shannon, David. "The Socialist Party before the First World War: An Analysis." *Mississippi Valley Historical Review* 38 (September 1951): 279–88.

Sims, Robert C. "Idaho's Criminal Syndicalism Act: One State's Response to Radical Labor." *Labor History* 15 (Fall 1974): 511–27.

Tyler, Robert. "I.W.W. in the Pacific N.W · Rebels of the Woods." *Oregon Historical Quarterly* 55 (March 1954): 3–44.

Vindex, Charles. "Radical Rule in Montana." *Montana The Magazine of Western History* 18 (Winter 1968): 3–17.

Weinstein, James. "Radicalism in the Midst of Normalcy." *Journal of American History* 52 (March 1966): 773–90.

Wessel, Thomas. "Wheat for the Soviet Masses: M. L. Wilson and the Montana Connection." *Montana, The Magazine of Western History* 31 (April 1981): 43–53.

Wetzel, Kurt. "The Defeat of Bill Dunne: An Episode in the Montana Red Scare." *Pacific Northwest Quarterly* 64 (January 1973): 12–20.

Whitfield, Stephen. "Autopsy Notes on American Socialism." *Reviews in American History* 3 (June 1975): 254–59.

Willis, Terry. "The Black Hole of Seattle: The Socialist Free Speech Movement, 1906–1907." *Pacific Northwest Quarterly* 91 (Summer 2000): 124–33.

Index